# The End of the Ages

**So...You Say You Want A Revelation?**

# KEN WINGATE

A WINGATE ARTHOUSE PRODUCTION

"Art That's Made for the Senses"

www.wingatearthouse.com

# Contents

# DEDICATION

Dedicated to:

My loving wife, Judy, who is always encouraging me in my writing and helping me find my voice.

My daughters, Elizabeth and Anna, for growing up to be the excellent people and the faithful believers that you are.

My sister, Annette, who was an angel who walked among us.

Pastors Mike and Kay Zello for our season of love and growth and for showing me, through living example, what doing right and good in the eyes of God really is.

# INTRODUCTION

Listening is a prerequisite to hearing. Hearing is a prerequisite to understanding. You must listen in order to hear. You must hear in order to understand. Listening requires attentiveness. Hearing requires openness. Understanding requires selflessness. Whether you are reading, attending a lecture, viewing a video, or having a life experience you are listening with your ears, eyes, spirit, and heart. You are listening with your whole being. But you must go beyond listening and hear what is evident. And then, in hearing, you will come to understanding.

It was November 21, 1981, when I had my epiphany. At least that is what I call it. I was lying in my bed in my apartment. Dawn was greeting me through the windows. I was twenty-two years old, and as I lay there alone, it simply became clear to me: God is.

I am not perfect. In the eyes of most Christian churches, my life has been a poor example of how a "Christian" should live. I have made some poor choices and bad decisions. I view poor choices as causing short-term personal suffering and bad decisions as causing long-term personal suffering. I have not committed any crimes, just personal and financial mistakes. I have hurt people, been hurt by people, and hurt myself in doing so. The lies I have told that have hurt others were driven by my insecurities, fear, depression, and the sheer desperation to survive and live another day. I am not proud of any of it.

But the two things I have never done are lie to myself or accept the lies of others. Those are the keys to a sincere search for God. You can lie to yourself, but God sees the lies. God sees through the facade and into the true intentions and motives of your soul. If you cannot be honest with yourself, you cannot be honest with God. That does not mean heaping undue condemnation upon yourself or demeaning yourself. It simply means being true and honest with yourself in accepting that your decisions, mistakes, and motives are what causes most of the chaos in your life. It is unnecessary to allow guilt to drive you down. Everything will be okay if you stay authentic within yourself to God with a sincere heart. In doing so, you will recognize who you are so that you can make the changes needed to be a better person. I will comment on that more in Chapter 6.

I have never been to seminary or attended classes on theology. In my search, I have been open in my discussions of God to a large and diverse assortment of church denominational leaders. The profession of music retail, live audio engineering, consulting, and installation, in which I spent over forty years, allowed me that luxury. My specialty in live audio was church sound systems so, I spent a lot of time working with churches associated with many of the mainstream denominations. I made sure to always have conversations about their doctrines. I wanted to understand their different views of salvation and damnation. Being open to hearing these differences provided me with an understanding and discernment to separate the man-made doctrines from my search to know and understand God.

Man-made doctrines have hindered many from knowing God. That is why I am writing this book. My hope is that in reading it you will begin your own personal search to know God as God is, not as how someone is telling you God is.

There are hundreds of gods that people worship throughout the world. I will not deny this. Out of the many, three of the largest religions believe in the same God. Followers of Judaism, Christianity, and Islam all believe in the God of Abraham. The followers of Judaism and Christianity believe in God through the lineage of Abraham to Isaac, his son born to him through Sarah, his wife. The followers of Islam believe in God through the lineage of Abraham to Ishmael, his son born to him through Hagar, Sarah's servant.

This God of Abraham is the same God of the Old Testament in which Judaism is founded. This is the same God that the New Testament in the Scriptures speaks of and that Christianity is based on. This is the same God that is found in the Qur'an, the foundational text of Islam. This is the same

God that the Christian Orthodox and Catholic religions are based upon. This is the same God that mainstream Christian denominations around the world are based on. This is the same God that many profess to believe in.

So, after looking into various other Eastern religions, my search brought me back to that same God, the God of Abraham, whom I have come to believe in and is found in the Scriptures. At that point, my objective was to find the truth of God and who God really is. This is where I found myself that morning as a twenty-two-year-old, lying in my bed in the apartment I was renting.

I do not believe that you have to attend church to have a personal relationship with God, but I do believe you have to establish a daily routine of reading the Scriptures, studying the Scriptures, and praying with a sincere heart to have that relationship. You have to be open. You have to be willing to set aside denominational doctrines and search for yourself. The Scriptures are found within the Bible that all of us know.

It is your perspective of the Scriptures that you must first change. To know God, you must know the Scriptures and not in just a one-sitting read. In reading the Scriptures, you do not have to spend hours at a time. You do not have to read chapters at a time. It is more important to read for understanding than for quantity. Your prayers do not have to be elaborate; they have to be sincere. Ask God to reveal the truth to you in the Scriptures. If you are open and sincere, God and the truth of the Scriptures will be revealed to you. You will receive your own personal revelations in doing so. The following are my revelations.

*NOTE: Throughout this book, any alternate text translations are presented in brackets directly beside the preferred text. I have chosen this method rather than using reference notes at the bottom of each page. Also, all verses are from the* New Revised Standard Version Updated Edition *translation except where noted.*

# PROLOGUE

**A BRIEF HISTORY OF THE BOOK
THAT IS CALLED THE BIBLE**

There are volumes of books available on this subject matter. I am not ignorant of how complex this subject is. My objective over the next few pages is to present a simple overview of the history of the Bible as I see it. The deeper you delve into this subject, the stronger your faith needs to be. There is nothing that human hands have touched that is perfect.

I will start with a note on the complexity of translating the languages in which the Bible (or the Scriptures, as I refer to it) was originally written. For you to understand the truth, you need to have at least this bit of understanding of the Scriptures.

Once I started searching for more understanding of God, the first thing I wanted to have some understanding of was the Scriptures. If the verses within the Scriptures were to lead me to understanding God and the truth, I needed to know where they came from and how they were compiled.

First, the Old Testament. When it all began, there were no typewriters, computers, or printing presses. There was not even paper or pens. The Scriptures all began by word of mouth, stories of old being handed down from generation to generation. Then scribes began to record the stories on plant fibers and animal skins. Later, papyrus became the most-used surface to record the Scriptures. As decades passed and writing surfaces progressed, these verses were passed on, translated, and reproduced by scribes and scholars on the most modern materials available.

By the time the New Testament came along, writing mediums such as parchment were readily available, and from that point it progressed along with the Old Testament.

The Old Testament was originally written in Classical Hebrew, along with some Aramaic. The New Testament was written primarily in Greek. That was all great for those times, but as humankind progressed, the teachings of the Scriptures became more popular, and as languages became more varied and diverse, these writings had to be translated into languages more people could understand.

I will not get into the many translations available today, but I will share with you a very simple example of the complexity of that process. Let's look at one of the most famous verses from the Scriptures: "The Lord's Prayer." Following is the Greek wording.

*NOTE: Greek wording and literal English translation via* www.biblehub.com.

> Matthew 6:9-13 [9] "οὕτως οὖν προσεύχεσθε ὑμεῖς Πάτερ ἡμῶν ὁ ἐν τοῖς οὐρανοῖς· Ἁγιασθήτω τὸ ὄνομά σου· [10] ἐλθάτω ἡ βασιλεία σου· γενηθήτω τὸ θέλημά σου, ὡς ἐν οὐρανῷ καὶ ἐπὶ γῆς· [11] Τὸν ἄρτον ἡμῶν τὸν ἐπιούσιον δὸς ἡμῖν σήμερον· [12] καὶ ἄφες ἡμῖν τὰ ὀφειλήματα ἡμῶν, ὡς καὶ ἡμεῖς ἀφήκαμεν τοῖς ὀφειλέταις ἡμῶν· [13] καὶ μὴ εἰσενέγκῃς ἡμᾶς εἰς πειρασμόν, ἀλλὰ ῥῦσαι ἡμᾶς ἀπὸ τοῦ πονηροῦ. ⟨Ὅτι σοῦ ἐστιν ἡ βασιλεία καὶ ἡ δύναμις καὶ ἡ δόξα εἰς τοὺς αἰῶνας. Ἀμήν⟩."

If you take that and translate it to literal English, it reads as follows:

> [9] "Thus therefore pray you: Father of us, who in the heavens, hallowed be the name of you. [10] Come the kingdom of You; be done the will of You, as in heaven, also upon earth. [11] The bread of us - daily grant us today. [12] And forgive us the debts of us, as also we forgive the debtors of us; [13] And not lead us into temptation, but deliver us from – evil. For Yours is the kingdom and the power and the glory for the ages. Amen."

As you can see, the literal English translation is not easy to read. So, in the process of translation, the translators must also apply proper English grammar rules and vocabulary addenda for it to have coherent word order. Samples of those translations follow.

*New Revised Standard Version Updated Edition* [9] "Pray, then, in this way: Our Father in heaven, may your name be revered as holy. [10] May your kingdom come. May your will be done on earth as it is in heaven. [11] Give us today our daily bread. [12] And forgive us our debts, as we also have forgiven our debtors. [13] And do not bring us to the time of trial, but rescue us from the evil one. Amen."

*New International Version* [9] "This, then, is how you should pray: Our Father in heaven, hallowed be your name, [10] your kingdom come, your will be done, on earth as it is in heaven. [11] Give us today our daily bread. [12] And forgive us our debts, as we also have forgiven our debtors. [13] And lead us not into temptation, but deliver us from the evil one. Amen"

*King James Version* [9] "After this manner therefore pray ye: Our Father which art in heaven, Hallowed be thy name. [10] Thy kingdom come, thy will be done in earth, as it is in heaven. [11] Give us this day our daily bread. [12] And forgive us our debts, as we forgive our debtors. [13] And lead us not into temptation, but deliver us from evil: For thine is the kingdom, and the power, and the glory, forever. Amen."

*New King James Version* [9] "In this manner, therefore, pray: Our Father in heaven, Hallowed be Your name. [10] Your kingdom come. Your will be done on earth as it is in heaven. [11] Give us this day our daily bread. [12] And forgive us our debts, as we forgive our debtors. [13] And do not lead us into temptation, but deliver us from the evil one. For Yours is the kingdom and the power and the glory forever. Amen."

*English Standard Version* [9] "Pray then like this: Our Father in heaven, hallowed be your name. [10] Your kingdom come, your will be done, on earth as it is in heaven. [11] Give us this day our daily bread, [12] and forgive us our debts, as we also have forgiven our debtors. [13] And lead us not into temptation, but deliver us from evil. Amen."

*New American Standard Bible* [9] "Pray, then, in this way: Our Father, who is in heaven, Hallowed be Your name. [10] Your kingdom come. Your will be done, on earth as it is in heaven. [11] Give us this day our daily bread. [12] And forgive us our debts, as we also have forgiven our debtors. [13] And do not lead us into temptation, but deliver us from evil. Amen."

The first thing you will notice is that the King James Version and the New King James Version are the only translations of these six that has the phrase, "For [Thine] Yours is the Kingdom and the power and the glory forever." There are various debates as to why this is so. One of them is that many older Greek transcripts have been found since the King James Bible was translated. Most of these older transcripts do not have the ending of the Lord's Prayer in them, so neither do their translations. This does not change the overall meaning or purpose of the prayer. It does not alter the subject matter. That is what is important.

Other than that, you can see from one translation to the other, that though words have been added and the verbiage arranged for an easier English reading, the substance or meaning of the prayer has not changed. They all point to the same basic principles within the prayer.

***

## THE INFLUENCE OF THE MALE GENDER THROUGHOUT THE BIBLE

I want to make this very clear: the following is my perspective concerning the history of the Scriptures and the process of them being handed down from century to century. But I share it with a sincere heart and belief that it has merit. I am confident God is not bothered by me sharing this.

Since the beginning of time as we have known it, the male gender has been the dominant gender. There are many arguments as to why. Some say that it is due to the sin Adam and Eve committed. Some look to nature and say that in the animal kingdom it is primarily the male that is dominant. Most mainstream religions teach the male is the head of the household. Then there are others who have mistakenly determined the female gender to be weaker and thus the male gender must be dominant. Whatever reason, history has focused upon the male as the dominant gender of the two.

Because of this, the male has also been the primary gender to chronicle religions through the ages. This is why so many doctrines and articles of beliefs are more prone to use male nouns and pronouns such as *he, him,* and *his* within their text. This is the way that it has been in most historical and religious circles. Even in the many different older translations of the Scriptures that I have read over the years, you will find this to be true.

There is a Greek word that I will note to you later on when we delve into Revelation. It appears in Revelation 12:10. The Greek word is *adelphoi.* Though many past English translations applied the term *brethren* or *brothers* to that word, it is meant to address both the male and the female genders. It is meant to address all faithful believers, both male and female. And yet, in the past, it was translated as *brethren* or *brothers,* denoting males. And yes, there are arguments on both sides of this translation issue, but I have come to agree on the side of the word denoting both male and female. Follow me on this because it is very important.

Genesis 1:26-27 Then God said, "Let us make humans [Hebrew *adam*: The Hebrew word for *man* (*adam*) is the generic term for mankind and becomes the proper name *Adam*] in our image, according to our likeness, and let them have dominion over the fish of the sea and over the birds of the air and over the cattle and over all the wild animals of the earth [Syriac: Hebrew *and over all the earth*] and over every creeping thing that creeps upon the earth."

So God created humans [Hebrew *adam*: The Hebrew word for *man* (*adam*) is the generic term for mankind and becomes the proper name *Adam*] in his image, in the image of God he created them [Hebrew *him*]; male and female he created them.

Genesis 2:20-23 The man gave names to all cattle and to the birds of the air and to every animal of the field, but for the man [or *for Adam*] there was not found a helper as his partner. So the Lord God caused a deep sleep to fall upon the man, and he slept; then he took one of his ribs and closed up its place with flesh. And the rib that the Lord God had taken from the man he made into a woman and brought her to the man. Then the man said, "This at last is bone of my bones and flesh of my flesh; this one shall be called Woman, for out of Man this one was taken."

I believe the story of Adam and Eve is not entirely accurate in the sense that they were the beginning. I believe the verses in Genesis 1:1-31 through Genesis 2:1-3 depict the creation of the universe and humankind more accurately than the verses found in Genesis 2:4-25. Let me be clear, I absolutely believe God created all the heavenly beings, the universe, the earth, and humankind. Period.

I see the "six days of creation" as not six literal days as we know it. Eternity has no time, and the days spoken of in Genesis 1 are simply a designation of events unfolding. Eternity is immeasurable. Within the existence of eternity there is no yesterday or tomorrow, there is only today. There is only the present (I will speak more on this in Chapter 13). If I believe God is eternal and has always been, why would I be fearful of the scientific fact that the earth is billions of years old? Billions of years is still today in eternity. Knowing that does not negate the truth that God created all of this, it simply negates the mistake of associating the "six days of creation" with the limited twenty-four-hour day we live by. It is a mistake that needs to be corrected.

I am convinced that the writer or writers of Genesis provide us with an account of the lineage of Israel for as far back as their ancestors were able to record it. I believe Adam and Eve existed within that lineage, but I do not believe that they were the first of humankind. I more strongly believe, as Genesis 1 notes, that God made humans (plural) and they date much earlier than the days of Adam and Eve. Let me explain my rationale behind this.

I believe God made all of this. I believe God is an intelligent spirit being far beyond our possible comprehension. I believe that God is eternal and has created all things, is creating all things, and will continue to create all things. I believe a God who is intellectually superior would not create a male alone and then after a period of time decide that this male needed a female partner. God is not ignorant. God does not make such human-like mistakes. In the beginning God created humans, both males and females, plural.

> Genesis 1:28 God blessed them, and God said to them, "Be fruitful and multiply and fill the earth and subdue it and have dominion over the fish of the sea and over the birds of the air and over every living thing that moves upon the earth."

I also do not believe that God created the male to be dominant over the female. Genesis 1:28 says, "God said to them." God was speaking to both male and female (and I believe it was multiple males and females). He spoke to them equally. I believe that God created them to live in harmony and as equals. I believe with all of my heart it was the male ego that contrived the male dominant factor. The free will of the male drove his ego to establish this imbalance of nature rather than to co-exist in harmony. That is what I see as the first true sin.

We have to accept that there are elements of the Scriptures that are not perfect. They cannot be "perfect." Though the Scriptures were inspired by God, they were written and translated by humans over thousands of years. God is infallible; man is not. Does knowing this negate the existence of God? No. Does knowing this cause me to question my faith in God? No. Why? Because the truth of God, the principles of God are still all there, written very clearly for us to read and understand. Arguments as to whether some stories in the Old Testament are parables rather than reality are irrelevant. The "Thread of Truth," as I have come to call it, is real and fluent through the Scriptures from Genesis to Revelation. I will share the "Thread of Truth" with you in Chapter 3.

The first step in anyone's life to building a relationship with God is simply believing. It is my hope that after reading this book, you will be willing to take that step and say that you believe. Believing in God is the easy part. Having faith in God is a whole other level of understanding. I will comment on this more in Chapter 8.

# GOD IS

God is.

If there is anything that I know from my sixty-six plus years of living on this earth, I know that God is.

I did not come to that realization while sitting in a church listening to a preacher. Nor did I do so while sitting in front of a television listening to one of the popular televangelists. It happened that morning as I was lying on my bed.

I then had to make a choice as to what to do with this revelation. So, I began to search for the truth. I wanted to know the truth and knew I had to find it myself. With this new realization that God is, I believed that I could find the truth by establishing a sincere relationship with God. After over forty years of reading, studying, and praying, I am presenting to you the important things I have learned. It is my hope that you will come to a similar conclusion and that you will grow in that truth. Seek the truth. Know the truth. Live the truth.

God is.

***

## GOD IS LOVE

1 John 4:7-21 Beloved, let us love one another, because love is from God; everyone who loves is born of God and knows God. Whoever does not love does not know God, for God is love. God's love was revealed among us in this way: God

sent his only Son into the world so that we might live through him. In this is love, not that we loved God but that he loved us and sent his Son to be the atoning sacrifice for our sins. Beloved, since God loved us so much, we also ought to love one another. No one has ever seen God; if we love one another, God abides in us, and his love is perfected in us.

By this we know that we abide in him and he in us, because he has given us of his Spirit. And we have seen and do testify that the Father has sent his Son as the Savior of the world. God abides in those who confess that Jesus is the Son of God, and they abide in God. So we have known and believe the love that God has for us.

God is love, and those who abide in love abide in God, and God abides in them. Love has been perfected among us in this: that we may have boldness on the day of judgment, because as he is, so are we in this world. There is no fear in love, but perfect love casts out fear; for fear has to do with punishment, and whoever fears has not reached perfection in love. We love [other ancient authorities add *him* or *God*] because he first loved us. Those who say, "I love God," and hate a brother or sister are liars, for those who do not love a brother or sister, whom they have seen, cannot love God, whom they have not seen. The commandment we have from him is this: those who love God must love their brothers and sisters also.

God loves us unconditionally. But to understand God's love, we must first understand the character of God.

From Genesis to Revelation, many characteristics are attributed to God. Some are positive like love, joy, gladness, pleasure, and compassion. Others are negative like anger, wrath, jealousy, grief, disappointment, regret, and sorrow. When we read these being attributed to God through the Scriptures, we are tempted to equate them with the human emotions we feel. We should not.

The very nature of God is holy and righteous. God's perfect, logical, rational, and practical character far exceeds our understanding. God's perspective is founded upon an absolutely flawless manner of justice toward the creation of humankind. We cannot understand God's form of justice because true justice among humankind does not exist on this earth. God's justice is impeccable. So, when presented with these characteristics of God throughout the Scriptures, we must not equate them to our human emotions, for they are not emotions when it comes to God; they are God's character. They are who God is. God has no emotions. God is not fickle, is not cynical, does not waver, and is not swayed by peer pressure or moods. God's character is flawless.

Human character is flawed by moods and emotions that cause us to go from rational to irrational and from practical to impractical with a turn of the switch. Moods and emotions cause us to go from love to hate, joy to sorrow, peace to conflict, patience to impatience, kindness to spite, goodness to wickedness, gentleness to brutality, faithfulness to faithlessness, and self-control to self-indulgence by simply what someone says or does to us. Some of us may have better control over our emotions and moods, but given the right situation, even the best heart can turn quickly.

So, when we read verses that note God's love, joy, gladness, pleasure, compassion, anger, wrath, jealousy, grief, disappointment, regret, or sorrow, we need to understand these characteristics to be justified and pure. They are not prone to the same emotional swings as in our nature. They are indisputable because they are derived from an all-seeing and all-knowing holy and righteous God.

In understanding this, when the Scriptures say that God is love and that God loves us, we know that it is indisputable and unconditional. We cannot do anything to earn God's love, nor can we do anything to stop

God from loving us. God's love is a bond between God as the creator and humankind, the creation. It cannot be severed or broken.

In hearing that God's love is unconditional, there are many who then question why bad things happen to good people or why anyone could possibly be eternally damned. It is simple: God is love. God loves us. In loving us, one of the greatest gifts God gave humankind is a free will, the ability to make our own choices and to live our own lives. What good would there be having humankind as a predestined creation: a creation in which God chooses who is righteous and who is unrighteous? That is not rational or practical from a God that has created all that exists.

In having free will, we are given the choice of receiving God's love or rejecting God's love. In having free will, we are given the choice to live a righteous life or live an unrighteous life. Having free will is a gift from a loving God, but it comes with responsibility. That responsibility is ours. God is not a dictator. God does not micro-manage our lives. We are responsible for our choices. Our choices cause bad things to happen to good people. It is our choices that cause us to be eternally damned. It is not God's fault. It is ours. It is the price of having the gift of a free will. A great example of this is found in the story of Cain and Abel. Let me explain.

> Genesis 4:1-16 Now the man knew his wife Eve, and she conceived and bore Cain, [In Hebrew *Cain* resembles the word for *produced*] saying, "I have produced a man with the help of the Lord." Next she bore his brother Abel. Now Abel was a keeper of sheep, and Cain a tiller of the ground. In the course of time Cain brought to the Lord an offering of the fruit of the ground, and Abel for his part brought of the firstlings of his flock, their fat portions. And the Lord had regard for Abel and his offering, but for Cain and his offering he had no regard. So Cain was very angry, and his countenance fell. The Lord said to Cain, "Why are you angry, and why has your countenance fallen? If you do well [or *what is right*], will you not be accepted? And if you do not do well

[or *what is right*], sin is lurking at the door; its desire is for you, but you must master it."

Cain said to his brother Abel, "Let us go out to the field." [Samaritan Pentateuch, Greek Septuagint, Syriac Peshitta, and Latin Vulgate: Hebrew Masoretic Text lacks *Let us go out to the field*] And when they were in the field, Cain rose up against his brother Abel and killed him. Then the Lord said to Cain, "Where is your brother Abel?" He said, "I do not know; am I my brother's keeper?" And the Lord said, "What have you done? Listen, your brother's blood is crying out to me from the ground! And now you are cursed from the ground, which has opened its mouth to receive your brother's blood from your hand. When you till the ground, it will no longer yield to you its strength; you will be a fugitive and a wanderer on the earth." Cain said to the Lord, "My punishment is greater than I can bear! Today you have driven me away from the soil, and I shall be hidden from your face; I shall be a fugitive and a wanderer on the earth, and anyone who meets me may kill me." Then the Lord said to him, "Not so! [Greek, Syriac Peshitta, and Latin Vulgate: Hebrew *Therefore*] Whoever kills Cain will suffer a sevenfold vengeance." And the Lord put a mark on Cain, so that no one who came upon him would kill him. Then Cain went away from the presence of the Lord and settled in the land of Nod, [that is, *wandering*] east of Eden.

Early in the Scriptures, we read about the story of Cain and Abel. Many miss the most important aspects of this story: the power of our free will, how it can destroy us and affect others, and just how God's love deals with each of us individually.

We are introduced to Cain and Abel as sons of Adam and Eve. Cain worked the land. Abel was a shepherd. When it came to providing an offering to God, a form of giving thanks, Cain brought some "fruit of the ground." But it notes that Abel "brought of the firstlings of his flock, their fat portions." Abel brought the first offspring born from his flock and chose the best portions. Abel's gesture was from a sincere heart of faith and thanksgiving. Cain simply brought some fruit. His expression did not show a sincere heart of thanksgiving. God honored Abel's offering because it came from a sincere heart of thanks. God did not honor the offering from Cain because it did not come from a sincere heart of thanks but more from obligation.

Because God knows our hearts, our motives, and our sincerity, God honored the offering of Abel greater than the offering of Cain because the heart of Abel was sincere, righteous, and faithful. Cain's heart was not. That is important to understand. God knows and sees all things. The judgment of God comes from knowing and seeing all things. You cannot lie to or deceive God.

That God did not honor Cain's offering does not mean that God loved Cain less than Abel. God loved them both. Because of this love, God approached Cain concerning the struggle he was having in his heart. Do you see that? Because God loved Cain, God approached Cain with concern and said, "Why are you angry, and why has your countenance fallen? If you do well [or *what is right*], will you not be accepted?" You see, out of love for Cain, God came to reason with him about what he was feeling. God took the time to share with Cain the most important principles in having a relationship with God: You must be sincere from your heart, and you must do what is right. In doing so, God expressed to Cain that if he did what was right, then he would be accepted. If he rejected the sinful thoughts in his heart and received the love God had for him, he would be accepted. God provided Cain with the solution to his struggle from the sin in his life. But God did not stop there. God informed Cain that "if you do not do well [or *what is right*], sin is lurking at the door; its desire is for you, but you must master it."

Do you see what God is doing? Do you understand that God is making it very clear to Cain that Cain is responsible for his actions. Cain could not blame his parents, his upbringing, peer pressure, or the culture around him. The sinful thoughts that had come into Cain's mind, heart, and spirit had to be dealt with by Cain. It was Cain's responsibility and no one else's. Cain had to deal with the sin that was beginning to consume his heart and thoughts, and he was responsible for mastering it and making a change.

Now, what happens next is very important in understanding how God deals with our individual free will. Even after God, out of love for him, approached Cain and appealed to him to resolve the conflict in his heart by recognizing and overcoming his sinful thoughts, Cain still murdered Abel. God did not stop Cain from murdering Abel, nor did God warn Abel that Cain was out to murder him. Some would immediately accuse God of not being loving in allowing Abel, a righteous man, to be murdered. Wrong.

Abel was a righteous man. He was recognized as such in the New Testament (Matthew 23:35, Luke 11:51, Hebrews 11:4, and Hebrews 12:24). Abel loved God and expressed his love to God by providing the best offerings he had. Abel was sincere in his devotion to God. There was nothing phony about his faith. God knew Abel's heart and knew how sincere his faith was. Abel was spiritually prepared to leave this life and receive his eternal blessing. So, in the eyes of God, Abel died to this flesh and was received into paradise for all of eternity. Abel gained an eternal blessed life in paradise by his death on this earth. Abel would struggle with this life no more. Abel would no longer face the worries of this world. Abel was now in the presence of his Creator in paradise. That is the eternal gift of love from God. Abel received his just reward for his love for God and his faith in God. And I can confidently assure you that Abel would not trade another second of this life for what he has experienced in heaven. Abel gained his life in losing it on this earth.

God then confronts Cain and proclaims to Cain the consequences of allowing his sin to overcome him and murder Abel. God proclaims to Cain that his work with the soil would no longer produce the abundance he was accustomed to and from that day forward, Cain would be a wanderer on this earth. Cain would never have a place to call home. He would be restless and discontented. But there was even a greater punishment that Cain faced and recognized as from God "I shall be hidden from your [God's] face." Cain had rejected the appeal and concern of the sin in his heart by a loving God. He had hardened his heart and turned from the word that God gave him. In doing so, he faced separation from a loving God for this life and all eternity.

But the story does not end there. In hearing the consequences of his sin and realizing the suffering he was going to face, Cain appealed to God for his life: "Anyone who meets me may kill me." Cain knew that this life was all that he had left before eternal damnation. He wanted the chance to at least live this life out before he met his final judgment. God's mercy provided protection for Cain from a premature death. God marked Cain so that he would be assured he would not die by another's hand. Cain would have to bear the consequences of his sin for the rest of his life and into eternity for his rejection of God's love. It was Cain's decision. It was Cain's responsibility. It was of no fault to God. "Cain went away from the presence of the Lord."

The story of Cain was later remembered in the books of 1 John and Jude.

> 1 John 3:11-12 For this is the message you have heard from the beginning, that we should love one another. We must not be like Cain, who was from the evil one and murdered his brother. And why did he murder him? Because his own deeds were evil and his brother's righteous.

> Jude 1:11 Woe to them! For they go the way of Cain and abandon themselves to Balaam's error for the sake of gain and perish in Korah's rebellion.

Here the writer of 1 John is emphasizing to us that love does not hate. Love does not envy. Love does not betray. The reason Cain murdered his brother was out of the evil of envy. Abel chose to receive God's love. Cain chose to reject God's love. Abel loved God in return. Cain did not. It was Cain's choice.

If God does not interfere with our free will, does that mean God will not intervene for us in personal matters? No. I can tell you of numerous times through my life when I know that God's angels and mercy intervened in my life. God hears the prayers of the faithful and will intervene if it leads us deeper into an understanding of God's love and will in our lives. That is not interfering with our free will since we are requesting intervention and it is addressing issues that draw us to a deeper understanding. But God does not always intervene if it does not benefit us spiritually. Paul taught us this in his Second Letter to the Corinthians.

> 2 Corinthians 12:7b-10 Therefore, to keep [other ancient authorities read *To keep*] me from being too elated, a thorn was given me in the flesh, a messenger of Satan to torment me, to keep me from being too elated [other ancient authorities lack *to keep me from being too elated*]. Three times I appealed to the Lord about this, that it would leave me, but he said to me, "My grace is sufficient for you, for power [other ancient authorities read *my power*] is made perfect in weakness." So I will boast all the more gladly of my weaknesses, so that the power of Christ may dwell in me. Therefore I am content with weaknesses, insults, hardships, persecutions, and calamities for the sake of Christ, for whenever I am weak, then I am strong.

Grace is the unconditional love of God for us. There are times in our lives when rather than intervening, God reminds us of that grace. God reminds us that there is always love for us to gain strength from in those dark times. To those who do not know God or have no understanding of the love of God, this would seem to be a frivolous response from a loving God. They see that as a cruel God. But to those of us who have experienced the grace of God in our lives and lived within its embrace, we know how powerful, how encouraging, and how much strength the grace of God gives us in times when it seems life is caving in around us. Maybe the answer will come later or maybe we see through the eyes of the Holy Spirit that the answer we wanted was not the right answer at all. But always and without fail, the grace of God embraces us and strengthens us in the midst of our need, forever reminding us that God's grace is sufficient for us.

So, we understand that God's love for us is unbreakable, unconditional, and unwavering. It is a love that we cannot fully comprehend because it is not based on human emotions. It is immovable and non-compromising. It is always there patiently waiting for us to receive it in our lives and walk in its truth.

The moment that we realize and understand that God loves us is what I call the Grace Revelation. It is a powerful moment. It is imperative to have a Grace Revelation for us to grasp the amazing provision of salvation that God has provided for us.

God is love. God loves us. If we abide in God's love, God's love will abide in us. God's love is perfect. It is a love we cannot fully understand because it is absolutely unconditional. It requires nothing more than us accepting it, receiving it, and living in it. In doing so, we will love. And where God's love is, hate cannot abide, for God's love cannot hate. This is what I call the perpetual motion of the love of God. It is always active from God to us, from us to God, and from us to others. God's love for humankind should have been enough through the ages, but God had an even greater expression of love for us to come.

> John 3:16-18 "For God so loved the world that he gave his only Son, so that everyone who believes in him may not perish but may have eternal life. Indeed, God did not send the Son into the world to condemn the world but in order that the world might be saved through him. Those who believe in him are not condemned, but those who do not believe are condemned already because they have not believed in the name of the only Son of God."

God's greatest expression of love for humankind came in the gift of the Beloved coming to this earth as the Messiah, Jesus Christ to give us the Gospel of the New Covenant, die on the cross, and rise from the dead for our salvation, redemption, and justification.

Through the life and teachings of Jesus, God expressed love for all of humankind providing us with the same compassion, consultation, instruction, and wisdom that was provided to Cain so that we might be given the unequivocally fair choice of accepting or rejecting God's love. Through the life, teachings, and death of Jesus, God gave humankind the ultimatum of our free will and the choices we make in this life. It is our choice to make.

During his life on this earth, Jesus provided us with many teachings to guide and direct us to having a personal relationship with God. Jesus proclaimed in Matthew 5:17, "Do not think that I have come to abolish the Law or the Prophets; I have come not to abolish but to fulfill." This was that very act of fulfilling the Law that provided all of humankind a means of salvation by believing and abiding by the teachings Jesus set forth.

Within those teachings, Jesus pointed to three very specific commandments in which all of the laws were founded upon. These commandments are the foundation of a faithful believer's life which we are to never discard.

Deuteronomy 6:4-7, Matthew 22:37, Mark 12:30, Luke 10:27 "Hear, O Israel: The Lord is our God, the Lord alone. You shall love the Lord your God with all your heart and with all your soul and with all your might. Keep these words that I am commanding you today in your heart. Recite them to your children and talk about them when you are at home and when you are away, when you lie down and when you rise."

Leviticus 19:18, Matthew 22:39, Mark 12:33, Luke 10:27 "And the second is like it: 'Love your neighbor as yourself.'"

Matthew 7:12, Luke 6:31 "So in everything, do to others what you would have them do to you, for this sums up the Law and the Prophets."

Jesus noted these verses as commandments meaning they were not to be taken lightly. They were to be a constant in a faithful believer's life. In the eyes of many, a commandment is a stern voice of conduct or demand. But it is not that way with God.

There are two principal thoughts when it comes to the word *commandment* in its original languages. The word *commandment*, pertaining to the laws of God, is the Hebrew word *Mitzvah* in the Old Testament and the Greek word *Entole* in the New Testament. Within the Jewish religious circles, as with most religious circles, there are the conservatives known as Orthodox who follow a stricter interpretation of the laws and the Liberals who follow a contemporary interpretation of the laws. Within the Orthodox community, the word *Mitzvah* is a stern law, ordinance, precept. Within the Liberal community, they see the word *Mitzvah* as an act of a divine good deed. The Greek word *Entole* in the New Testament is viewed quite similarly in the Christian religious circles with the conservatives viewing *Entole* as a strict demand and the liberals viewing it as more of a request. As I reviewed these two perspectives, I was drawn to conclude a more balanced perspective, and I feel this is good and right.

Everything that is within the Scriptures is based solely on the fact that God loves us. God's love for us who believe and have faith in the salvation of Jesus convinces me that these commandments are loving instructions rather than demands or good deeds. God provides us with these loving instructions to protect us from ourselves, selfish ambitions, and the enticements of sin. In adhering to love God and love our neighbors as we do ourselves, we will be kept from the enticement of sin and Satan's lies. These loving instructions are there to protect us. God has provided us with these instructions just as God, out of love, went to Cain to provide him with resolutions for his conflict. It is all here provided to us by a loving God.

It all points back to the simple act of love and making love a major priority in our lives. For God is love and those who abide in the love of God, love God in return. It is that perpetual motion of love I spoke of. The instruction to love God reminds us that we always need God. That is not an option. With God we have everything. Without God we have nothing.

So that commandment to love God is better viewed as God's love for us by providing loving instruction for our own good and the good of others. It is not a demand nor is it to be taken lightly as a deed, but we need to recognize these words as God loving us and desiring to protect us from the evil in this world. If we follow these instructions, we will find our lives to be fuller and filled with grace. If we reject them, we will find ourselves lost just like Cain.

In loving others, we are demonstrating God's love. For God's love is active not passive. If our hearts are open to God's love and the gift of salvation through Jesus Christ, those that we demonstrate that love to will realize God's love for them in a real way. They in turn will love God and also love others. That should be the sole motive of our heart. The motive of our heart in doing what is right in the eyes of God should always be based upon the love God has for us and our love for God. This is the perpetual motion of God's love.

So, if God is love, why do good people suffer? Suffering occurs when the perpetual motion of God's love is interrupted by sin and evil. When we open ourselves up to sin and evil, the consequences can be minimal or devastating. The selfish and greedy ambition of our flesh can cause many to suffer. That is our fault. That is our responsibility. You cannot blame God for what we are responsible for. Just as you cannot blame God for Cain murdering Abel. We have been warned just as Cain was. We have been given the choice to do right or fall to our sin. The consequences are on us.

The very design of humankind is based on our free will. Each of us is responsible for our individual actions. God does not micro-manage us as individuals. As individuals, when we allow peer pressure or fear to persuade us to follow a group or mass of people, then suddenly we have a corporate body doing what is wrong in the eyes of God. That corporate body can cause many to suffer. Again, it goes back to the perpetual motion of God's love being severed and the consequences that follow. God cannot be blamed for that. It is our responsibility.

One evening, an elderly Cherokee brave told his grandson about a battle that goes on inside each of us. He said, "My son, there is a battle between two 'wolves' inside us all. One is bad. It provokes anger, envy, jealousy, sorrow, regret, greed, arrogance, self-pity, guilt, resentment, inferiority, lies, false pride, superiority, and ego. The other is good. It produces joy, peace, love, hope, serenity, humility, kindness, benevolence, empathy, generosity, truth, compassion, and faith."

The grandson thought about it for a while and then asked his grandfather, "Which wolf wins?"

His grandfather replied, "The one that you feed."

I end this section concerning God's love with a very popular American Indian parable about the two wolves inside us all. The reason this parable is so popular is because it holds a very simple yet profound truth to this life in more ways than one. I want to draw our attention to its association with God's love.

In the story of Cain and Abel, God expressed love for Cain by coming to him concerning his anger. God appealed to Cain concerning that anger. God promised Cain forgiveness in that if Cain would do what was right, he would be accepted. God warned Cain that he must master the sin that was in his life. He must overcome it. Cain chose to feed the sin in his life rather than feed the love God had shown him.

God has done the same for each and every one of us via the Scriptures, providing us with expressions of love and reassurance that if we do what is right according to the life, teachings and death of Jesus, we will be accepted. It is all in the Scriptures if we read them and study them. If we feed the love that we have for God rather than feed the love we have for this world, we will do well.

1 John 5:3 For the love of God is this, that we obey his commandments. And his commandments are not

burdensome, for whatever is born of God conquers the world. And this is the victory that conquers the world, our faith.

The loving instructions God has provided for us are not burdensome and provide us with resolutions for all of our struggles on this earth. That is how much God loves us. All we have to do is receive that love and live according to the truth of that love.

When we reject feeding the sin that tempts us, God's peace and love will abide in us. When we feed the sin that tempts us, we separate ourselves from that peace and sever the perpetual motion of God's love causing us and possibly others hurt.

Philippians 1:6 I am confident of this, that the one who began a good work in you will continue to complete [or *perfect*] it until the day of Jesus Christ.

God's will for all of us is to do what is right and good and hold fast to our faith while sharing the love of God with all. In doing so, God promises us that the work that is begun in us will be completed to perfection, just as Abel had completed the work God had given him to do and was taken up into Paradise upon his death on this earth. God's love for us does not dwell on whether we live one year or one hundred years on this earth. God is only concerned with us embracing the love and truth that Jesus taught and sharing it with others. That is our calling. That is God's will for each and every one of us.

God is love. If we receive that love, embrace it, and share it with others, our lives will be filled with peace and contentment. If we reject that love, the perpetual motion of God's love will be severed, and it will cost us and possibly others around us hurt. That is the free will we have been given by a loving God. Our choice of what we feed in our lives determines if we live in peace or conflict. It is our choice to make.

## GOD IS FORGIVING

Psalm 103:8-12 The Lord is merciful and gracious, slow to anger and abounding in steadfast love. He will not always accuse, nor will he keep his anger forever. He does not deal with us according to our sins nor repay us according to our iniquities. For as the heavens are high above the earth, so great is his steadfast love toward those who fear him; as far as the east is from the west, so far he removes our transgressions from us.

Isaiah 59:1-2 See, the Lord's arm is not too short to save, nor his ear too dull to hear. Rather, your iniquities have been barriers between you and your God, and your sins have hidden his face from you so that he does not hear.

John 21:15-19 When they had finished breakfast, Jesus said to Simon Peter, "Simon son of John, do you love me more than these?" He said to him, "Yes, Lord; you know that I love you." Jesus said to him, "Feed my lambs." A second time he said to him, "Simon son of John, do you love me?" He said to him, "Yes, Lord; you know that I love you." Jesus said to him, "Tend my sheep." He said to him the third time, "Simon son of John, do you love me?" Peter felt hurt because he said to him the third time, "Do you love me?" And he said to him, "Lord, you know everything; you know that I love you." Jesus said to him, "Feed my sheep. Very truly, I tell you, when you were younger, you used to fasten your own belt and to go wherever you wished. But when you grow old, you will stretch out your hands, and someone else will fasten a belt around you and take you where you do not wish to go." (He said this to indicate the kind of death by which he would glorify God.) After this he said to him, "Follow me."

In addressing God's love for us, I would be remiss if I did not share the precious gift God has provided in forgiveness. In my studies and in my heart, I believe in the salvation and forgiveness that God has provided for us. I believe that Jesus Christ came to this earth, gave us the Word, died on the cross, and rose from the dead for our salvation, redemption, and justification. I believe that anyone who calls upon the name of Jesus Christ as their Lord and Savior, confesses their sins, obeys the Word, and does what is right in the eyes of God will be saved. Following is my favorite story of forgiveness.

It is recorded, right before Jesus was arrested, in all four Gospels (Mathew 26:31-35, Mark 14:29-31, Luke 22:34, and John 13:38) that Jesus declared to Peter that Peter would deny knowing Jesus three times before the cock crowed. It is also recorded in all four Gospels the instance in which Peter denied knowing Jesus, just as Jesus had told him he would (Matthew 26:69-75, Mark 14:66-72, Luke 22:54-62, and John 18:15-27).

The verses in John 21:15-19 are so very important in grasping God's forgiveness. Knowing that Peter had denied Him, Jesus confronted Peter after His resurrection. In this dialogue exchange, Jesus asks Peter three different times, "Do you love me?" In an immensely compassionate exchange of love, Jesus assures Peter that he has been forgiven of his three denials. Peter denying Jesus was devastating to Peter's faith. He thought that he was strong but when faced with the reality of the circumstances in front of his peers, Peter failed by fearing for his own life. Jesus knew and understood this and made sure to acknowledge to Peter that he was forgiven in this gracious dialogue exchange while, at the same time, letting Peter know that eventually he would be faced with death again for his faith in Jesus but at that time he would not fail. What a powerful example of God's loving forgiveness and understanding.

This exchange of dialogue is also a strong reminder to Peter and to all of us that we are to forgive even as we have been forgiven as we will discuss later in this section.

1 John 1:5-10 This is the message we have heard from him and proclaim to you, that God is light and in him there is no darkness at all. If we say that we have fellowship with him while we are walking in darkness, we lie and do not do what is true; but if we walk in the light as he himself is in the light, we have fellowship with one another, and the blood of Jesus his Son cleanses us from all sin. If we say that we have no sin, we deceive ourselves, and the truth is not in us. If we confess our sins, he who is faithful and just will forgive us our sins and cleanse us from all unrighteousness. If we say that we have not sinned, we make him a liar, and his word is not in us.

1 John 2:1-2 My little children, I am writing these things to you so that you may not sin. But if anyone does sin, we have an advocate with the Father, Jesus Christ the righteous, and he is the atoning sacrifice for our sins, and not for ours only but also for the sins of the whole world.

1 Samuel 15:22 And Samuel said, "Has the Lord as great delight in burnt offerings and sacrifices as in obedience to the voice of the Lord? Surely, to obey is better than sacrifice and to heed than the fat of rams."

It is true, as stated in 1 Samuel 15:22, "Surely, to obey is better than sacrifice and to heed than the fat of rams." Or, it is better to do what is right and good in the eyes of God than to have to ask for forgiveness. And, at all costs, we should try to do so. But during those times when we find ourselves having fallen into sin and in need of the forgiveness God has promised, we know that all we have to do is approach God with a sincere heart and be forgiven.

As I have shared, God knows our hearts. God knows the truth within us and if we are sincere in our confession of our sins. We cannot lie to God. As Jesus illustrated with this parable found in Luke.

> Luke 18:9-14 He also told this parable to some who trusted in themselves that they were righteous and regarded others with contempt: "Two men went up to the temple to pray, one a Pharisee and the other a tax collector. The Pharisee, standing by himself, was praying thus, 'God, I thank you that I am not like other people: thieves, rogues, adulterers, or even like this tax collector. I fast twice a week; I give a tenth of all my income.' But the tax collector, standing far off, would not even lift up his eyes to heaven but was beating his breast and saying, 'God, be merciful to me, a sinner!' I tell you, this man went down to his home justified rather than the other, for all who exalt themselves will be humbled, but all who humble themselves will be exalted."

God sees past all of the faults and weaknesses and sees the purity of our hearts, our motives, and the truth within us. That is how God knows us and how we will know ourselves in eternity.

God deals with each of us individually when we sin. The Spirit of God within us provides a spiritual check when we have made a poor choice or bad decision. It is always best to deal with it at that time than to let it eat at us and cause more hurt. That is what we must strive for. That is the goal we have in this life. God's wish is for us to do what is right. But God knows there will be times when our flesh will be weak and we fall. It is those times when we are assured by God's Word that forgiveness awaits us if we pray with a humble and sincere heart of repentance. If we do, our prayers will be heard and we will be forgiven.

Always remember the following character teachings and instructions when you are seeking forgiveness. They are signs of a broken and contrite heart.

We must be merciful:

Matthew 5:7 Blessed are the merciful, for they will receive mercy.

We must forgive even as we are forgiven:

Matthew 6:12 And forgive us our debts, as we also have forgiven our debtors.

Mark 11:25 "Whenever you stand praying, forgive, if you have anything against anyone, so that your Father in heaven may also forgive you your trespasses."

We must be willing to forgive...always:

Matthew 18:21-22 Then Peter came and said to him, "Lord, if my brother or sister sins against me, how often should I forgive? As many as seven times?" Jesus said to him, "Not seven times, but, I tell you, seventy-seven [or *seventy times seven*] times."

Luke 17:3-4 "Be on your guard! If a brother or sister sins, you must rebuke the offender, and if there is repentance, you must forgive. And if the same person sins against you seven times a day and turns back to you seven times and says, 'I repent,' you must forgive."

For we must remember that God forgives and forgets. It is important that our faith in God extends to God's forgiveness. So, when we ask for forgiveness with a sincere and contrite heart, we know that God not only forgives us the sin but also forgets that sin and we are no longer accountable for that sin through the redemptive work of Jesus Christ. There may be earthly consequences that we may have to endure for the sin, but forgiveness from God cleanses us from being accountable to God for that sin.

When God forgives sin, that sin will no longer carry any condemnation from God. That sin may carry natural or personal consequences that may last for a time or for years. It is a burden we must carry, but God's grace and mercy will help us endure. The devil may use memories or the consequences to weigh us down, but God sees them no more. God's grace is sufficient to sustain us in those times. Have faith in this truth, and do not let guilt and condemnation keep you oppressed. Move forward doing what is right and good in God's eyes.

***

## GOD IS JUST

Matthew 20:1-16 "For the kingdom of heaven is like a landowner who went out early in the morning to hire laborers for his vineyard. After agreeing with the laborers for a denarius for the day, he sent them into his vineyard. When he went out about nine o'clock, he saw others standing idle in the marketplace, and he said to them, 'You also go into the vineyard, and I will pay you whatever is right.' So they went. When he went out again about noon and about three o'clock, he did the same. And about five o'clock he went out and found others standing around, and he said to them, 'Why are you standing here idle all day?' They said to him, 'Because no one has hired us.' He said to them, 'You also go into the vineyard.' When evening came, the owner of the vineyard said to his manager, 'Call the laborers and give them their pay, beginning with the last and then going to the first.' When those hired about five o'clock came, each of them received a denarius. Now when the first came, they thought they would receive more; but each of them also received a denarius. And when they received it, they grumbled against the landowner, saying, 'These last worked only one hour, and you have made them equal to us who have borne the burden of the day and the scorching heat.' But he replied to one of them, 'Friend, I am doing you no wrong; did you not agree with me for a denarius? Take what belongs to you and go; I choose to give to this last the same as I give to you. Am I not allowed to do what I choose with what belongs to me? Or are you envious because I am generous?' [Greek *is your eye evil because I am good?*] So the last will be first, and the first will be last [other ancient authorities add *for many are called, but few are chosen*]."


There is no way we can truly understand how just God is.

Dictionary.com defines *just* as the following: "Guided by truth, reason, justice, and fairness. Done or made according to principle; equitable; proper. In keeping with truth or fact; true; correct. Given or awarded rightly; deserved, as a sentence, punishment, or reward. In accordance with standards or requirements; proper or right. Righteous, actual, real, or genuine."

We do not know or understand what pure justice is on this earth. Our minds and lives have been so corrupted with injustice that our understanding is warped. Our judicial system is so corrupted with ignorance, favoritism, and bias. Why? Because all that are involved in the system are fallible human beings. They are not God, and they are not perfect. Our judicial system is so corrupt and biased that it cannot even take a document that was written within the last 250 years and agree on what it says. It is a sad state of affairs.

Because we have experienced only this flawed form of justice, it is impossible for us to truly understand that God is just and that God's justice is pure and perfect. Each and every one of us will be judged by a perfect God administering perfect justice. How can this be? Because we will be judged by our deepest and true inner thoughts and motives. We will not be judged by corrupted evidence, biased opinions, racism, deceptive lies, and favored status. White privilege will have no place at the judgment seat of God. God's judgment will be based solely upon what is in the depth of our souls, the motives of our hearts, and the purity of our humility.

God is an intelligent being with wisdom that goes beyond our comprehension. The universe and all its magnificence cannot compare to all that God is. We look at the vastness of this universe and wonder. God created it all. God's judgment for the unrighteous may seem harsh, but it is just. God has expressed love for all of humankind by providing a means of salvation and forgiveness through the life, death, and resurrection of Jesus Christ. All God asks in return is for us to do what is right and good. Why do we think it is so harsh for there to be eternal punishment for those who do not do what is right in the eyes of God? It is our fault if we do wrong. We are to blame. God does not send anyone into eternal punishment. It is of our own doing. God desires for all of us to live in a state of grace. Choosing not to do so is all on us. Choosing to rebel and deny God's salvation is all on us. God's judgment is just.

> Revelation 15:3 And they sing the song of Moses, the servant [Greek *slave*] of God, and the song of the Lamb: "Great and amazing are your deeds, Lord God the Almighty! Just and true are your ways, King of the nations [other ancient authorities read *the ages*]!"

> Revelation 16:4-7 The third angel poured his bowl into the rivers and the springs of water, and they became blood. And I heard the angel of the waters say, "You are just, O Holy One, who are and were, for you have judged these things; because they shed the blood of saints and prophets, you have given them blood to drink. It is what they deserve!" And I

heard the altar respond, "Yes, O Lord God, the Almighty, your judgments are true and just!"

Revelation 19:1-2 After this I heard what seemed to be the loud voice of a great multitude in heaven, saying, "Hallelujah! Salvation and glory and power to our God, for his judgments are true and just; he has judged the great whore [or *prostitute*] who corrupted the earth with her prostitution, and he has avenged on her the blood of his servants [Greek *slaves*]."

All of the angels and heavenly beings know and understand the purity of God's justice. They have, are, and will continuously proclaim the just actions of God through all eternity. As we discussed earlier concerning God's love and character, there is nothing fallible in the character of God or the just acts of God. We will all stand in awe of God when we pass from this life into eternity. All will bow to God's pure justice and receive a rightful judgment.

Exodus 33:19 And he said, "I will make all my goodness pass before you and will proclaim before you the name, 'The Lord,' [Hebrew *YHWH*] and I will be gracious to whom I will be gracious and will show mercy on whom I will show mercy."

Romans 9:14-16 What then are we to say? Is there injustice on God's part? By no means! For he says to Moses, "I will have mercy on whom I have mercy, and I will have compassion on whom I have compassion." So it depends not on human will or exertion but on God who shows mercy."

God's justice comes from God's all-knowing character. It is here where God's mercy reigns. God, knowing our hearts and our true motives, judges with justice and mercy. We are not called to live a good life; we are called to live a righteous life via the Presence of the Holy Spirit and the Spirit of Jesus Christ living in us. As individuals we will be judged according to how we live that life. There will be those who, in God knowing all things, will be bathed in God's mercy and enter into eternal blessings. But not all. For God will choose those who will receive mercy at that time.

***

## GOD IS SPIRIT

John 4:23-24 "But the hour is coming and is now here when the true worshipers will worship the Father in spirit and truth, for the Father seeks such as these to worship him. God is spirit, and those who worship him must worship in spirit and truth."

All of the heavenly beings are spirits. All of the angels are spirits. When we pass over into eternity, we will receive a spirit body. It will be flawless. We will have knowledge and understanding of all things. The veil will be removed, the mystery of God will be revealed, and we will have understanding of all that has happened.

1 John 3:1-2 See what love the Father has given us, that we should be called children of God, and that is what we are. The reason the world does not know us is that it did not know him. Beloved, we are God's children now; what we will be has not yet been revealed. What we do know is this: when he [or *it*] is revealed, we will be like him, for we will see him as he is.

Our eternal bodies will be spirit bodies. There will be no gender or race. There will be no flesh and bones. We will be a spirit being in the company of the Creator, the Beloved, and the Presence. We will be servants of God and will live in peace and harmony. Death will be no more. This is the promise for all who believe and have accepted the eternal salvation that God has provided.

> Matthew 22:29-30 Jesus answered them, "You are wrong because you know neither the scriptures nor the power of God. For in the resurrection people neither marry nor are given in marriage but are like angels of God [other ancient authorities lack *of God*] in heaven."

> 1 Corinthians 15:50-55 What I am saying, brothers and sisters, is this: flesh and blood cannot inherit the kingdom of God, nor does the perishable inherit the imperishable. Look, I will tell you a mystery! We will not all die, [Greek *fall asleep*] but we will all be changed, in a moment, in the twinkling of an eye, at the last trumpet. For the trumpet will sound, and the dead will be raised imperishable, and we will be changed. For this perishable body must put on imperishability, and this mortal body must put on immortality. When this perishable body puts on imperishability and this mortal body puts on immortality, then the saying that is written will be fulfilled: "Death has been swallowed up in victory. Where, O death, is your victory? Where, O death, is your sting?"

In knowing the Scriptures and what they say and in knowing that God is far superior than we can conceive in our limited brains, I believe it is quite clear that God is not made of flesh and bones. God is spirit. And I am certain that when we pass over into eternity, we will be in absolute awe of what we will see and experience.

As God being spirit, we as faithful believers become one with each other and with God through the Presence of the Holy Spirit. Let me explain.

> Matthew 19:4-6 and Mark 10:7-9 Jesus speaking to the Pharisees answered, "Have you not read that the one who made them at the beginning 'made them male and female,' and said, 'For this reason a man shall leave his father and mother and be joined to his wife, and the two shall become one flesh'? So they are no longer two but one flesh. Therefore what God has joined together, let no one separate."

In these verses, Jesus portrays the consummation of a marriage to the joining of two into one flesh ("So they are no longer two but one flesh"). Obviously, the two do not literally become one flesh. They are not suddenly conjoined. They become one in the Spirit.

> John 13:34-35 I give you a new commandment, that you love one another. Just as I have loved you, you also should love one another. By this everyone will know that you are my disciples, if you have love for one another."

The Presence of the Holy Spirit in our lives nurtures and sustains the love we have for one another as faithful believers. The love of the Beloved for faithful believers is always present within those who allow this Presence to be active in their lives. It is through the Presence of the Holy Spirit that we "love one another" and we "become one." It is through the Presence of the Holy Spirit that we are able to "love our neighbor as we do ourselves." It is through the Presence of the Holy Spirit that we are able to "do to others as we would have them do to us." It is through the Presence of the Holy Spirit that we are able to "love God with all of our heart, soul, and mind." With the Presence of the Holy Spirit in our lives the love of God shines through.

John 10:30 Jesus speaking to the elders of the Jewish faith: "The Father and I are one."

John 14:8-11 Philip said to him, "Lord, show us the Father, and we will be satisfied." Jesus said to him, "Have I been with you all this time, Philip, and you still do not know me? Whoever has seen me has seen the Father. How can you say, 'Show us the Father'? Do you not believe that I am in the Father and the Father is in me? The words that I say to you I do not speak on my own, but the Father who dwells in me does his works. Believe me that I am in the Father and the Father is in me, but if you do not, then believe [other ancient authorities add *me*] because of the works themselves.

John 14:18-20 "I will not leave you orphaned; I am coming to you. In a little while the world will no longer see me, but you will see me; because I live, you also will live. On that day you will know that I am in my Father, and you in me, and I in you."

John 17:10-11 "All mine are yours, and yours are mine, and I have been glorified in them. And now I am no longer in the world, but they are in the world, and I am coming to you. Holy Father, protect them in your name that you have given me, so that they may be one, as we are one.

John 17:20-26 "I ask not only on behalf of these but also on behalf of those who believe in me through their word, that they may all be one. As you, Father, are in me and I am in you, may they also be in us [other ancient authorities read *be one in us*], so that the world may believe that you have sent me. The glory that you have given me I have given them, so that they may be one, as we are one, I in them and you in me, that they may become completely one, so that the world may know that you have sent me and have loved them even as you have loved me. Father, I desire that those also, whom you have given me, may be with me where I am, to see my glory, which you have given me because you loved me before the foundation of the world.

"Righteous Father, the world does not know you, but I know you, and these know that you have sent me. I made your name known to them, and I will make it known, so that the love with which you have loved me may be in them and I in them."

The word *one* that is used here is the Greek word *heis*.

heis: One - Original Word: εἷς - KJV: a(-n, -ny, certain), + abundantly, man, one (another), only, other, some - NASB: one, first, one thing, alone, individual, one man, someone

Word Origin: [a primary numeral] - to be united most closely (in will, spirit), John 10:30; John 17:11, 21-23

When Jesus is speaking of being "one" with the Father, He is not speaking of being literally "one" as in "one in the same." In all the previous verses noted Jesus prays "that they [His disciples] may be one, as we are one." And, "that they may all be one. As you, Father, are in me and I am in you, may they also be in us, so that the world may believe that you have sent me." If we believe, if we are faithful, if we are disciples and followers of the teachings of Jesus Christ, then through the Presence of the Holy Spirit in us we become one with other faithful believers, the Beloved, and the Creator. The Presence is the unifying entity in the Deity. The Presence abides in all faithful believers who live according to the Gospel of Jesus Christ and do what is right and good in the eyes of God. The Presence cannot abide in a vessel that is full of lies and deception because the Presence *is* truth and truth cannot exist within a heart that lies.

The Presence of the Holy Spirit is the provision given to faithful believers which unites us in spirit with other faithful believers and with God. This union of the spirit is a powerful force within the life of faithful believers. Without the Presence of the Holy Spirit in our lives it is impossible to become united in spirit with other faithful believers and with God. The Presence is the unifying advocate of love and truth, the two most important elements of our spiritual lives. Without them we are spiritually dead.

***

## GOD IS THEY

1 Corinthians 13:9-12 For we know only in part, and we prophesy only in part, but when the complete comes, the partial will come to an end. When I was a child, I spoke like a child, I thought like a child, I reasoned like a child. When I became an adult, I put an end to childish ways. For now we see only a reflection, as in a mirror, but then we will see face to face. Now I know only in part; then I will know fully, even as I have been fully known.

This is not a new revelation. I ask that, as you continue reading this, keep the above scripture in mind: "For now we see only a reflection, as in a mirror, but then we will see face to face. Now I know only in part; then I will know fully, even as I have been fully known."

The Catholic Church and most of the mainstream Protestant churches around the world believe in the Holy Trinity: God the Father, Son, and Holy Spirit. That is not disputed. They teach that the Holy Trinity is three in one with an often-ambiguous explanation of what "three in one" means, emphasizing that it is one of the mysteries of God. From my over forty years of reading the Scriptures and meditating on them through prayer and fellowship with the Holy Spirit, I have come to accept that God; the Holy Trinity are one Deity comprised of three separate spirit entities; the Creator, the Beloved, and the Presence. What follows is how I came to that conclusion.

> John 4:23-24 Jesus speaking to the Samaritan woman at the well: "But the hour is coming and is now here when the true worshipers will worship the Father in spirit and truth, for the Father seeks such as these to worship him. God is spirit, and those who worship him must worship in spirit and truth."

First and foremost, as we have just discussed in the previous section, we have to realize and understand the truth that God is spirit. The Deity of God is spirit. God does not exist within a physical form as we exist. God is spirit. I fully believe this spirit form is tangible but not of flesh and blood. Jesus states this plainly to the Samaritan woman at the well: "God is spirit."

Some may argue that the spirit composition of God could be just one spirit being, but that still does not make sense according to the Scriptures.

> John 3:11 Jesus speaking to Nicodemus: "Very truly, I tell you, we speak of what we know and testify to what we have seen, yet you [the Greek word for *you* here is plural] do not receive our testimony."

Here Jesus is speaking to Nicodemus and he is speaking in plural throughout, "we speak," "we know and testify," "you [the Jewish elders] do not," and "our testimony." Now many would believe that Jesus is speaking of Him and the disciples when He says, "we" and "our" but this does not follow the structure of the conversation Jesus is having with Nicodemus.

First, Jesus is confronting Nicodemus with the subject matter of spiritual things versus the earthly thought behavior of the Jewish elders. Throughout John 3:1-21 Jesus is speaking to Nicodemus about spiritual or heavenly things and even challenges him in the midst of the conversation with, "Are you the teacher of Israel, and yet you do not understand these things? Very truly, I tell you, we speak of what we know and testify to what we have seen, yet you do not receive our testimony. If I have told you about earthly things and you do not believe, how can you believe if I tell you about heavenly things?"

So, who is Jesus referring to in speaking in plural? He is not referring to the disciples. At this stage of the ministry of Jesus, the disciples were following Jesus, but they did not have a clue to what was really going on. They were not spiritually in tune with all that the life of Jesus truly meant. The disciples' eyes had still not been open to all that was happening. They were unaware of the full purpose of the life of Jesus. The disciples' understanding would not come to fullness until after the ascension of Jesus Christ and the fulfillment of the Advocate, the Presence of the Holy Spirit, coming down from heaven upon them. So, clearly, Jesus was not speaking of Him and the disciples when He states, "we speak of what we know and testify to what we have seen, yet you do not receive our testimony." Jesus is clearly speaking of the plan of salvation brought forth by the Deity of God. Jesus is referring to the Deity of the Holy Trinity, as "we" and "our." Separate spirit entities.

Even further into John, look at what Jesus says.

John 5:31-38 "If I testify about myself, my testimony is not true. There is another who testifies on my behalf, and I know that his testimony to me is true. You sent messengers to John, and he testified to the truth. Not that I accept such human testimony, but I say these things so that you may be saved. He was a burning and shining lamp, and you were willing to rejoice for a while in his light. But I have a testimony greater than John's. The works that the Father has given me to complete, the very works that I am doing, testify on my behalf that the Father has sent me. And the Father who sent me has himself testified on my behalf. You have never heard his voice or seen his form, and you do not have his word abiding in you, because you do not believe him whom he has sent."

Jesus clearly distinguishes His existence from the existence of the Father. They are two different entities with two different roles within the Deity. Two different roles, not vying roles but roles that work within each other for the same purpose.

Again, hear what Jesus is saying.

John 8:12-18 Again Jesus spoke to them, saying, "I am the light of the world. Whoever follows me will never walk in darkness but will have the light of life." Then the Pharisees said to him, "You are testifying on your own behalf; your testimony is not valid." Jesus answered, "Even if I testify on my own behalf, my testimony is valid because I know where I have come from and where I am going, but you do not know where I come from or where I am going. You judge by human standards [Greek *according to the flesh*]; I judge no one. Yet even if I do judge, my judgment is valid, for it is not I alone who judge but I and the Father [other ancient authorities read *he*] who sent me. In your law it is written that the testimony of two witnesses is valid. I testify on my own behalf, and the Father who sent me testifies on my behalf."

John 14:22-23 Judas (not Iscariot) said to him, "Lord, how is it that you will reveal yourself to us and not to the world?" Jesus answered him, "Those who love me will keep my word, and my Father will love them, and we will come to them and make our home with them."

Within these verses, Jesus clearly distinguishes Himself from the Father. Two separate spirit entities. Listen to what Jesus said: "Those who love me will keep my word, and my Father will love them, and we will come to them and make our home with them." "...and *we* will come to them and make *our* home with them." This cannot be spoken more clearly.

John 14:15-17 "If you love me, you will keep [other ancient authorities read *me, keep*] my commandments. And I will ask the Father, and he will give you another Advocate [or *Helper* or *Comforter*], to be with you forever. This is the Spirit of truth, whom the world cannot receive because it neither sees him nor knows him. You know him because he abides with you, and he will be [other ancient authorities read *he is*] in [or *among*] you.

John 14:25-27 "I have said these things to you while I am still with you. But the Advocate [or *Helper* or *Comforter*], the Holy Spirit, whom the Father will send in my name, will teach you everything and remind you of all that I have said to you. Peace I leave with you; my peace I give to you. I do not give to you as the world gives. Do not let your hearts be troubled, and do not let them be afraid."

John 16:12-15 "I still have many things to say to you, but you cannot bear them now. When the Spirit of truth comes, he will guide you into all the truth, for he will not speak on his own but will speak whatever he hears, and he will declare to you the things that are to come. He will glorify me because

he will take what is mine and declare it to you. All that the
Father has is mine. For this reason I said that he will take what
is mine and declare it to you."

Within these verses, Jesus proclaims to the disciples of the coming of
the Presence of the Holy Spirit. As He addresses the disciples, Jesus clearly
introduces the Presence of the Holy Spirit as a separate entity within the
Deity of God whose purpose is to guide, counsel, and comfort the faithful.
This is the spirit of truth that abides in all who believe and are faithful.

Take note of what Jesus says in John 14:25-27: "The Advocate...will
teach you everything and remind you of all that I have said to you." This
is important concerning the power and the work of the Holy Spirit. The
Presence of the Holy Spirit in our lives is the greatest source of feeding
us what we need to say or do and the right time to say or do it. If we are
sensitive to the Holy Spirit, we will never be without the proper words or
actions God wants us to proclaim at any given time.

Genesis 1:2 NIV Now the earth was formless and empty,
darkness was over the surface of the deep, and the Spirit of
God was hovering over the waters.

From the very beginning of creation the Spirit of God, the Presence of
the Holy Spirit, has always been noted as separate from the Creator. From
Genesis to Revelation this holds true. The Presence of the Holy Spirit
completes the third spirit entity in the Deity of God.

John 3:10-12 Jesus answered him, "Are you the teacher of
Israel, and yet you do not understand these things? Very truly,
I tell you, we speak of what we know and testify to what we
have seen, yet you [The Greek word for *you* here and in 3:12 is
plural] do not receive our testimony. If I have told you about
earthly things and you do not believe, how can you believe if
I tell you about heavenly things?"

1 Corinthians 3:1-3a And so, brothers and sisters, I could not speak to you as spiritual people but rather as fleshly, as infants in Christ. I fed you with milk, not solid food, for you were not ready for solid food. Even now you are still not ready, for you are still fleshly.

God does not change, but as we learn, our understanding of God must grow. When Jesus Christ came to this earth, He challenged everyone to grow in their spiritual understanding of God. Every time the disciples, Pharisees, Sadducees, or scribes thought they had Him figured out, Jesus would throw them a curve to challenge them to think differently. God expects the same of us today.

It is time for faithful believers to grow up in their spiritual understanding and see God as God is. We have come to view God as more of a superhuman or super artificial intelligence rather than the all-powerful Creator of our planet, galaxy, and universe. We have come to view heaven as if it is just outside of our galaxy and that is so wrong to think like that. God is so much more than we can understand in our limited intelligence.

God is an all-powerful and omnipresent spirit Deity comprised of three separate entities: the Creator, the Beloved, and the Presence, which are one in absolute omnipotence, understanding, and operation. They each have Their specific role within the Holy Trinity, but They are one in Their collective spirit of action. There is a divine order within the Holy Trinity that operates in perfect unity, harmony, understanding, and peace toward Their purpose.

They are not human beings made of flesh, bone, and blood. They are spirit and reign in majesty. They are merciful and just in all Their ways. They love us with an unconditional love that transcends any form of love that we understand. But They are also a God of accountability to which we all will be answerable to on the day of judgment. We are called to love God with all of our heart, mind, soul, and strength. God calls us to love our neighbor as we do ourselves. These are the loving instructions we have been given.

God desires for us to believe and share Their love with all we come in contact, not just by spoken word, but with actions and compassion. If we do not do so, we are doing a disservice to those who are searching for truth and to the very Gospel we believe. God is They, and They are one Deity.

That being said, as we move forward with our study here and in Revelation, I will refer to Jesus Christ the Messiah, the man who came to this earth, gave us the Word, died on the cross, and rose from the dead for our salvation, redemption, and justification, in my commentary by using the pronouns of He/Him/His. This will keep with a continuity alongside the Scriptures as Jesus being male while He walked the earth.

But, as I am comfortable with it and have explained above in referring to God, I will use the pronouns They/Them/Their as I am speaking of God the Deity the Holy Trinity of the Creator, the Beloved, and the Presence through this writing. But, as I will not alter the Scripture verses, you will still see He/Him/His in the verses from the Scriptures as they have always been.

The Creator the one who imparts life and is committed to it; a progenitor (an ancestor in the direct line, a biologically ancestral form) with intimate connection and relationship to creation.

The Beloved The love of God incarnate. The absolute embodiment of true love. The Mediator that has provided salvation, redemption, and justification for all who believe and are faithful.

The Presence the Advocate (one who defends or maintains a cause or proposal). Our guide, counsellor, and comforter. The source of truth. The source of true love that makes us one with all faithful believers and God.

***

## GOD IS NEITHER MALE OR FEMALE

Mark 12:24-25 Jesus said to them, "Is not this the reason you are wrong, that you know neither the scriptures nor the power of God? For when people rise from the dead, they neither marry nor are given in marriage but are like angels in heaven."


1 Corinthians 2:9-10 and Isaiah 64:4 But, as it is written, "What no eye has seen, nor ear heard, nor the human heart conceived, what God has prepared for those who love him"— God has revealed to us through the Spirit, for the Spirit searches everything, even the depths of God.


1 Corinthians 13:11-12 When I was a child, I spoke like a child, I thought like a child, I reasoned like a child. When I became an adult, I put an end to childish ways. For now we see only a reflection, as in a mirror, but then we will see face to face. Now I know only in part; then I will know fully, even as I have been fully known.


1 Corinthians 15:53-55 For this perishable body must put on imperishability, and this mortal body must put on immortality. When this perishable body puts on imperishability and this mortal body puts on immortality, then the saying that is written will be fulfilled: "Death has been swallowed up in victory." "Where, O death, is your victory? Where, O death, is your sting?"


1 John 3:1-2 See what love the Father has given us, that we should be called children of God, and that is what we are. The reason the world does not know us is that it did not know him. Beloved, we are God's children now; what we will be has

not yet been revealed. What we do know is this: when he [or *it*] is revealed, we will be like him, for we will see him as he is.

This too is not a new revelation. There are no gender identities in heaven. God is God. The angels are angels. And we will be the children of God, "like angels." There will be no marrying or given in marriage in heaven. We will all be as one in the presence of our God and all of the heavenly hosts. It was humankind, primarily the male gender on this earth who chronicled the Bible and assigned the gender of male to all the heavenly beings; only because that is what they rationalized that they were, not because God said they were. Jesus clarifies this misconception in the verses from Mark 12:24-25.

Let me clarify that there is absolutely no question that the Beloved Jesus Christ was born and came into this world as a male. The Creator sent the Beloved to this world as the Messiah, Jesus Christ for the salvation of all people. That was necessary in the fulfillment of the prophecies. The Messiah in the Old Testament was always prophesied as a male that was to come. So, the Beloved had to come to this earth as a male. At the same time Jesus came as a man, He more importantly came to provide salvation, redemption, and justification for all humankind. *All* of humankind. In His teachings and sermons, Jesus emphasized a powerful message of inclusion to all genders and races. He preached a gospel that broke down walls of conservative and traditional thoughts. He came as a gift to the world not just to the male gender or Jewish race but to all. But I am not addressing the birth, life, death, and resurrection of the man Jesus Christ in this section. In this section I am addressing the Deity of God as the Creator, the Beloved, and the Presence that abide in Heaven.

Have you ever noticed that throughout the Bible, none of the angels or creatures are identified as females? All are identified as males. In all of the visions that are documented in the Old and New Testament, all of the heavenly beings are identified as male. Does this mean that only males are given heavenly duties? Are our minds and perspective of God and heaven that narrow and foolish?

After Jesus was resurrected, the Scriptures record that Mary did not recognize Jesus when she looked upon Him. She only recognized Him after

He spoke to her (John 20:11-18). The two disciples walking to Emmaus did not recognize Jesus at all while He walked with them and talked to them. It was not until He left their side and they discussed the manner in which He had spoken that they realized it was Jesus (Luke 24:13-35). When Jesus appeared before the disciples, the doors were locked, and yet there He stood (John 20:19-23). When some of the disciples left to go fishing all night, just after daybreak Jesus appeared on the shore and spoke to them. Once again, they did not recognize Him immediately (John 21:1-14). In pointing out these four verses, all I am saying is this: The body in which Jesus rose in was not the same body that He died in, and the only form of recognition to which they all responded was the way in which He spoke to them. But even then, He was still not in His eternal heavenly spirit form.

The writer of 1 Corinthians 13:11-12 encouraged us to understand that what we will experience in heaven is far beyond what we are able to comprehend with the finite minds we possess here on earth. When we pass into eternity, we will obtain knowledge and understanding of all that is. There will no longer be questions. We will have all of the answers. We will be complete in the presence of our God.

Jesus made clear in the Scriptures that there are no genders in heaven. All are spirit beings, tangible and with absolute knowledge and understanding, but with no gender. There are no physical identifying attributes in the eternal spirit body that is present in heaven. "We will know ourselves fully, even as we have been fully known" by God (1 Corinthians 13:12 paraphrased). But there will be no gender distinction.

You may ask yourself, *What about Jesus calling the Creator "Father?"* There is no denying that. So, let's look at that word in its fullest sense.

> Patēr - *patér* – *father*; one who *imparts* life and is *committed* to it; a progenitor (an ancestor in the direct line - a biologically ancestral form), bringing into being to pass on *the potential for likeness*.

*patér* ("father") is used of our heavenly *Father*. He imparts life, from physical birth to the gift of eternal life through the *second* birth (regeneration, being born again). Through ongoing sanctification, the believer more and more *resembles* their heavenly Father

*patér* ("father") refers to a begetter, originator, progenitor – one in "intimate connection and relationship" (Gesenius).

Israel looked at Abraham as being their father. Jesus tried to make them understand, more precisely, that the Creator was their Father, the source of their lives, the "one who *imparts* life and is *committed* to it." So, Jesus is not referring to the Creator as Father in the sense of being a male figure, the "Father" is indicative of being the source of our lives. This clarifies the statement that Jesus made in saying:

Matthew 23:9 "And call no one your father on earth, for you have one Father, the one in heaven."

Call no one else father, *or* call no one else your Creator, for the Creator is the only *true* imparter of life that is fully committed to it *if* we believe and accept that truth.

So, we see Father as being a title of position rather than an indication of gender. That is important.

And then there is God's wisdom.

Throughout the Old and New Testaments, in many verses and even in the teachings of Jesus, the wisdom of God is noted of feminine persuasion. The highest form of intellect from God is denoted as feminine. In the Old Testament, the Hebrew word for wisdom is *Chokmah*. It appears approximately 149 times in various verses. It is a feminine noun.

chokmah: wisdom, skill, wisely - Original Word: - □□□□□□□
Part of Speech: Noun Feminine

KJV: skilful, wisdom, wisely, wit - NASB: wisdom, skill, wisely, wits'

In Proverbs 4:3-9 Solomon remembers a time when he was a child and King David, his father, instructed him to "get wisdom."

Proverbs 4:3-9 When I was a son with my father (King David), tender and my mother's favorite, he taught me and said to me, "Let your heart hold fast my words; keep my commandments and live. Get wisdom; get insight: do not forget nor turn away from the words of my mouth. Do not forsake her, and she will keep you; love her, and she will guard you. The beginning of wisdom is this: get wisdom, and whatever else you get, get insight. Prize her highly, and she will exalt you; she will honor you if you embrace her. She will place on your head a fair garland; she will bestow on you a beautiful crown."

In the New Testament, the Greek word for wisdom is *Sophia*. It appears approximately fifty-one times in various verses. It is a feminine noun.

sophia: Wisdom - Original Word: σοφία - Part of Speech: Noun, Feminine

KJV: wisdom - NASB: wisdom, cleverness, learning

In Matthew 11:18-19 and Luke 7:33-35 Jesus speaks of God's wisdom.

Matthew 11:18-19 "For John came neither eating nor drinking, and they say, 'He has a demon'; the Son of Man came eating and drinking, and they say, 'Look, a glutton and a drunkard, a friend of tax collectors and sinners!' Yet wisdom is vindicated by her deeds [other ancient authorities read *children*]."

Luke 7:33-35 "For John the Baptist has come eating no bread and drinking no wine, and you say, 'He has a demon'; the Son of Man has come eating and drinking, and you say, 'Look, a glutton and a drunkard, a friend of tax collectors and sinners!' Nevertheless, wisdom is vindicated by all her children."

I encourage you to study the Scriptures yourself from cover to cover and you will see that what I have stated is accurate. In 1 Corinthians 3:19a, Paul goes on to even state, "For the wisdom of this world is foolishness with God." And so, we learn that *true* wisdom is the convergence of human knowledge and spiritual understanding. Without spiritual understanding there is no wisdom. True wisdom can be appropriated only through the study of the Scriptures and the Presence of the Holy Spirit within us. I will often comment when it is appropriate, "Science says that there is intelligent life out there, somewhere. I agree with that. God is that intelligent life."

I want to share a very sad truth with you. The reason I feel we should step away from using male pronouns for God. This is not a feminist perspective or a take on our modern culture. This is simple truth.

According to Statista, 90 percent of the perpetrators in sexual abuse are male. 98 percent of mass murders are carried out by males. Out of 21,504 homicides in 2023, 14,327 offenders were males, 1,898 offenders were female, and 5,279 were unsolved as to who the offender was.

According to the FBI, 80 percent of all robberies were performed by males, and 80 percent of violent crimes were performed by males.

According to the Office of Justice Programs, 75 percent of white-collar offenders are male.

When it comes to the seven deadly sins that God abhors the most pride, greed, lust, envy, gluttony, anger, and apathy it is the male gender that commits the greatest majority of these sins. It is these very sins that has caused and is causing most of the struggles, sorrow, and death that we are experiencing all around the world throughout history and at this present time. Males, ruling the governments of the world, murdering innocent people, raping females (children and adults alike), creating chaos, and refusing to work together for the betterment of humanity. Humankind's rejection of God has brought us to such as this.

Why do I make this point? It is my opinion, referring to a loving, merciful, and forgiving God as He/Him/His is a disservice to Their immense love for this creation. No wonder so many find it hard to view God as the loving, merciful, and forgiving God that They are. One cannot help but associate God with the human male ego, when referring to God as He/Him/His, especially in this day and age.

I believe it is time we grew up spiritually and acknowledged these truths. I strongly believe it is time we present God in this fullness of understanding. God is far greater than we can understand. God is far vaster in Their wisdom and perfection than we can understand. God is so much larger than our imaginations can comprehend. The greatest fault of the modern church is placing God and the love of God in a box and determining that God sees things as we do. That is a lie. God is so much more forgiving, so much more loving, so much more compassionate, so much more just, and so much more understanding than we are. Why? Because God is the only One who absolutely knows each one of us and the true motives and intentions of our hearts. Even at our worst, God loves us and is willing to forgive us if we only will accept Their love for us.

There are many who, from their years of studies of the Scriptures, know the truth that God is neither a male or female but is genderless. But they refuse to speak up. They justify it by saying it is not worth it, it is a moot point, it is not necessary for our faith, and it will just confuse people. I do not agree with this philosophy.

1 Corinthians 3:1-3 And so, brothers and sisters, I could not speak to you as spiritual people but rather as fleshly, as infants in Christ. I fed you with milk, not solid food, for you were not ready for solid food. Even now you are still not ready, for you are still fleshly. For as long as there is jealousy and quarreling [other ancient authorities add *and dissensions*] among you, are you not fleshly and behaving according to human inclinations?

It is time we spoke up about what we know is true concerning God and the Scriptures. It is time we laid aside doctrinal and denominational differences and focused solely on the foundational principles of the teachings of Jesus within the Scriptures and throw away the man-made doctrines.

The truth be known, if you, with a committed and open heart of faith in God, sincerely follow the powerful teachings of Jesus found in the Gospel of John along with the follow-up assurances found in the book of First John, you will do right in the eyes of God and be saved. If you commit your life to following the very simple truth found in those two writings, you can set the rest of the Scriptures aside. I am not saying that reading the rest of the Scriptures is not profitable to edifying your spirit, I am saying the gift of love and salvation for all of humankind is found in those two writings. Those writings alone are enough to change the world. To achieve a life that is committed to walking in the truths within those writings is a righteous life and pleasing in the eyes of God. Those two writings are pure salvation that is stripped of all the man-made doctrines and denominational hearsay.

God is love. God is forgiving. God is just. God is spirit. God is They. God is genderless.

Hebrews 13:8-9 Jesus Christ is the same yesterday and today and forever. Do not be carried away by all kinds of strange teachings, for it is good for the heart to be strengthened by grace, not by regulations about food [Greek *not by foods* (or laws made by man)] which have not benefited those who observe them.

The pureness of the Scriptures has been perverted for the cause and profit of the contemporary church. Don't look to the brick-and-mortar church as your source of truth or growth. All you need to do is to look to the Scriptures God has provided for us, though written by the hand of man, handed down and translated by the hand of man, and presented to us with all the flaws of humanity within them, the truth that God wants us to see and live by is still there. God loves Their creation and that love is so superior to any love that can be found on this earth. Live your life for that love, and you will do well.

There is a very important truth that we all have to remember in all of this concerning God: God's greatest concern is our eternal soul. God's perspective is always eternal. God's only interest for each of us on this earth during our lives here is whether we accept Their love and plan of salvation. Everything else that this world offers us is irrelevant in God's eyes. It is just a distraction for us from seeing what the truth is. That is the spiritual battle for our soul between God and Satan.

God loves us and wants us to believe and have faith that there is an eternity that awaits all of us. Where we spend that eternity is up to us. C.S. Lewis said it best, "If you live for the next world, you get this one in the deal; but if you live only for this world, you lose them both."

***

## A FINAL THOUGHT

What do you really believe about God? Let us break it down to very basic logic. If you profess to be a believer and you are basing your belief and faith on the book that is known as The Holy Bible, it does not matter which mainstream translation you might read. In principle, they all say the same thing. So, let us go with that basic premise.

Let me say here, I am addressing only those who profess the Christian faith. I am not judging anyone outside of that faith. God is the judge of all. I do not have enough understanding outside of the Christian faith to address what is believed about any other gods.

To get back to my logic, let us say you belong to any of the mainstream religious sects, be it Catholic, Greek Orthodox, or any primary Protestant church such as Lutheran, Presbyterian, Methodist, Baptist, Pentecostal, Seventh Day, or Independent. The basic core of beliefs in all of these sects is the same. There is the Holy Trinity, which is God the Creator, the Beloved, and the Presence. That being said, the core of beliefs is that the Creator created the earth and sent Jesus Christ the Beloved, as the Messiah, to this earth to provide salvation, redemption, and justification for all who believe, and then provided the Presence of the Holy Spirit to all who believe to be our guide, our counselor, and our comforter. This is the foundation of all Christian faith.

Now, if that is what we say we believe, that we believe in the God of The Holy Bible; if we believe that God is the Almighty, the Great Creator, the Divine Justice, the First and the Last, the Beginning and the Ending, the Alpha and Omega, and the Great I Am; if we believe that God is our Provider, our Protector, our Healer, our Righteousness, our Sanctifier, our Peace, the God who is there, and our Shepherd, then we must not, we cannot put our restricted limitations on who God is with our finite minds and knowledge. God is infallible, limitless, and wiser than all of us put together. Why do we put limits on a God who has no limits?

We claim that God is eternal, that They were, are, and always will be. That means eternally. Forever. They never have not existed. Do you get that? We cannot comprehend that. And there are those who claim we are the only creation when the Scriptures plainly state that before humankind existed, God had created other beings. And from what I believe, God is still creating outside of our universe. Why would you limit such a magnificent and awesome God? Why would you be so closed and narrow-minded?

If we say that God is love and has prepared for us a paradise that is so amazing to behold, why do we cling so tightly to this earth? There is an old saying, "Everybody wants to go to Heaven, but nobody wants to die." Why would we be so eager to be here when, if we truly believe what we say, there is such a wondrous home waiting for us in eternity? If we believe in such a loving God and we are doing what is right and good, why do we live contrary to that? Why are we not living in such a way that expresses that security and makes others want to believe also. The disciples surely did. The Early Church lived that way. I am not saying we should wish for death, but we should definitely be living in anticipation of our eternal blessing and seeing the wondrous glory that awaits us in the presence of our loving God.

We are simply passing through this life on our way to the next. We are immortal and eternal; we just have not received our spirit body yet. Make this real in your life. God created humankind. God is not a human. God far exceeds anything that we can comprehend. We are the creation, not God. We owe our existence to God. So, in this life we have two choices: to believe in God and live like we believe in God or not believe in God and live like we do not believe in God. Don't get stuck being lukewarm. It is that simple. It is my hope that you will choose to believe.

# THE WORLD IS ON FIRE

"The world is on fire." We have heard this common catchphrase over the last century concerning global warming, but there is more to it than that. It is a sign of the times. It is a warning. The acceleration of technology has created a flame of communication, both good and bad, to spread around the world like wildfire. Prior to the advent of the modern newspaper in the 1600s, the telephone in the 1880s, the radio in the 1920s, and the television in the 1930s, news was slow to spread. The world was much larger, and local communities shaped people's perspective of the world. Prior to those innovations, to hear of world events took weeks, months, years, and to some, never, due to the logistics of their communities and homes.

As communications technology progressed, the world began to shrink. We began receiving newspapers at our door step each morning. We were not only able to make a local phone call on our telephones; we could place long-distance calls across the country and even to other countries on the other side of the world. The radio airwaves began to expand, and soon we could hear news from around the globe. The television went from broadcasting only from daybreak to late night to broadcasting twenty-four hours a day with programs and shows that covered a range of interests.

Over the last thirty-five years, technology has progressed at a rate much faster than ever anticipated. The newspaper, along with any other form of paper reading, has become obsolete to many. The cell phone has exploded in use and become our digital reading source—telephone, radio, and television, all wrapped up into one single small device. We receive personal messages, photographs, videos, entertainment, and news instantly. We can video chat with someone halfway around the world in real-time to find out what is happening. You would think that with all of these resources in a much smaller world, humankind would be able to live more harmoniously. Yet, it does not. Why?

I have been working with computers since 1979 when my employer bought an IBM computer for the company to track our inventory, payables, and receivables. I created the inventory system and entered all of the pertinent information of description, costs, and selling prices. It was exciting using that relatively new technology.

From there, my work in professional audio technology saw a continued advancement. I purchased my first cell phone in 1995. I continued using computers throughout my professional work life, and in 1998, I purchased my first home computer. Since then, I have always had one or two computers for my personal use.

I have watched the growth of the internet along with all of the technology that has followed through the years. What caught my spiritual attention, though, was the sudden growth of virtual reality, deep fakes, and artificial intelligence. Evil has raised its head with the advancement of these technologies and has made itself known. I am certain that all who read this book are aware of the lies and deception that these technologies have thrust into our lives. You read and hear about them on the news on a daily basis. Identity theft has become an epidemic. You have to be excessively careful with your email and internet activity.

I see the growing technology of artificial intelligence as the infrastructure for the "image of the beast" spoken of in Revelation. The "image of the beast" described in Revelation possesses the ability to know who is doing what, communicate and listen as a human, reason, think, deceive, create a cashless society, produce a "brand" that would be required for anyone to buy, sell, or trade, and even cause death to those who are not obedient. Sixty years ago, many of us would never believe this could even happen in our lifetime. But it has. We will discuss this more when we get to the section of Chapter 16 concerning the "image of the beast."

These technologies have progressed the deception of "the lie." Through the last several decades the "lie" became "white lies." "White Lies" became "untruths." "Untruths" became "embellishments of the truth." "Embellishments of the truth" became "misinformation."

Misinformation has become "fake news." With each softening of the delusion and twisted verbiage along with the technology to deceive, the lines between truth and lies have become massively blurred. It has become harder to discern what is true. This is how the lie has disguised itself and has created such confusion among us. If we are unable to discern the truth from the lie, evil has won. I encourage you to seek the truth and resist the lie.

Research this yourself. I Googled the following questions.

*How many fact-checking websites are available on the internet?* I found lists ranging from 126 to 439 different fact-checking websites. Duke University's "Duke Reporters' Lab" has established the most thorough research on this subject. These fact-checking websites were solely created to help discern what is true and what is a lie on the internet. Think about that. Lies and deception have become so prevalent that we need websites to help us determine what is truth.

*How many deep-fake images and videos are circulating on the internet?* There are many reports concerning this subject matter. IBM reports that deep-fake images increased from three thousand in 2019 to over one million by March of 2020. University of Buffalo reports have deep-fakes surpassing eight-million at the end of 2025.

*How many artificial intelligence images and videos are circulating on the internet?* Again, there are multiple reports on this subject matter. Everypixel.com has a journal noting that over fifteen-billion AI images and videos are circulating on the internet at the end of 2025.

All these deceptive fake images and fake videos have created this turmoil. Why? Because they are all part of the lie. No wonder we find ourselves questioning everything. No wonder we are so desperate to find truth.

There is no question the good that technology provides us in the medical field along with the physical comfort, entertainment, and the "smart" security it has brought to us within our homes, but the acceleration of that technology has also brought upon us an avalanche of evil. In our quest to progress and create to be "the newest," "most innovative," or "most realistic," that acceleration has brought about a resource for evil for which we were not technologically prepared. The world is on fire from these lies disguised as truth. The advent of the "image of the beast" is upon us.

The need to demonstrate the love of Jesus has never been greater. The need to know our loving God has never been greater. With each day the end of the ages grows nearer.

Since the beginning of my search to know God over the last forty-plus years, I concentrated on finding the truth. In doing so, I became more and more focused on God's plan for humanity. I had four questions I wanted answered. I wanted to know: Why are we created? What makes us different from all of the rest of God's creations? What is our purpose? Where will it all lead?

I want to provide you with the answers that I have found to those questions. I hope that you will also search the Scriptures and find the answers to the questions you have. That is the challenge. Seek the truth. Know the truth. Live the truth.

# THE THREAD OF TRUTH

From the Tree of Life and river at the beginning of the Scriptures (Genesis 2:8-10) to the Tree of Life and river at the end of the Scriptures (Revelation 22:1-5) runs, what I call, the Thread of Truth for eternal life. The fundamental character and principle of a faithful believer was established by God early in the Scriptures when God declared to Cain, "If you do what is right, will you not be accepted?" (Genesis 4:7).

That truth is woven throughout the Scriptures from beginning to end. The question you might ask is, "What is right in the eyes of God?" That is answered by Jesus in the Scriptures when it states in Matthew and Luke: "In everything do to others as you would have them do to you, for this is the Law and the Prophets" (Matthew 7:12 and Luke 6:31).

Jesus further expounds on this truth in Matthew, Mark, and Luke by stating, "'Love the Lord your God with all your heart and with all your soul and with all your mind.' This is the greatest and first commandment. And a second is like it: 'You shall love your neighbor as yourself.' On these two commandments hang all the Law and the Prophets" (Matthew 22:37-40, Mark 12:30-31, and Luke 10:27).

We all know what is right, but it is only those who do what is right in the eyes of God who are deemed righteous. We are not just talking about being a good person; we are talking about doing what is right. That is two different distinctions of character. A person who does what is right in the eyes of God will be blessed with eternal life in the presence of God. A good person may find themselves lacking when they stand in judgment. I will address this issue more in Chapters 4 and 5.

I hope you will seek to do what is right and what is good in the eyes of God for this is the very foundation of life as a faithful believer. Whether you are at home, at work, among family, among strangers, on a bus or a plane, at the grocery store, at the gas station, wherever you may be, in your actions, from your heart, do what is right and good in the eyes of God. This is our calling. It cannot be anything less.

***

As mentioned in my prior paragraphs, the "Thread of Truth" is woven through the Scriptures from Genesis where we find the Tree of Life and the river watering the garden to Revelation where the Tree of Life and the river once again appear. In Genesis 2:8-10 and 3:22-24, we are introduced to the Tree of Life and the river.

> Genesis 2:8-10 - NIV Now the Lord God had planted a garden in the east, in Eden; and there he put the man he had formed. The Lord God made all kinds of trees grow out of the ground—trees that were pleasing to the eye and good for food. In the middle of the garden were the <u>tree of life</u> and the tree of the knowledge of good and evil. A <u>river</u> watering the garden flowed from Eden; from there it was separated into four headwaters.

> Genesis 3:22-24 - NIV And the Lord God said, "The man has now become like one of us, knowing good and evil. He must not be allowed to reach out his hand and take also from the *tree of life* and eat, and live forever." So the Lord God banished him from the Garden of Eden to work the ground from which he had been taken. After he drove the man out, he placed on the east side of the Garden of Eden cherubim

and a flaming sword flashing back and forth to guard the way
to the *tree of life.*

In Genesis 4:6-7, we are presented the first verse of the "Thread of
Truth." From this moment on, it weaves itself throughout the Scriptures
all the way to the end of Revelation.

> Genesis 4:6-7 - NIV Then the Lord said to Cain, "Why are
> you angry? Why is your face downcast? If you do *what is
> right,* will you not be accepted? But if you do not do what
> is right, sin is crouching at your door; it desires to have you,
> but you must rule over it."

> Genesis 6:9 - NIV This is the account of Noah and his family.
> Noah was a *righteous* man, blameless among the people of his
> time, and he walked faithfully with God.

> Genesis 15:6 - NIV Abram believed the Lord, and he credited
> it to him as *righteousness.*

> Genesis 18:18-19 - NIV Abraham will surely become a great
> and powerful nation, and all nations on earth will be blessed
> through him. For I have chosen him, so that he will direct his
> children and his household after him to keep the way of the
> Lord by doing *what is right* and just, so that the Lord will
> bring about for Abraham what he has promised him.

Exodus 15:26 - NIV He said, "If you listen carefully to the Lord your God and do *what is right* in his eyes, if you pay attention to his commands and keep all his decrees, I will not bring on you any of the diseases I brought on the Egyptians, for I am the Lord, who heals you."

Deuteronomy 6:18 - NIV Do *what is right* and good in the Lord's sight, so that it may go well with you and you may go in and take over the good land the Lord promised on oath to your ancestors.

Deuteronomy 6:24-25 - NRSVUE "Then the Lord commanded us to observe all these statutes, to fear the Lord our God, for our lasting good, so as to keep us alive, as is now the case. If we diligently observe this entire commandment before the Lord our God, as he has commanded us, *we will be in the right.*"

Deuteronomy 12:24-25 - NIV You must not eat the blood; pour it out on the ground like water. Do not eat it, so that it may go well with you and your children after you, because you will be doing *what is right* in the eyes of the Lord.

Deuteronomy 12:28 - NIV Be careful to obey all these regulations I am giving you, so that it may always go well with you and your children after you, because you will be doing *what is good and right* in the eyes of the Lord your God.

Deuteronomy 13:17b-18 - NIV Then the Lord will turn from his fierce anger, will show you mercy, and will have compassion on you. He will increase your numbers, as he promised on oath to your ancestors because you obey the Lord your God by keeping all his commands that I am giving you today and doing *what is right* in his eyes.

Deuteronomy 21:8-9 - NIV "Accept this atonement for your people Israel, whom you have redeemed, Lord, and do not hold your people guilty of the blood of an innocent person." Then the bloodshed will be atoned for, and you will have purged from yourselves the guilt of shedding innocent blood, since you have done *what is right* in the eyes of the Lord.

1 Samuel 12:23 - NIV As for me, far be it from me that I should sin against the Lord by failing to pray for you. And I will teach you the way that is *good and right*.

2 Samuel 8:15 - NIV David reigned over all Israel, doing *what was just and right* for all his people.

1 Kings 3:9 - NIV So give your servant a discerning heart to govern your people and to *distinguish between right and wrong*. For who is able to govern this great people of yours?

1 Kings 3:6 - NIV Solomon answered, "You have shown great kindness to your servant, my father David, because he was faithful to you and *righteous* and upright in heart. You have continued this great kindness to him and have given him a son to sit on his throne this very day."

1 Kings 8:35-36 - NIV When the heavens are shut up and there is no rain because your people have sinned against you, and when they pray toward this place and give praise to your name and turn from their sin because you have afflicted them, then hear from heaven and forgive the sin of your servants, your people Israel. Teach them the *right* way to live, and send rain on the land you gave your people for an inheritance.

1 Kings 11:33 - NIV  "I will do this because they have forsaken me and worshiped Ashtoreth the goddess of the Sidonians, Chemosh the god of the Moabites, and Molek the god of the Ammonites, and have not walked in obedience to me, nor done *what is right* in my eyes, nor kept my decrees and laws as David, Solomon's father, did."

1 Kings 11:38 - NIV "If you do whatever I command you and walk in obedience to me and do *what is right* in my eyes by obeying my decrees and commands, as David my servant did, I will be with you. I will build you a dynasty as enduring as the one I built for David and will give Israel to you."

1 Kings 14:8 - NIV "I tore the kingdom away from the house of David and gave it to you, but you have not been like my servant David, who kept my commands and followed me with all his heart, doing only *what was right* in my eyes."

1 Kings 15:5 - NIV For David had done *what was right* in the eyes of the Lord and had not failed to keep any of the Lord's commands all the days of his life—except in the case of Uriah the Hittite.

1 Kings 15:11 - NIV Asa did *what was right* in the eyes of the Lord, as his father David had done.

1 Kings 22:43 - NIV In everything he followed the ways of his father Asa and did not stray from them; he did *what was right* in the eyes of the Lord. The high places, however, were not removed, and the people continued to offer sacrifices and burn incense there.

2 Kings 10:30 - NIV The Lord said to Jehu, "Because you have done well in accomplishing *what is right* in my eyes and have done to the house of Ahab all I had in mind to do, your descendants will sit on the throne of Israel to the fourth generation."

2 Kings 12:2 - NIV Joash did *what was right* in the eyes of the Lord all the years Jehoiada the priest instructed him.

2 Kings 14:3 - NIV He [Amaziah] did *what was right* in the eyes of the Lord, but not as his father David had done. In everything he followed the example of his father Joash.

2 Kings 15:3 - NIV He [Azariah] did *what was right* in the eyes of the Lord, just as his father Amaziah had done.

2 Kings 15:34 - NIV He [Jotham] did *what was right* in the eyes of the Lord, just as his father Uzziah had done.

2 Kings 18:3 - NIV He [Hezekiah] did *what was right* in the eyes of the Lord, just as his father David had done.

2 Kings 22:2 - NIV He [Josiah] did *what was right* in the eyes of the Lord and followed completely the ways of his father David, not turning aside to the right or to the left.

1 Chronicles 18:14 - NIV David reigned over all Israel, doing *what was just and right* for all his people.

2 Chronicles 6:26-27 - NIV When the heavens are shut up and there is no rain because your people have sinned against you, and when they pray toward this place and give praise to your name and turn from their sin because you have afflicted

them, then hear from heaven and forgive the sin of your servants, your people Israel. Teach them the *right* way to live, and send rain on the land you gave your people for an inheritance.

2 Chronicles 14:2 - NIV Asa did *what was good and right* in the eyes of the Lord his God.

2 Chronicles 20:32 - NIV He [Jehoshaphat] followed the ways of his father Asa and did not stray from them; he did *what was right* in the eyes of the Lord.

2 Chronicles 24:2 - NIV Joash did *what was right* in the eyes of the Lord all the years of Jehoiada the priest.

2 Chronicles 25:2 - NIV He [Amaziah] did *what was right* in the eyes of the Lord, but not wholeheartedly.

2 Chronicles 26:4 - NIV He [Uzziah] did *what was right* in the eyes of the Lord, just as his father Amaziah had done.

2 Chronicles 27:2 - NIV He [Jotham] did *what was right* in the eyes of the Lord, just as his father Uzziah had done, but unlike him he did not enter the temple of the Lord. The people, however, continued their corrupt practices.

2 Chronicles 29:2 - NIV He [Hezekiah] did *what was right* in the eyes of the Lord, just as his father David had done.

2 Chronicles 31:20 - NIV This is what Hezekiah did throughout Judah, doing *what was good and right* and faithful before the Lord his God.

2 Chronicles 34:2 - NIV He [Josiah] did *what was right* in the eyes of the Lord and followed the ways of his father David, not turning aside to the right or to the left.

Nehemiah 9:13- NIV You came down on Mount Sinai; you spoke to them from heaven. You gave them regulations and laws that are *just and right*, and decrees and commands that are good.

Job 17:9 - NIV "Nevertheless, the *righteous* will hold to their ways, and those with clean hands will grow stronger."

Job 32:7-9 - NIV "I thought, 'Age should speak; advanced years should teach wisdom.' But it is the spirit in a person, the breath of the Almighty, that gives them understanding. It is not only the old who are wise, not only the aged who understand *what is right*."

Job 34:4 - NIV "Let us discern for ourselves *what is right*; let us learn together what is good."

Psalm 1:6 - NIV For the Lord watches over the way of the *righteous*, but the way of the wicked leads to destruction.

Psalm 11:5 - NIV The Lord examines the *righteous*, but the wicked, those who love violence, he hates with a passion.

Psalm 15:1-2 - NRSVUE O Lord, who may abide in your tent? Who may dwell on your holy hill? Those who walk blamelessly and *do what is right* and speak the truth from their heart.

Psalm 18:24 - NIV The Lord has rewarded me according to my *righteousness*, according to the cleanness of my hands in his sight.

Psalm 19:8 - NIV The precepts of the Lord are *right*, giving joy to the heart. The commands of the Lord are radiant, giving light to the eyes.

Psalm 23:1-3 - NIV The Lord is my shepherd, I lack nothing. He makes me lie down in green pastures, he leads me beside quiet waters, he refreshes my soul. He guides me along the *right* paths for his name's sake.

Psalm 25:9 - NIV He guides the humble in *what is right* and teaches them his way.

Psalm 32:11 - NIV Rejoice in the Lord and be glad, you *righteous*; sing, all you who are upright in heart!

Psalm 33:4 - NIV For the word of the Lord is *right and true*; he is faithful in all he does.

Psalm 34:15 - NIV The eyes of the Lord are on the *righteous*, and his ears are attentive to their cry.

Psalm 37:25 - NIV I was young and now I am old, yet I have never seen the *righteous* forsaken or their children begging bread.

Psalm 37:39 - NIV The salvation of the *righteous* comes from the Lord; he is their stronghold in time of trouble.

Psalm 51:4 - NIV Against you, you only, have I sinned and done what is evil in your sight; so *you are right* in your verdict and justified when you judge.

Psalm 51:10 - NRSVUE Create in me a clean heart, O God, and put a new and *right spirit* within me.

Psalm 64:10 - NIV The *righteous* will rejoice in the Lord and take refuge in him; all the upright in heart will glory in him!

Psalm 99:4 - NIV The King is mighty, he loves justice— you have established equity; in Jacob you have done *what is just and right*.

Psalm 106:3 - NIV Blessed are those who act justly, who always do *what is right*.

Psalm 119:137 - NIV You are righteous, Lord, and your laws are *right*.

Psalm 146:8 - NIV The Lord gives sight to the blind, the Lord lifts up those who are bowed down, the Lord loves the *righteous*.

Proverbs 1:1-6 - NIV The proverbs of Solomon son of David, king of Israel: for gaining wisdom and instruction; for understanding words of insight; for receiving instruction in prudent behavior, doing *what is right* and just and fair; for giving prudence to those who are simple, knowledge and discretion to the young—let the wise listen and add to their learning, and let the discerning get guidance—for understanding proverbs and parables, the sayings and riddles of the wise.

Proverbs 2:9-11 - NIV Then you will understand *what is right* and just and fair—every good path. For wisdom will enter your heart, and knowledge will be pleasant to your soul. Discretion will protect you, and understanding will guard you.

Proverbs 2:20 - NIV Thus you will walk in the ways of the good and keep to the paths of the *righteous*.

Proverbs 8:6 - NIV Listen, for I have trustworthy things to say; I open my lips to speak *what is right*.

Proverbs 8:9 - NIV To the discerning all of them are *right*; they are upright to those who have found knowledge.

Proverbs 10:16 - NRSVUE The wages of the *righteous* is life, but the earnings of the wicked are sin and death.

Proverbs 16:13 - NIV Kings take pleasure in honest lips; they value the one who speaks *what is right.*

Proverbs 20:11 - NRSVUE Even children make themselves known by their acts, by whether *what they do is pure and right.*

Proverbs 21:3 - NIV To do *what is right* and just is more acceptable to the Lord than sacrifice.

Proverbs 21:7 - NIV The violence of the wicked will drag them away, for they refuse to do *what is right.*

Proverbs 23:15-16 - NIV My son, if your heart is wise, then my heart will be glad indeed; my inmost being will rejoice when your lips speak *what is right.*

Proverbs 23:19 - NIV Listen, my son, and be wise, and set your heart on the *right* path.

Proverbs 28:5 - NIV Evildoers do not understand *what is right*, but those who seek the Lord understand it fully.

Isaiah 1:17 - NIV Learn to do *right*; seek justice. Defend the oppressed. Take up the cause of the fatherless; plead the case of the widow.

Isaiah 7:14-15 - NIV Therefore the Lord himself will give you a sign: The virgin will conceive and give birth to a son, and will call him Immanuel. He will be eating curds and honey when he knows enough to reject the wrong and *choose the right*.

Isaiah 16:5 - NIV Then a throne shall be established in steadfast love in the tent of David, and on it shall sit in faithfulness a ruler who seeks justice and is swift to do *what is right*.

Isaiah 26:7 - NIV The path of the *righteous* is level; you, the Upright One, make the way of the *righteous* smooth.

Isaiah 28:26 - NIV His God instructs him and teaches him the *right* way.

Isaiah 33:14b-16 - NIV Who of us can dwell with the consuming fire? Who of us can dwell with everlasting burning?" Those who walk *righteously* and speak *what is right*, who reject gain from extortion and keep their hands from accepting bribes, who stop their ears against plots of murder and shut their eyes against contemplating evil—they are the ones who will dwell on the heights, whose refuge will be the mountain fortress. Their bread will be supplied, and water will not fail them.

Isaiah 40:13-14 - NIV Who can fathom the Spirit of the Lord, or instruct the Lord as his counselor? Whom did the Lord consult to enlighten him, and who taught him the *right* way? Who was it that taught him knowledge, or showed him the path of understanding?

Isaiah 45:19 - NIV "I have not spoken in secret, from somewhere in a land of darkness; I have not said to Jacob's descendants, 'Seek me in vain.' I, the Lord, speak the truth; I declare *what is right*."

Isaiah 51:7 - NIV "Hear me, you who know *what is right*, you people who have taken my instruction to heart: Do not fear the reproach of mere mortals or be terrified by their insults.

Isaiah 53:11 - NIV After he has suffered, he will see the light of life and be satisfied; by his knowledge my *righteous* servant will justify many, and he will bear their iniquities.

Isaiah 56:1- NIV This is what the Lord says: "Maintain justice and do *what is right*, for my salvation is close at hand and my righteousness will soon be revealed.

Isaiah 58:2 - NIV For day after day they seek me out; they seem eager to know my ways, as if they were a nation that does *what is right* and has not forsaken the commands of its God. They ask me for just decisions and seem eager for God to come near them.

Isaiah 64:5a - NIV You come to the help of those who gladly do *right*, who remember your ways.

Jeremiah 8:6 - NIV I have listened attentively, but they do not say *what is right*. None of them repent of their wickedness, saying, "What have I done?" Each pursues their own course like a horse charging into battle.

Jeremiah 22:3 - NIV This is what the Lord says: Do *what is just and right*. Rescue from the hand of the oppressor the one who has been robbed. Do no wrong or violence to the foreigner, the fatherless or the widow, and do not shed innocent blood in this place.

Jeremiah 22:15 - NIV Does it make you a king to have more and more cedar? Did not your father have food and drink? He did *what was right* and just, so all went well with him.

Jeremiah 23:5 - NIV "The days are coming," declares the Lord, "when I will raise up for David a righteous Branch, a King who will reign wisely and do *what is just and right* in the land."

Jeremiah 33:15 - NIV "In those days and at that time I will make a righteous Branch sprout from David's line; he will do *what is just and right* in the land."

Jeremiah 34:15 - NRSVUE You yourselves recently repented and did *what was right* in my sight by proclaiming liberty to one another, and you made a covenant before me in the house that is called by my name,

Ezekiel 18:19 - NIV "Yet you ask, 'Why does the son not share the guilt of his father?' Since the son has done *what is just and right* and has been careful to keep all my decrees, he will surely live."

Ezekiel 18:21 - NIV "But if a wicked person turns away from all the sins they have committed and keeps all my decrees and does *what is just and right*, that person will surely live; they will not die."

Ezekiel 18:27 - NIV But if a wicked person turns away from the wickedness they have committed and does *what is just and right*, they will save their life.

Ezekiel 33:14-16 - NIV "And if I say to a wicked person, 'You will surely die,' but they then turn away from their sin and do *what is just and right*— if they give back what they took in pledge for a loan, return what they have stolen, follow the decrees that give life, and do no evil—that person will surely live; they will not die. None of the sins that person has committed will be remembered against them. They have done <u>what is just and right</u>; they will surely live."

Ezekiel 33:19 - NIV And if a wicked person turns away from their wickedness and does *what is just and right*, they will live by doing so.

Ezekiel 45:9 - NIV "This is what the Sovereign Lord says: You have gone far enough, princes of Israel! Give up your violence and oppression and do *what is just and right*. Stop dispossessing my people, declares the Sovereign Lord."

Daniel 4:27 - NIV "Therefore, Your Majesty, be pleased to accept my advice: Renounce your sins by doing *what is right*, and your wickedness by being kind to the oppressed. It may be that then your prosperity will continue."

Daniel 4:37 - NIV "Now I, Nebuchadnezzar, praise and exalt and glorify the King of heaven, because everything he does is *right* and all his ways are just. And those who walk in pride he is able to humble."

Hosea 14:9 - NIV Who is wise? Let them realize these things. Who is discerning? Let them understand. The ways of the Lord are *right*; the *righteous* walk in them, but the rebellious stumble in them.

Malachi 3:18 - NIV And you will again see the distinction between the *righteous* and the wicked, between those who serve God and those who do not.

Matthew 5:6 - NIV "Blessed are those who hunger and thirst for *righteousness*, for they will be filled."

Matthew 7:12 - NRSVUE "*In everything* do to others as you would have them do to you, for this is the Law and the Prophets."

Matthew 11:19 - NIV "The Son of Man came eating and drinking, and they say, 'Here is a glutton and a drunkard, a friend of tax collectors and sinners.' But wisdom is proved *right* by her deeds."

Matthew 13:43 - NIV "Then the *righteous* will shine like the sun in the kingdom of their Father. Whoever has ears, let them hear."

Matthew 22:34-40 - NRSVUE When the Pharisees heard that he had silenced the Sadducees, they gathered together, 35 and one of them, an expert in the law, asked him a question to test him. "Teacher, which commandment in the law is the greatest?" He said to him, " *'You shall love the Lord your God with all your heart and with all your soul and with all your mind.'* This is the greatest and first commandment. And a second is like it: *'You shall love your neighbor as yourself.'* On these two commandments hang all the Law and the Prophets."

Matthew 25:46 - NIV "Then they will go away to eternal punishment, but the *righteous* to eternal life."

Mark 12:28-31 - NRSVUE One of the scribes came near and heard them disputing with one another, and seeing that he answered them well he asked him, "Which commandment is the first of all?" Jesus answered, "The first is, 'Hear, O Israel: the Lord our God, the Lord is one; *you shall love the Lord your God with all your heart and with all your soul and with all your mind and with all your strength.'* The second is this, *'You shall love your neighbor as yourself.' There is no other commandment greater than these."*

Luke 1:5-6 - NIV In the time of Herod king of Judea there was a priest named Zechariah, who belonged to the priestly division of Abijah; his wife Elizabeth was also a descendant of Aaron. Both of them were *righteous* in the sight of God, observing all the Lord's commands and decrees blamelessly.

Luke 2:25 - NIV Now there was a man in Jerusalem called Simeon, who was *righteous* and devout. He was waiting for the consolation of Israel, and the Holy Spirit was on him.

Luke 6:31 - NRSVUE *"Do to others* as you would have them do to you."

Luke 10:25-28 - NRSVUE An expert in the law stood up to test Jesus. "Teacher," he said, *"what must I do to inherit eternal life?"* He [Jesus] said to him, "What is written in the law? What do you read there?" He [the Scribe] answered, *"You shall love the Lord your God with all your heart and with all your soul and with all your strength and with all your mind and your neighbor as yourself."* And he [Jesus] said to him, *"You have given the right answer; do this, and you will live."*

Luke 12:57-59 - NIV "Why don't you judge for yourselves *what is right*? As you are going with your adversary to the magistrate, try hard to be reconciled on the way, or your adversary may drag you off to the judge, and the judge turn you over to the officer, and the officer throw you into prison.

I tell you, you will not get out until you have paid the last penny."


Luke 20:21 - NIV So the spies questioned him: "Teacher, we know that you speak and teach *what is right*, and that you do not show partiality but teach the way of God in accordance with the truth."


Acts 8:21 - NIV "You have no part or share in this ministry, because your heart *is not right* before God."


Acts 10:34-35 - NIV Then Peter began to speak: "I now realize how true it is that God does not show favoritism but accepts from every nation the one who fears him and does *what is right*."


Romans 1:17 - NIV For in the gospel the righteousness of God is revealed—a righteousness that is by faith from first to last, just as it is written: "The *righteous* will live by faith."


Romans 12:17 - NIV Do not repay anyone evil for evil. Be careful to do *what is right* in the eyes of everyone.


Romans 13:3 - NIV For rulers hold no terror for those who do *right*, but for those who do wrong. Do you want to be free from fear of the one in authority? Then do *what is right* and you will be commended.

1 Corinthians 7:35 - NIV I am saying this for your own good, not to restrict you, but that you may live in a *right* way in undivided devotion to the Lord.

2 Corinthians 8:21 - NIV For we are taking pains to do *what is right*, not only in the eyes of the Lord but also in the eyes of man.

2 Corinthians 13:7 - NRSVUE But we pray to God that you may not do anything wrong—not that we may appear to have met the test but that you may do *what is right*, though we may seem to have failed.

Galatians 6:9 - NIV So let us not grow weary in doing *what is right*, for we will reap at harvest time, if we do not give up.

Ephesians 5:9 - NRSVUE for the fruit of the light is found in all *that is good and right* and true.

Ephesians 6:1 - NIV Children, obey your parents in the Lord, for *this is right*.

Philippians 4:8 - NIV Finally, brothers and sisters, whatever is true, whatever is noble, *whatever is right*, whatever is pure, whatever is lovely, whatever is admirable—if anything is excellent or praiseworthy—think about such things.

Colossians 4:1 - NIV Masters, provide your slaves with *what is right* and fair, because you know that you also have a Master in heaven.

2 Thessalonians 3:13 - NIV Brothers and sisters, do not be weary in doing *what is right*.

1 Timothy 2:3 - NRSVUE *This is right* and acceptable before God our Savior.

Hebrews 11:4 - NIV By faith Abel brought God a better offering than Cain did. By faith he was commended as *righteous*, when God spoke well of his offerings. And by faith Abel still speaks, even though he is dead.

James 2:8 - NIV If you really keep the royal law found in Scripture, "Love your neighbor as yourself," you are doing *right*.

James 2:24 - NIV You see that a person is considered *righteous* by what they do and not by faith alone.

1 Peter 2:15 - NRSVUE For it is God's will that by *doing right* you should silence the ignorance of the foolish.

1 Peter 3:14 - NIV But even if you should suffer for *what is right*, you are blessed. "Do not fear their threats; do not be frightened."

1 John 2:29 - NIV If you know that he is *righteous*, you know that everyone who does *what is right* has been born of him.

1 John 3:7 - NIV Dear children, do not let anyone lead you astray. The one who does *what is right is righteous*, just as he is *righteous*.

1 John 3:10 - NIV This is how we know who the children of God are and who the children of the devil are: Anyone who *does not do what is right* is not God's child, nor is anyone who does not love their brother and sister.

The "Thread of Truth" ends as we are presented with the river of the water of life and the Tree of Life found in the new heaven and new earth.

Revelation 22:1-5 - NIV Then the angel showed me the *river of the water of life*, as clear as crystal, flowing from the throne of God and of the Lamb down the middle of the great street of the city. On each side of the river stood the *tree of life*, bearing twelve crops of fruit, yielding its fruit every month. And the leaves of the tree are for the healing of the nations. No longer will there be any curse. The throne of God and of the Lamb will be in the city, and his servants will serve him. They will see his face, and his name will be on their foreheads. There will be no more night. They will not need the light of a lamp or the light of the sun, for the Lord God will give them light. And they will reign for ever and ever.

Revelation 22:11 - NIV Let the one who does wrong continue to do wrong; let the vile person continue to be vile; *let the one who does right* continue *to do right*; and let the holy person continue to be holy.

Revelation 22:14 - NIV Blessed are those who wash their robes, that they may have *the right to the tree of life* and may go through the gates into the city.

# WHAT IS DOING RIGHT IN THE EYES OF GOD?

Psalm 15:1-5 O Lord, who may abide in your tent? Who may dwell on your holy hill? Those who walk blamelessly and do what is right and speak the truth from their heart; who do not slander with their tongue and do no evil to their friends nor heap shame upon their neighbors; in whose eyes the wicked are despised but who honor those who fear the Lord; who stand by their oath even to their hurt; who do not lend money at interest and do not take a bribe against the innocent. Those who do these things shall never be moved.

Isaiah 58:6-9a Is not this the fast that I choose: to loose the bonds of injustice, to undo the straps of the yoke, to let the oppressed go free, and to break every yoke? Is it not to share your bread with the hungry and bring the homeless poor into your house; when you see the naked, to cover them and not to hide yourself from your own kin? Then your light shall break forth like the dawn, and your healing shall spring up quickly; your vindicator [or *vindication*] shall go before you; the glory

of the Lord shall be your rear guard. Then you shall call, and
the Lord will answer; you shall cry for help, and he will say,
"Here I am."

What is doing right in the eyes of God? In the early 1990s I lived in
Maryland. I attended a church in Montgomery County just outside of the
southeast Washington, DC, line. I loved that church. Pastors Mike and
Kay Zello were the most authentic people I had ever met in a church. In
my eyes, they were the real deal. The church was associated with a drug
and alcohol rehab center. We provided food where needed, we reached
out to the neighborhoods in southeast DC, and we bused in children
and adults to attend the church. We took care of the hurting and helped
out with finances wherever we could. We did all the things that I felt in
my heart were those things that pleased God. I had never experienced a
church like that and have never since. We were not a megachurch with
a multi-million-dollar facility. We were around two hundred strong in a
simple brick building. Our real strength came from our love for God and
doing what was right and good in Their eyes.

One day at church, Pastor Mike came up to me and asked me if I had my
toolbox with me. I said I did. He told me to grab my toolbox and go with
him in his car to the southeast DC neighborhood we often visited. When
we got there, he opened the trunk of the car and there were bicycle parts
and tire fix-it kits. He took a sign out of his car that read, "Bicycle Repair
Shop," and he stuck it into the ground. For the next four or more hours, we
sat on the street curb and repaired all the bicycles that the neighborhood
children brought to us. We did the best we could with all that we had to
make those bicycles ride again. At the end of our time there, we sat and
watched all those children riding their bikes up and down the street and
on the sidewalks. They were happy and having a blast. That is when Pastor
Mike looked at me, then pointed toward the children, and said, "That is
the love of Jesus." So, I say to you: that is doing what is right in the eyes of
God.

I could tell you one story after another about what happened during my
time at that church, and they all come back to that same message: Sharing
the love of Jesus by our actions. That is why, to this day, I will always

treasure those years. It was those years that laid the foundation of all that I believe now. What is good, what is right, what is pleasing to the God whom I love so much.

Pastors Mike and Kay were offered the opportunity to be a part of an international ministry for the drug and alcohol abuse organization I spoke of earlier. It was their life's purpose, so they moved on to that great work. I moved on with my life.

I wish I could tell you that I lived a perfect life from that point on, but that would not be true. I still struggled with insecurities and making poor choices and bad decisions. But, as I said earlier, I never lied to myself or to God. I never took God's grace or mercy for granted. I never allowed myself to think that I had arrived spiritually. I kept searching and growing, wanting to know more, wanting to have a deeper relationship with God. I wanted to understand what was happening in the world around me as it related to the Scriptures.

I have not attended a church consistently since that time. Many would say that my struggles came from my not attending church regularly, but I know that is not the case. I tried attending other churches, but I never felt the sincerity or commitment to do what is right and good in the eyes of God as I did at that church in Maryland. I never felt the presence of a genuine love for God.

For a few years after that period, I would occasionally see Pastors Mike and Kay. Pastor Kay would always refer to our time together during those years as "a very special season of love and growing." That is the truth. It has now been twenty or more years since I have seen Pastors Mike and Kay Zello, but I think of them often. That is why I name them in the dedication of this book.

You can find churches in every city of our country. In some cities, you can find churches within blocks of each other. I know of a city that literally has three churches on the same block. Hartford Institute estimates there are roughly 350,000 religious congregations (churches) in the United States. Of those, about 314,000 are Protestant and other Christian churches, and 24,000 are Catholic and Orthodox churches. Non-Christian religious congregations are estimated at about 12,000. Yet, our country is in a serious state of pain. There are people hurting, homeless, and hopeless. Everywhere we look, we see anger, bitterness, and division. The spirits of confusion and deception run rampant across our land. I have a problem with that. God has a problem with that.

If the Church, as a single body, would stop trying to dictate peoples' lives, stop trying to legislate morality, stop rubbing shoulders with unrighteous politicians, and do what it was called to do, do what is right and good in the eyes of God, our country would not be in the shape that it is in. The Church has to stop lying to itself and God and go back to the basics of doing what is right, demonstrating the love of Jesus instead of whipping people with self-righteous rhetoric. The love of Jesus is our only hope. The only side we are called to be on is God's side, which is pro-love and nothing else.

The modern religious right movement has damaged and caused more hurt to the name of God than any other movement in history. It has lost its true purpose and vision. No wonder so many have turned away from the Church. No wonder so many are lost. No wonder so many are hurting, homeless, and hopeless. And it is the fault of this movement and no one else. The Church was called to administer the love of Jesus to the lost. The Church was called to make itself available to the hurting, homeless, and hopeless. The Church was called to be the walking and active member of the body of Jesus. Over the last fifty years, it has failed miserably, and our country is paying dearly for it. The spirit of the false prophet is alive and well behind the pulpits of many of our churches, rejecting the Spirit of God and being a stench to the nostrils of God.

Being conservative has nothing to do with being a believer or having faith in God. It is contrary to the acts that God requires of us in doing what is right and good. Being conservative is adhering to the ideals and hypocrisy of religious laws. The same type of laws that Jesus came to free us from. The same type of laws that Martin Luther declared were wrong within the Catholic church. And so, the Protestant church was established to free believers from those legalistic forms of laws for repentance and establish that we are justified by our faith. And now these are the same religious laws that the modern religious right movement is trying to oppress us with.

Jesus came to free us from those forms of laws and to liberate us from the bondage of sin. The life of a true believer that is repentant and has faith in

God is free and liberated from all sins by the works of Jesus. That does not give us the freedom to go out and indulge in sin. It gives us the freedom to live a full life by doing what is right and good in the eyes of God. In doing so, we will not be captive to the sins of our past but be liberated by the grace and mercies of a loving God.

Doing what is right and good in the eyes of God will not bring you fame, fortune, a megachurch, or popular television show, but it will bring you the peace that comes with sharing the love of Jesus with a hurting world. It will bring you the assurance that the God who created all things and gives you your every breath loves you and is pleased with the person you have become.

At the age of sixty-six, after years of searching, reading, and praying, I have found that peace. I wish it had not taken so long. I wish I could have learned my lessons earlier, but at least I have now come to understand what is truly important and what I can do that is right and good in the eyes of a God who loves me and has stood beside me through so many years of poor choices and bad decisions. My past is now my past and not my present. That is the place God wants us all to reach. The past has to be left behind, and our present has to move forward.

Following are some of my favorite verses, which express those things that are right and good in the eyes of God along with the rewards They have for us in eternity if we do so.

> Micah 6:6-8 With what shall I come before the Lord and bow myself before God on high? Shall I come before him with burnt offerings, with calves a year old? Will the Lord be pleased with thousands of rams, with ten thousands of rivers of oil? Shall I give my firstborn for my transgression, the fruit of my body for the sin of my soul?" He has told you, O mortal, what is good, and what does the Lord require of you but to do justice and to love kindness and to walk humbly with your God?

Matthew 25:35-40 "...for I was hungry and you gave me food, I was thirsty and you gave me something to drink, I was a stranger and you welcomed me, I was naked and you gave me clothing, I was sick and you took care of me, I was in prison and you visited me.' Then the righteous will answer him, 'Lord, when was it that we saw you hungry and gave you food or thirsty and gave you something to drink? And when was it that we saw you a stranger and welcomed you or naked and gave you clothing? And when was it that we saw you sick or in prison and visited you?' And the king will answer them, 'Truly I tell you, just as you did it to one of the least of these brothers and sisters of mine, you did it to me.'"

John 13:34-35 I give you a new commandment, that you love one another. Just as I have loved you, you also should love one another. By this everyone will know that you are my disciples, if you have love for one another.

Luke 3:10-14 – John the Baptist Teaching His Followers – And the crowds asked him [John the Baptist], "What, then, should we do?" In reply he said to them, "Whoever has two coats must share with anyone who has none, and whoever has food must do likewise." Even tax collectors came to be baptized, and they asked him, "Teacher, what should we do?" He said to them, "Collect no more than the amount prescribed for you." Soldiers also asked him, "And we, what should we do?" He said to them, "Do not extort money from anyone by threats or false accusation, and be satisfied with your wages."

Romans 12:9-21 Let love be genuine; hate what is evil; hold fast to what is good; love one another with mutual affection; outdo one another in showing honor. Do not lag in zeal; be ardent in spirit; serve the Lord. Rejoice in hope; be patient in affliction; persevere in prayer. Contribute to the needs of the saints; pursue hospitality to strangers.

Bless those who persecute you; bless and do not curse them. Rejoice with those who rejoice; weep with those who weep. Live in harmony with one another; do not be arrogant, but associate with the lowly; [or *give yourselves to humble tasks*] do not claim to be wiser than you are. Do not repay anyone evil for evil, but take thought for what is noble in the sight of all. If it is possible, so far as it depends on you, live peaceably with all. Beloved, never avenge yourselves, but leave room for the wrath of God, [Greek <u>the wrath</u>] for it is written, "Vengeance is mine; I will repay, says the Lord." Instead, "if your enemies are hungry, feed them; if they are thirsty, give them something to drink, for by doing this you will heap burning coals on their heads." Do not be overcome by evil, but overcome evil with good.

1 John 3:11-24 For this is the message you have heard from the beginning, that we should love one another. We must not be like Cain, who was from the evil one and murdered his brother. And why did he murder him? Because his own deeds were evil and his brother's righteous. Do not be astonished, brothers and sisters, that the world hates you. We know that we have passed from death to life because we love the brothers and sisters. Whoever does not love abides in death. All who hate a brother or sister are murderers, and you know that murderers do not have eternal life abiding in them. We know

love by this, that he laid down his life for us—and we ought to lay down our lives for the brothers and sisters. How does God's love abide in anyone who has the world's goods and sees a brother or sister in need and yet refuses help?

Little children, let us love not in word or speech but in deed and truth. And by this we will know that we are from the truth and will reassure our hearts before him whenever our hearts condemn us, for God is greater than our hearts, and he knows everything.

Beloved, if our hearts do not condemn us, we have boldness before God, and we receive from him whatever we ask, because we obey his commandments and do what pleases him. And this is his commandment, that we should believe in the name of his Son Jesus Christ and love one another, just as he has commanded us. All who obey his commandments abide in him, and he abides in them. And by this we know that he abides in us, by the Spirit that he has given us.

1 John 4:7-21 Beloved, let us love one another, because love is from God; everyone who loves is born of God and knows God. Whoever does not love does not know God, for God is love. God's love was revealed among us in this way: God sent his only Son into the world so that we might live through him. In this is love, not that we loved God but that he loved us and sent his Son to be the atoning sacrifice for our sins. Beloved, since God loved us so much, we also ought to love one another. No one has ever seen God; if we love one another, God abides in us, and his love is perfected in us.

By this we know that we abide in him and he in us, because he has given us of his Spirit. And we have seen and do testify that the Father has sent his Son as the Savior of the world. God abides in those who confess that Jesus is the Son of God, and they abide in God. So we have known and believe the love that God has for us.

God is love, and those who abide in love abide in God, and God abides in them. Love has been perfected among us in this: that we may have boldness on the day of judgment, because as he is, so are we in this world. There is no fear in love, but perfect love casts out fear; for fear has to do with punishment, and whoever fears has not reached perfection in love. We love [Other ancient authorities add *him* or *God*] because he first loved us. Those who say, "I love God," and hate a brother or sister are liars, for those who do not love a brother or sister, whom they have seen, cannot love God, whom they have not seen. The commandment we have from him is this: those who love God must love their brothers and sisters also.

1 Corinthians 13:13 speaks the truth that we are to live by: Love is the greatest of all gifts. To show the love of Jesus is what is right and good in the eyes of God.

1 Corinthians 13:13 And now faith, hope, and love remain, these three, and the greatest of these is love.

Galatians 5:22-26 records the fruit of that love which is the love of Jesus in us. This love produces the remaining fruit of the Spirit as we grow spiritually in Jesus.

In 1 John 2:3-6 and 1 John 2:15-17, we find a clarification of who the love of God abides in.

> Galatians 5:22-26 By contrast, the fruit of the Spirit is love, joy, peace, patience, kindness, generosity, faithfulness, gentleness, and self-control. There is no law against such things. And those who belong to Christ [Other ancient authorities read Christ Jesus] have crucified the flesh with its passions and desires. If we live by the Spirit, let us also be guided by the Spirit. Let us not become conceited, competing against one another, envying one another.

> 1 John 2:3-6 Now by this we know that we have come to know him, if we obey his commandments. Whoever says, "I have come to know him," but does not obey his commandments is a liar, and in such a person the truth does not exist; but whoever obeys his word, truly in this person the love of God has reached perfection. By this we know that we are in him: whoever says, "I abide in him," ought to walk in the same way as he walked.

> 1 John 2:15-17 Do not love the world or the things in the world. The love of the Father is not in those who love the world, for all that is in the world—the desire of the flesh, the desire of the eyes, the pride in riches—comes not from the Father but from the world. And the world and its desire [or *the desire for it*] are passing away, but those who do the will of God abide forever.

Following are some of the eternal rewards we are promised in doing what is right and good.

Revelation 2:7b "To everyone who conquers, I will give permission to eat from the tree of life that is in the paradise of God."


Revelation 2:10b-11 "Be faithful until death, and I will give you the crown of life. Whoever conquers will not be harmed by the second death."


Revelation 2:17b "To everyone who conquers I will give some of the hidden manna, and I will give a white stone, and on the white stone is written a new name that no one knows except the one who receives it."


Revelation 2:26-28 "To everyone who conquers and continues to do my works to the end, I will give authority over the nations, to rule [or *to shepherd*] them with an iron scepter, as when clay pots are shattered—"even as I also received authority from my Father. To the one who conquers I will also give the morning star."


Revelation 3:5 "If you conquer, you will be clothed like them in white robes, and I will not erase your name from the book of life; I will confess your name before my Father and before his angels."

Revelation 3:12 "If you conquer, I will make you a pillar in the temple of my God; you will never go out of it. I will write on you the name of my God and the name of the city of my God, the new Jerusalem that comes down from my God out of heaven, and my own new name."

Revelation 3:20-21 "Listen! I am standing at the door, knocking; if you hear my voice and open the door, I will come in and eat with you, and you with me. To the one who conquers I will give a place with me on my throne, just as I myself conquered and sat down with my Father on his throne."

I want to share this thought concerning doing what is right in the eyes of God versus the constant appeal from churches and ministries asking for funds and donations for their church building or ministry: God would rather we give one-hundred percent of ourselves to the teachings of Jesus Christ than to give ten percent of our earnings to a brick-and-mortar building. God is more concerned with the condition of our hearts and souls than our financial giving. Don't get me wrong, a compassionate heart following the teachings of Jesus Christ will give of their resources but they will give according to where the Presence of the Holy Spirit leads them. We are justified by our faith in Jesus Christ and His teachings not by our financial giving. We should always be aware of the Presence of the Holy Spirit in our lives as to what we are to do with our financial resources. Be aware of that.

# WHAT IS SIN?

Genesis 4:6-7 NIV 1984 Then the Lord said to Cain, "Why are you angry? Why is your face downcast? If you do what is right, will you not be accepted? But if you do not do what is right, sin is crouching at your door; it desires to have you, but you must master it."

What is sin? Genesis 4:6-7 addresses the two opposing choices in our lives. We have our free will to make choices. If we believe in the salvation God has provided and do what is right in Their eyes, we will be accepted. If we do not do what is right, sin is in our lives. But the really deep part of these two verses is in verse 7: "It desires to have you, but you must master it."

God looks at all of us as individuals. We will all be judged as individuals. When we pass from this life into eternity, we will be the only ones responsible for our actions. "You must master it." No blaming our parents, our brothers or sisters, our peers, or our work life. We are responsible for mastering the sins in our life. No excuses. We may think that we can get away with sin and keep going, but that is not the case. That shows a callous and unrepentant heart. We are accountable for the sins in our lives, so we are the ones that have to seek forgiveness for them from God and from those we have offended.

There are denominations and churches that will tell you what sin is and how to act. That is not serving God with a pure and righteous heart. That is legalistic religion. If we submit to the Spirit of God, seek the truth, know the truth, and live the truth, we will know when sin is crouching at our door. That is when it needs to be dealt with, at that moment. That is what is right.

There is sin that is obvious to all of us. The Scriptures make it clear what the obvious sins are that separate us from God and cause us and those around us spiritual harm. Following are verses that address those sins.

Mark 7:21-23 [Jesus said to the disciples] "For it is from within, from the human heart, that evil intentions come: sexual immorality, theft, murder, adultery, avarice, wickedness, deceit, debauchery, envy, slander, pride, folly. All these evil things come from within, and they defile a person."

Galatians 5:16-21 Live by the Spirit, I say, and do not gratify the desires of the flesh. For what the flesh desires is opposed to the Spirit, and what the Spirit desires is opposed to the flesh, for these are opposed to each other, to prevent you from doing what you want. But if you are led by the Spirit, you are not subject to the law. Now the works of the flesh are obvious: sexual immorality, impurity, debauchery, idolatry, sorcery, enmities, strife, jealousy, anger, quarrels, dissensions, factions, envy [other ancient authorities add *murder*], drunkenness, carousing, and things like these. I am warning you, as I warned you before: those who do such things will not inherit the kingdom of God.

2 Timothy 3:1-9 You must understand this, that in the last days distressing times will come. For people will be lovers of themselves, lovers of money, boasters, arrogant, abusive, disobedient to their parents, ungrateful, unholy, unfeeling, implacable, slanderers, profligates, brutes, haters of good, treacherous, reckless, swollen with conceit, lovers of pleasure

rather than lovers of God, holding to the outward form of godliness but denying its power. Avoid them! For among them are those who make their way into households and captivate immature women, overwhelmed by their sins and swayed by all kinds of desires, who are always studying yet never able to recognize truth. As Jannes and Jambres opposed Moses, so these people, of corrupt mind and counterfeit faith, also oppose the truth. But they will not make much progress because, as in the case of those two men [Greek lacks *two men*], their folly will become plain to everyone.

Jesus identifies some of the more obvious sins, as we will read about in Chapter 14 in our discussion of Revelation. Let us now look at the other types of sin, which are not so obvious. These are the sins that God cares about the most because these are the sins that cause hurt and pain, not only to ourselves but to others.

Sin can be found in the flaunting of our personal freedoms. There are many denominational doctrines that tell you how to behave and the things that you can and cannot do. They tell you what sins are and that you are not to participate in them. These doctrines are legalistic in their belief and so produce followers who are more controlled in their religious worship rather than free in their spirit. They have an appearance of righteousness on their outside, but they are filthy on the inside. These doctrines instruct their followers as to how to dress and act. Some doctrines state that smoking cigarettes or marijuana, drinking any form of alcohol, wearing makeup or jewelry, or the practice of women wearing pants is sin. There are activities that you are not to participate in, such as sports, dancing, celebrating holidays, or going to the beach. Other doctrines will tell you that all of these are perfectly fine as faithful believers.

As I have stated, God deals with each of us as individuals. In so doing, you may have freedoms in Jesus that others may not agree with. Flaunting those freedoms can hurt those whose faith is not as strong, who are struggling with sin, and need our loving support rather than being subjected to our freedoms.

The writer of Romans addressed this very issue. At that time, there were those who felt that eating the meat of animals that had been used as a sacrifice was wrong. There were also those who felt drinking wine was wrong. Other faithful believers felt that neither of these actions were a sin.

Romans 14:13-23 provides us with the loving attitude in which we should have as faithful believers in these situations. This is the love of Jesus and what is pleasing in the eyes of God. We should never flaunt or display our personal freedoms to the harm of those who are weaker. That is wrong. That is an act of pride. We should always defer to the loving act of humility rather than parade our freedoms. In doing so, we will find peace within.

Remember: Any of these freedoms, when practiced in excess and paraded around, can become sin in our lives. Anything that becomes more important to us over the salvation and growth of another's spiritual life is a danger to our own souls. Romans 14:23b provides us with a very clear definition of what sin is: "For whatever does not proceed from faith [or *conviction*] is sin." Let that always be our guide.

Matthew 12:36-37 "I tell you, on the day of judgment you will have to give an account for every careless word you utter, for by your words you will be justified, and by your words you will be condemned."

Romans 14:13-23 Let us therefore no longer pass judgment on one another, but resolve instead never to put a stumbling block or hindrance in the way of a brother or sister. I know and am persuaded in the Lord Jesus that nothing is unclean in itself, but it is unclean for anyone who considers it unclean. If your brother or sister is distressed by what you eat, you are no longer walking in love. Do not let what you eat cause the ruin of one for whom Christ died. So do not let your good be slandered. For the kingdom of God is not food and drink but righteousness and peace and joy in the Holy Spirit. The one who serves Christ in this way is acceptable to God and has human approval. Let us then pursue what makes for peace and for mutual upbuilding. Do not, for the sake of food, destroy the work of God. Everything is indeed clean, but it is wrong to make someone stumble by what you eat; it is good not to eat meat or drink wine or do anything that makes your brother or sister stumble [Other ancient authorities add *or be upset or be weakened*]. Hold the conviction that you have as your own before God. Blessed are those who do not condemn themselves because of what they approve. But those who have doubts are condemned if they eat because they do not act from faith, [or *conviction*] for whatever does not proceed from faith [or *conviction*] is sin.

***

Sin can also be found in the depths of our personal emotions and motives. Bitterness, anger, resentment, regrets, frustrations, and sexual impurities are like cancer. They can eat away at our spirits and cause much harm to ourselves and those around us.

I am not saying that we will never experience these emotions. We cannot help but experience them within our lives. But it is our responsibility to not allow them to overcome us and cause hurt to others. We can reach this objective by always reminding ourselves that God's grace is sufficient. By God's grace, along with the fruit of the Spirit within us, we can overcome these emotions and allow the grace of God to permeate us. Their grace will help us to overcome those emotions and provide us peace within.

In Matthew 5, Jesus dealt with some of these emotions and instructed us the better way to resolve them. In my life, this is the area that has caused me the most hurt and destruction. Allowing God's grace to overcome my emotions has been tough for me. I have become better over the last ten years as I have fought to draw closer to God. But it has not been easy. As I have stated, God knows my heart and knows my sincerity in seeking to be better. God is loving and has always let me know They are with me by providing Their peace within my heart. It is that peace that assures me that I am ever drawing closer to overcoming in this life.

Matthew 5:21-26 "You have heard that it was said to those of ancient times, 'You shall not murder,' and 'whoever murders shall be liable to judgment.' But I say to you that if you are angry with a brother or sister [other ancient authorities add *without cause*], you will be liable to judgment, and if you insult [Greek *say Raca to ...Raca is an obscure term of abuse*] a brother or sister, you will be liable to the council, and if you

105

say, 'You fool,' you will be liable to the hell [Greek *Gehenna*] of fire. So when you are offering your gift at the altar, if you remember that your brother or sister has something against you, leave your gift there before the altar and go; first be reconciled to your brother or sister, and then come and offer your gift. Come to terms quickly with your accuser while you are on the way to court [Greek lacks *to court*] with him, or your accuser may hand you over to the judge and the judge to the guard, and you will be thrown into prison. Truly I tell you, you will never get out until you have paid the last penny."

Matthew 5:38-42 "You have heard that it was said, 'An eye for an eye and a tooth for a tooth.' But I say to you: Do not resist an evildoer. But if anyone strikes you on the right cheek, turn the other also, and if anyone wants to sue you and take your shirt, give your coat as well, and if anyone forces you to go one mile, go also the second mile. Give to the one who asks of you, and do not refuse anyone who wants to borrow from you."

Matthew 5:43-48 "You have heard that it was said, 'You shall love your neighbor and hate your enemy.' But I say to you: Love your enemies and pray for those who persecute you, so that you may be children of your Father in heaven, for he makes his sun rise on the evil and on the good and sends rain on the righteous and on the unrighteous. For if you love those who love you, what reward do you have? Do not even the tax collectors do the same? And if you greet only your brothers and sisters, what more are you doing than others? Do not even the gentiles do the same? Be perfect, therefore, as your heavenly Father is perfect."

***

Sin can be found in the motives of our actions and non-actions. Because God knows the true motives of our hearts, They know why we do and do not do things. When Jesus walked the earth, He often times would have conflict with the Pharisees, scribes, and Sadducees, the leaders of the Jewish religion. These conflicts arose due to Jesus knowing the motives in their hearts versus their outward appearance and acts.

In Matthew 23, Jesus confronts them with their hypocrisies. I have selected two particular verses from that chapter to illustrate this point. Though from all outward appearances, the scribes [experts in the sacred Mosaic Law] and Pharisees were righteous men; in knowing their hearts, Jesus called them out for the motives and filth in their hearts. They were full of pride and arrogance on the inside. Their acts were all based on their social status and religious legalism rather than a compassionate heart.

This is where a "good person" can be most deceiving. Just because a person performs acts of goodness, kindness, and generosity, does not mean that they are doing so from a spiritually humble heart. They may very well be performing good acts due to a sense of pride, a feeling of superiority, or a need to be boastful. These are all characteristics of a prideful and arrogant heart which is not a proper attitude for someone with a sincere understanding of God. I will deal more with these characteristics later when I share what I call "The Righteous Secret" in Chapter 6.

Matthew 23:25-26 "Woe to you, scribes and Pharisees, hypocrites! For you clean the outside of the cup and of the plate, but inside they are full of greed and self-indulgence. You blind Pharisee! First clean the inside of the cup and of the plate, [other ancient authorities lack *and of the plate*] so that the outside also may become clean."

Matthew 23:27-28 "Woe to you, scribes and Pharisees, hypocrites! For you are like whitewashed tombs, which on the outside look beautiful but inside are full of the bones of the dead and of all kinds of uncleanness. So you also on the outside look righteous to others, but inside you are full of hypocrisy and lawlessness."

***

As we can perform acts of goodness and yet be hypocrites within, we can also be super religious on the outside, yet totally self-centered on the inside.

We are justified by our faith in God and the salvation They have provided through Jesus. There is no question about that. At the same time, the growth in our faith will produce good works. As we continue to know God and to understand Them more, the love of Jesus grows in us. This love produces works of compassion and kindness as we read in the prior chapter concerning doing what is right and good in the eyes of God. Just as Matthew 25:35-40 shared those things that Jesus spoke of as being what is right for a faithful believer to do, Matthew 25:41-46 shares with us those things that apathy produces. Apathy has no place in a faithful believer's heart.

I shared my story with you concerning the bicycle repair work that Pastor Mike and I performed on that summer day so that you would understand that as faithful believers we are called to action. It is a much more effective testimony to the world in sharing the love of Jesus by acts of love, compassion, and kindness than it is to preach a sermon or pass legislation. The world has heard enough about the love of Jesus. We must make a greater effort to show His love.

Until the majority of the money taken into the American churches goes to the direct need of the hurting, homeless, and hopeless, the religion it preaches is useless. It is flawed with hypocrisy. The American church needs to turn away from the hypocrisy of legislating morality and return to the acts of love that Jesus called us to. If the modern "Religious Right" movement were to spend as much energy and resources on feeding the hungry, providing water to drink, welcoming strangers and immigrants into our homes, clothing the poor, teaching the less privileged, and visiting the sick, shut-ins, and prisons as they do lobbying for legislative changes and cramming moral standards down the throats of our country, then our statistics of crime, racism, and murders would decrease and we would see a powerful move in the love of Jesus. Love produces love. Hatred and oppression produce hatred and oppression.

Remember, just as 1 Timothy 6:10a teaches us that the love of money and the sins of self-indulgence and greed are the source of all sorts of evil, the love of Jesus is the source of all sorts of good.

> Matthew 25:41-46 "Then he will say to those at his left hand, 'You who are accursed, depart from me into the eternal fire prepared for the devil and his angels, for I was hungry and you gave me no food, I was thirsty and you gave me nothing to drink, I was a stranger and you did not welcome me, naked and you did not give me clothing, sick and in prison and you did not visit me.' Then they also will answer, 'Lord, when was it that we saw you hungry or thirsty or a stranger or naked or sick or in prison and did not take care of you?' Then he will answer them, 'Truly I tell you, just as you did not do it to one of the least of these, you did not do it to me.' And these will go away into eternal punishment."

> John 12:47-50 "I do not judge anyone who hears my words and does not keep them, for I came not to judge the world but to save the world. The one who rejects me and does not receive my words has a judge; on the last day the word that I have spoken will serve as judge, for I have not spoken on

my own, but the Father who sent me has himself given me a commandment about what to say and what to speak. And I know that his commandment is eternal life. What I speak, therefore, I speak just as the Father has told me."

In recognizing the sin in our lives, we must always remember the forgiveness that is provided to us by the life, death, and resurrection of Jesus Christ as we discussed in Chapter One. Never allow Satan the upper hand of oppression with guilt or condemnation. Forgiveness is waiting for a sincere and repentant heart. All we have to do is ask for it.

# GOD KNOWS OUR HEARTS

1 Samuel 13:13-14 Samuel said to Saul, "You have done foolishly; you have not kept the commandment of the Lord your God, which he commanded you. The Lord would have established your kingdom over Israel forever, but now your kingdom will not continue; the Lord has sought out a man after his own heart, and the Lord has appointed him to be ruler over his people because you have not kept what the Lord commanded you."

John 2:24-25 But Jesus on his part would not entrust himself to them, because he knew all people and needed no one to testify about anyone, for he himself knew what was in everyone.

Acts 13:21-22 "Then they asked for a king, and God gave them Saul son of Kish, a man of the tribe of Benjamin, who reigned for forty years. When he had removed him, he made David their king. In his testimony about him he said, 'I have found David, son of Jesse, to be a man after my heart, who will carry out all my wishes.'"

God knows our hearts. The story of David, a humble shepherd promoted to king of Israel, is an amazing one. David was not perfect and fell to his fleshly desires, but he never lied to himself or to God. He understood that God knows the heart of man. This is why David was found to be a man after God's own heart. When David was called out for his sins, he humbled himself and sincerely sought the forgiveness of God. For David, it was never an outward act of religion, it was an inward act of humility and sincerity when he cried out to God.

I have spoken multiple times of God knowing our hearts, motives, and inward thoughts throughout this writing. I hope that you have learned that God knows the truth within you. That is so important to understand. Lies are not an option with Them. You cannot deceive God for They see the unseen and know the unknown.

Revelation 20:11-13 states, "Then I saw a great white throne and the one who sat on it; the earth and the heaven fled from his [Greek *the*] presence, and no place was found for them. And I saw the dead, great and small, standing before the throne, and books were opened. Also another book was opened, the book of life. And the dead were judged according to their works, as recorded in the books. And the sea gave up the dead who were in it, Death and Hades gave up the dead who were in them, and all were judged according to what they had done." Those "books" contain all of our actions, our non-actions, all of our motives and intentions. For the righteous, the sincere moments of seeking God's forgiveness and doing what is right are all there along with having their names found in the Book of Life. But for those who have denied God and turned away from the salvation God has provided or have not been sincere in their belief and faith, the books will proclaim the unrighteous secrets of their hearts, and their names will not be found in the Book of Life. Again, you can get away with lying to yourselves and to others, but you will not get away with lying to God.

Psalms 24:3-4 Who shall ascend the hill of the Lord? And who shall stand in his holy place? Those who have clean hands and pure hearts, who do not lift up their souls to what is false and do not swear deceitfully.

Jeremiah 23:24 "Who can hide in secret places so that I cannot see them?" says the Lord. "Do I not fill heaven and earth?" says the Lord.

Matthew 10:26 "So have no fear of them, for nothing is covered up that will not be uncovered and nothing secret that will not become known."

Mark 4:22 "For there is nothing hidden, except to be disclosed; nor is anything secret, except to come to light."

Luke 8:17 "For nothing is hidden that will not be disclosed, nor is anything secret that will not become known and come to light."

Luke 12:2-3 "Nothing is covered up that will not be uncovered and nothing secret that will not become known. Therefore whatever you have said in the dark will be heard in the light, and what you have whispered behind closed doors will be proclaimed from the housetops. "

Romans 2:12-16 All who have sinned apart from the law will also perish apart from the law, and all who have sinned under the law will be judged in accordance with the law. For it is not the hearers of the law who are righteous in God's sight but the doers of the law who will be justified. When gentiles, who do not possess the law, by nature do [or *law by nature, do*] what the law requires, these, though not having the law, are a law to themselves. They show that what the law requires is written on their hearts, as their own conscience also bears witness, and their conflicting thoughts will accuse or perhaps excuse them on the day when, according to my gospel, God through Christ Jesus judges the secret thoughts of all.

John 9:35-41 Jesus heard that they had driven him out, and when he found him he said, "Do you believe in the Son of Man?" [Other ancient authorities read *the Son of God*] *He answered, "And who is he, sir?* [or *Lord*] Tell me, so that I may believe in him." Jesus said to him, "You have seen him, and the one speaking with you is he." He said, "Lord, [or *Sir*] I believe." And he worshiped him. Jesus said, "I came into this world for judgment, so that those who do not see may see and those who do see may become blind." Some of the Pharisees who were with him heard this and said to him, "Surely we are not blind, are we?" Jesus said to them, "If you were blind, you would not have sin. But now that you say, 'We see,' your sin remains."

***

There is another aspect of this that I call "The Righteous Secret." Besides God seeing the secret sins in our lives, They also see the righteous acts that we perform in secret. This is an attribute that we are called to practice in our spiritual lives. It is called humility. God detests a proud and arrogant heart. Our righteous acts are only justified when they are motivated by our love for God. Self-righteous acts are never justified. As I addressed in the previous chapter, sin can be found in the motives behind our actions. Being a spiritual show-off is not pleasing to God. Spiritual acts performed on display for all to see is calling attention to self rather than a worship of God.

Proverbs 16:18 Pride goes before destruction and a haughty spirit before a fall.

Matthew 23:12 "All who exalt themselves will be humbled, and all who humble themselves will be exalted."

During the Sermon on the Mount, Jesus provides us with what I have come to call, "The Righteous Secret." This teaching demonstrates a characteristic of humility, which God desires of us. If we believe that God is, that God knows all things, and that God sees all things, then humbling ourselves in worship in our secret actions and places strengthens our faith and acknowledges to God that we know They see all things. Seeking humankind's recognition for doing good is a selfish act and not pleasing to God.

Also, in keeping with a humble heart while performing good acts in secret, we should never expect some amazing material gain from God. I have found, in these turbulent times, having the peace of God abide in me is a more powerful gift than material gain. God's peace is a wondrous gift and should be cherished dearly for it is greater than gold or silver. The idea of receiving material gain from God for financial or righteous acts should never be a motive from your heart. I am not saying that God does not provide these forms of blessings, for all good things come from above (James 1:17). I am saying that if your motive for giving is receiving back, then that is an improper motive. That is a selfish motive.

Matthew 6:2-4 "So whenever you give alms, do not sound a trumpet before you, as the hypocrites do in the synagogues and in the streets, so that they may be praised by others. Truly I tell you, they have received their reward. But when you give alms, do not let your left hand know what your right hand is doing, so that your alms may be done in secret, and your Father who sees in secret will reward you [other ancient authorities add *openly*]."

Matthew 6:5-6 "And whenever you pray, do not be like the hypocrites, for they love to stand and pray in the synagogues and at the street corners, so that they may be seen by others. Truly I tell you, they have received their reward. But whenever you pray, go into your room and shut the door and pray to your Father who is in secret, and your Father who sees in secret will reward you [other ancient authorities add *openly*]."

Matthew 6:16-18 "And whenever you fast, do not look somber, like the hypocrites, for they mark their faces to show others that they are fasting. Truly I tell you, they have received their reward. But when you fast, put oil on your head and wash your face, so that your fasting may be seen not by others but by your Father who is in secret, and your Father who sees in secret will reward you [other ancient authorities add *openly*]."

***

Matthew 5:7 "Blessed are the merciful, for they will receive mercy."

There is a character attribute of God that we should never abuse, neglect, or negate. The mercy of God is a very powerful attribute to which They have absolute control. It is a quality that we all should seek and cherish because as faithful believers we know "it depends not on human will or exertion but on God who shows mercy" (Romans 9:16).

Grace is the unconditional love of God for Their creation, but the mercy of God is conditional and solely provided by Their choosing. I know, in my own life, God has been very merciful to me. I may very well have left this earth many years ago if not for God's mercy. I am fully convinced that God will always have mercy upon those who come to Them with a totally broken and sincere heart. God will never turn away an honest heart that is seeking Them.

During these turbulent times, especially here in the United States, I cringe whenever I hear someone say, "God Bless America." I love my country, and I am grateful to God for having given me life in this country. But with all that is happening across this land that we call the United States, I say it is much more appropriate that we should be on our knees, humble and begging for God to have mercy on America. We need it.

Exodus 33:17-19 The Lord said to Moses, "I will also do this thing that you have asked, for you have found favor in my sight, and I know you by name." Moses [Hebrew *He*] said, "Please show me your glory." And he said, "I will make all my goodness pass before you and will proclaim before you the name, 'The Lord,' [The word "Lord" when spelled with capital letters stands for the divine name, *YHWH*, which is here connected with the verb *hayah*, "to be"] and I will be gracious to whom I will be gracious and will show mercy on whom I will show mercy."

Romans 9:14-15 What then are we to say? Is there injustice on God's part? By no means! For he says to Moses, "I will have mercy on whom I have mercy, and I will have compassion on whom I have compassion."

# REMEMBER THOSE FOUR QUESTIONS?

Remember those four questions? I will now share with you the answers I have found in my search for the truth. You may find entirely different answers in your search. To me that only confirms that God is and They deal with each and every one of us individually.

**Why Were We Created and What Makes Us Different?**

Why were we created and what makes us different from the other creations of God? This earth, this life is not what we are ultimately here for. God does not exist for our pleasure and needs. We were created to exist for God. We are not God's first creation, nor are we the last creation. But we are unique among God's creations.

All the creations before us were present in heaven with God. These creations were capable of seeing and interacting with Them. With humankind, God chose to make a creation that not only had free will but was also set apart in a universe of its own. God wanted a creation that had to believe and have faith in Them without being able to physically see or interact with Them. We are not in Their physical presence to behold Them. We can only believe by having faith in Them. We have to choose to believe and love Them without seeing Them. This is the kind of creation that God chose to make in us. That is why we were created and what makes us different. Having to believe and have faith without physically seeing God or being in Their physical presence.

In the beginning of this creation, God did deal with humankind directly, as They dealt with Cain and the rest of humankind in the early part of creation. As humankind grew and progressed forward, God used angels and anointed prophets to speak to and guide this creation. The prophets proclaimed to humankind that there would be a Messiah to come to fulfill the Word of God and provide a plan of salvation for all humanity. Jesus Christ the Messiah was born and fulfilled all the work that was given to Him to do.

So, Jesus came to this earth and walked among us, God in the flesh. Even then, He was rejected because Jesus did not come as a power-hungry king to rid Israel of all its troubles and annihilate its enemies. Jesus came as a humble man who taught love, inclusion, and obedience to a loving God. He came to alter humankind's perception of who and what God really is. He came to help humankind understand that God does not change, but that our understanding of Them must always progress if we love Them and desire to know Them better. Progressive understanding of God comes from growth in our faith. Every time the disciples thought they had Jesus figured out, He would do something radical to alter their perception. The Pharisees, Sadducees, and scribes wanted Jesus to adhere to their conservative and traditional ways, but He would not. Jesus wanted His disciples and all that came after them to understand that God's thinking, God's perspective, and God's purpose is so far beyond human comprehension. God is much greater. We cannot put our limitations on a God that has no limits. God has not changed; we must change so that we may begin to understand Their ways better. In following God's will, Jesus fulfilled His purposed in His life, death, and resurrection on this earth.

Now God's purpose for humankind and being different, being justified by faith and not by sight had been completed. God sent the Presence of the Holy Spirit to rest upon all faithful believers to guide them in their lives. But humankind would no longer be in the physical presence of God until the end of the ages. We were now alone in all of God's creations in having to make a free choice to believe and have faith in Them without physically seeing Them. That is why we were created. That is why we are different.

That is why we are here. We are here to choose to love God, to love our neighbor as we do ourselves, and to grow in our understanding of God. Everything else is superfluous.

## What Is Our Purpose?

What is our purpose? I can say this: Each of us has a purpose, and it is not predestined. When God created humankind, They did not predetermine who would live eternally in heaven and who would be eternally damned to suffering. What would make that creative? There is no logic or rational thought behind that thinking. I am fully convinced and know by my faith that God is totally logical and rational in Their plan and purpose for us. That goes for anything They have done. We have a free will to choose to love God and do what is right in Their eyes or to deny God's existence. It is that simple: Our purpose in this life is to make that one choice.

Now, because God knows all things and everything that is to come, They know what choice we will make, but it will still be our choice. It will still be our determination and not Theirs. But They will know. A friend once explained it to me like this. This life is like a maze that we are walking through. We can see only what is directly in front of us. But from God's perspective, They are able to see where we all come out. That is not predestination; that is simply all-knowing. That is why I believe that no one dies before their time. God holds everyone's breath in Their hands from the moment that we take our very first breath until we take our last. We will not be lost in the maze without God knowing. Some of us simply take a shorter route. Let me provide some examples concerning this.

Cain was not predestined to kill Abel. Cain chose to allow envy and bitterness to dwell in his heart. God addressed these issues with Cain, but Cain declined to listen to God. He chose to murder.

The Pharoah of Egypt was not predestined to oppress the children of Israel in the time of Moses. The Pharoah chose to do evil and sin against God. God then used Pharoah to fulfill Their objective in freeing Israel.

Judas was not predestined to be evil and betray Jesus Christ. Judas chose to do evil because of greed and the desire to have riches. God then used Judas to fulfill Their objective in the betrayal and death of Jesus Christ.

We are not predestined. We have a free will to choose. Our choices will lead us as to how God may use us in Their plan for the purpose and completion of this creation. God has an overall plan for this creation, and it will come to pass.

Getting back to our primary purpose as humankind, it all goes back to what Jesus said in Matthew 22:37-40: "'Love the Lord your God with all your heart and with all your soul and with all your mind.' [Deuteronomy 6:5] This is the first and greatest commandment. And the second is like it: 'Love your neighbor as yourself.' [Leviticus 19:18] All the Law and the Prophets hang on these two commandments."

In God's eyes, that is our only purpose. That is all that we will be judged on when we face Them in eternity. To choose to believe and have faith while loving our neighbor as ourselves. It is not complicated. We have made it complicated by our selfish and indulgent behavior. That is not God's fault; it is ours.

**Where Will It Lead?**

Where will it lead? As we will see in our discussion of Revelation, eventually it will lead to the judgment of all humankind and the destruction of this universe and earth.

God is in control of Their plan, not ours. I do not like when people say, "Everything happens for a reason." That is a lie. That takes the blame off us and assumingly directs it to God or someone else. It makes us feel better. The truth is, rather: "There is a reason for everything that happens." That keeps the blame where it belongs. Cause and effect. Our choices and our decisions bring on us what may happen in our own lives.

Now, do not take this out of context. Sometimes we may have to face something that we have no control over. I have had several friends and family who have battled cancer. Yes, for some, it may have been their choices of earlier lifestyle habits that caused the cancer, but for others, it simply happened. Cancer is a merciless disease. Those type of instances and others that we know are a curveball some of us are thrown and have to deal with in this life. During those times, faith in God and leaning on God's grace will always bring peace. I can guarantee you that.

Besides that, we have no control over the family or the social status we are born into. Those are things that are a part of life we have no control over. That does not give us an excuse to do wrong and not believe in God. If we submit to the Presence of the Holy Spirit, we will be given the strength to overcome any obstacles that this life brings us.

My point is this: Most of the times in our lives, our financial, physical, and relationship struggles are brought on by our own poor choices and bad decisions. So, to say that God is in control as a blanket statement is not true. That is another way of diverting the blame. God is in control of Their plan, and that plan is the direction in which humankind is all headed, eventually. As individuals, we have to get in God's plan and stay there. We cannot expect Them to follow our plan.

# THE DIFFERENCE BETWEEN BELIEVING AND HAVING FAITH

John 1:11-13 He came to what was his own, [or *to his own home*] and his own people did not accept him. But to all who received him, who believed in his name, he gave power to become children of God, who were born, not of blood or of the will of the flesh or of the will of man, but of God.

Luke 18:7-8 "And will not God grant justice to his chosen ones who cry to him day and night? Will he delay long in helping them? I tell you, he will quickly grant justice to them. And yet, when the Son of Man comes, will he find faith on earth?"

James 2:19 You believe that God is one; you do well. Even the demons believe—and shudder.

There is a difference between believing in God and having faith in God.

Believing in God is the easy part. Having faith in God is a whole other level of understanding. Believing is the first step to everyone's relationship with God. It all has to start with believing. In the New Revised Standard Version Updated Edition translation of the New Testament, you will only find the term *Christian* used three times. You will find the term *believers* used twenty-six times. You will find the word *believe* used 222 times. You will find the word *faith* used 280 times. I prefer calling myself a "faithful believer" over "Christian" out of my respect for what Jesus did and all that He accomplished while on this earth. I believe and I have faith, which are two different things.

Anyone can believe in humankind, their country, the world, and the universe. To believe is just accepting that something is real. We can have hope in all of those things, though those things can also crush our hope. But we can believe in, have faith in, and hope in God for They will never let us down. There is absolutely nothing on this earth that we can have faith in, except God. Why? Because everything that exists on this earth outside of God is fallible. God is infallible.

We can say that we believe in God, but what kind of God do we believe in? The God we learned about in Sunday School? The God we heard some preacher tell us about in church? The God the televangelist told us about on our television? What God do we believe in?

Believing comes from knowledge; faith comes from understanding. We decide in our hearts and choose to believe that God is. We then seek to know who God is by reading the Scriptures. Within the Scriptures we learn about God the Creator, the Beloved, and the Presence. We seek the truth, then we know the truth, and then we live the truth. Believing begins with us seeking the truth and faith is where we begin living the truth.

In John 20:29 Jesus said to Thomas, "Have you believed because you have seen me? Blessed are those who have not seen and yet have come to believe." Believing is the beginning. Faith comes next.

> Hebrews 11:1 – NIV 1984 Now faith is being sure of what we hope for and certain of what we do not see.

*Merriam-Webster* defines the word *sure* as "marked by or given to feelings of confident certainty, characterized by a lack of wavering or hesitation, the admitting of no doubt, indisputable." It defines *certain* as "fixed, settled, dependable, reliable, known or proved to be true: indisputable." So, faith is a much deeper relationship with God than the simple believing that there is a God.

Believing is when we open our heart to know God. Having faith in God is to know without question, without doubt, without wavering, that you know with all certainty, with all surety, with all confidence, that God is.

Our faith cannot be based on the book we call the Bible. If so, it can be destroyed quite handily by anyone that has understanding. The Bible contains stories of old, words of encouragement, the life of Jesus, and the breath of God within its pages, but it cannot be the source of our faith. "So faith [or *trust*] comes from what is heard, and what is heard comes through the word of Christ [or *about Christ*; other ancient authorities read *of God*]" (Romans 10:17 NRSVUE). This verse is the essence of pure faith. Faith comes from communion with God in the Scriptures and in prayer. What we hear Them tell us through the Scriptures and through the Spirit is a combination of both. But first and foremost, it begins with the spirit within us believing that God is. Then comes faith through us seeking God with a pure heart.

Hebrews 11 goes on to list those who had steadfast faith in God before a single word was physically written of the Bible. Abel, Enoch, Noah, Abraham, Isaac, Jacob, Moses on and on, their initial belief was solely based upon their willingness to open their heart to God. Afterward, they were all found righteous in the eyes of God for the faith they displayed in God. Then they had their revelation of God, but only after they had chosen to extend their belief and have faith in God for their own lives. Yes, they had heard stories of God from their ancestors, but they did not have the Bible to lean on. Through those stories they believed. They proved their faith by turning their lives over to God. Then the Presence of the Holy Spirit comes to strengthen and encourage.

This is how my faith in God was birthed. I chose to believe and then my faith grew stronger. Since that time, the things that I have seen and all that I have experienced have absolutely and unequivocally convinced me that God is. Having that confidence, I know that if you open yourself to believe in God, your faith will grow with the assurance that They will reveal Themself to you. And through prayer, reading the Scriptures, and communion with Them, you will see the truth, know the truth, and live the truth.

As you have noticed through this writing, I use the term *faithful believers*. Jesus makes a valid distinction in Luke 18:7-8: "And yet, when the Son of Man comes, will he find faith on earth?" Hebrews 11 is called the faith chapter and for good reason. It lists Old Testament faithful believers who "though they were commended for their faith, did not receive what was promised, since God had provided something better so that they would not, apart from us, be made perfect" (Hebrews 11:1-40).

These people were not commended for simply believing in God. They were commended for their faith in God. In Luke 18:7-8, Jesus reiterates that it is faith in God, faith in the teachings of Jesus Christ, that differentiates those who are committed to God and those who simply "believe." Faith is mandatory in a true believer's life.

# WHAT I BELIEVE

John 3:16-21 For God so loved the world that he gave his only Son, so that everyone who believes in him may not perish but may have eternal life. Indeed, God did not send the Son into the world to condemn the world but in order that the world might be saved through him. Those who believe in him are not condemned, but those who do not believe are condemned already because they have not believed in the name of the only Son of God. And this is the judgment, that the light has come into the world, and people loved darkness rather than light because their deeds were evil. For all who do evil hate the light and do not come to the light, so that their deeds may not be exposed. But those who do what is true come to the light, so that it may be clearly seen that their deeds have been done in God.

I believe in God, one Holy Deity comprised of three spirit entities: the Creator, the Beloved, and the Presence.

I believe that the Creator sent the Beloved to this earth as the Messiah, Jesus Christ for the salvation of all people.

I believe Jesus Christ was born to the Virgin Mary by the Presence of the Holy Spirit.

I believe that Jesus Christ walked this earth, gave us the Word, died on the cross, and rose from the dead for our salvation, redemption, and justification if we believe.

I believe Jesus Christ rose from the dead and walked the earth for forty days appearing to the disciples and many others, teaching them and instructing them to wait upon the Presence of the Holy Spirit.

I believe that Jesus Christ then ascended back into heaven to return to the side of the Creator at which time the Creator poured out the Presence of the Holy Spirit upon all the faithful believers from that day until now, according to the prophecy stated in Joel 2:28-32.

I believe that the Presence of the Holy Spirit is our guide, our counselor, and our comforter.

I believe that all people who call upon the name of Jesus Christ, confess their sin, obey the Word, and do what is right in the eyes of God will be saved.

I believe that one day, Jesus Christ will return to this earth and gather all the faithful believers, both from the dead and the living, and provide us a new home where we will abide in the company of God the Creator, the Beloved, and the Presence for all eternity.

I believe that those who do not believe and are unfaithful will be cast into eternal punishment and suffering, forever separated from the presence of a loving God.

I believe that in our lives on this earth as we seek the truth of God there needs to come a time when our past life of sins will be our past and not our present. If we, by faith, are committing our lives to God, there needs to be that point in which all the sins that once overcame us becomes our past, and our present abides in the knowledge and understanding of a loving God. That does not mean we have reached perfection; it simply means that we know, understand, and do what is right and good in the eyes of God by faith.

# THE END BEGINS

Isaiah 14:24 The Lord of hosts has sworn: "As I have designed, so shall it be, and as I have planned, so shall it come to pass."

Matthew 16:1-3 The Pharisees and Sadducees came, and to test Jesus [Greek *him*] they asked him to show them a sign from heaven. He answered them, "When it is evening, you say, 'It will be fair weather, for the sky is red.' And in the morning, 'It will be stormy today, for the sky is red and threatening.' You know how to interpret the appearance of the sky, but you cannot interpret the signs of the times." [Other ancient authorities lack *When it is . . . of the times*]

The end begins.

As there was a beginning, there will be an end. God has a plan for this creation and humankind. As I stated early on God does not micro-manage our individual lives but as a whole, this creation moves forward according to God's plan and purpose. Once again, the Scriptures lay this out plainly for all of us to see. There will be an end to all of this.

Since the early years of my reading and studying the Scriptures, I was drawn to the concept of the end of the ages. Not in a morbid way, but as a subject that interested me highly. Whether you believe in the concepts or not, all of us have heard the terms, *Second Coming of Jesus, Rapture* (though that actual word is not in the Scriptures), and *Armageddon*, all of which pertain to the end of the ages. So, I really anticipated reading the Book of Revelation. In fact, the first time I read it, I spent the entire day reading it straight through. I was looking for answers to the four questions I had. The Book of Revelation provides us with those answers or at least directs us to those answers.

Let me say here: We have all heard of the concept of the world ending. Whether it was from going to church, casual conversation, television, movies, or other modes of communication and media, we have all heard that God has a plan for the end of this world. And though we have heard about it all our lives—and in truth, throughout the history of humankind since the life of Jesus—it has obviously not happened. I understand the doubting heart. I understand why so many have lost their faith. I can say this: There is an order to God. God's order is both logical and rational. It is my hope that I can give you a glimpse of that order as we move forward and that you will gain a better understanding.

Before I had read the Book of Revelation, I thought that it was written in chronological order. I thought that I would be able to read it and understand it from start to finish, but I did not, primarily because it is not written in chronological order, or at least it has not been translated in chronological order. It is not even in any logical order with many of the visions being concurrent.

Revelation is a series of visions. It is a puzzle. I am confident of these two things: The writer experienced these visions, and the Spirit of God was the source of them. The visions are circumstances and events that are past, present, and future to the writer. Some of the visions, though seen separately by the writer, occur concurrently. All of this makes for a most fascinating read, though confusing at times. So, my objective, in this project, is to present a logical order to the events as I see them, so that there is a more sensible flow to them, at least from my perspective, studies, and understanding.

There will be some who will be critical of what I am presenting. That is okay. I am not bastardizing the Scriptures. I am not making the Scriptures say anything that they are not already saying. I am not taking a single stand-alone verse and creating a doctrine out of it like so many churches have done. What I am doing is sharing with you a very logical and rational perspective of how I see God and how I see the end of the ages unfold. I am doing this with a comprehensive understanding of the Scriptures from beginning to end, a complete perspective. As an assurance, Chapter 12 is a complete Table of Contents for Revelation, which provides you with a list of all the chapters and verses and the pages on which they can be found. Not a single verse has been removed or replaced.

We are individuals, and that is how God sees us. God does not see a denomination, church building, or any form of group. We are seen strictly as individuals. In the end, as stated in earlier chapters, we will all be judged according to our individual selves, our spiritual being, our personal motives, the truth that cannot be hidden. As I have read the Scriptures, this is one of the revelations God has given me. The Scriptures can show you your own revelation, but you have to make the effort to read and study them. You have to search for it within the Scriptures. God will give you that revelation if you search for it with a pure and sincere heart. I can promise you that.

So, I reached the point in my studies where I asked myself, "What would be the best way to logically approach the understanding of the events in the Book of Revelation?" I concluded that there would be only one correct way to do that, by using the very words of Jesus when He was approached with the same question by the disciples.

The Gospels of Matthew, Mark, and Luke all tell the story of the life of Jesus. The Gospel of John is a beautiful documentation of humankind's salvation through Jesus. It does not address the end of the ages like the other three. Most of Matthew, Mark, and Luke tell the same story pertaining to the end of the ages, with just slight nuances. One might share more detail than the others concerning specific events, but in searching for the specific question about the end of the ages, they all say, almost verbatim, the same thing. Let's review those particular verses.

***

In the verses of Luke 17:22-37, Jesus makes a very important proclamation to the disciples. This is one of the primary passages in which many denominations speak of what is called "the Rapture." They paint a picture that Jesus will suddenly return and gather those who will go to heaven, then disappear into heaven with them. But that is not what is being said here, not when it is incorporated with all of the rest of the Scriptures. I will comment on this more within the study of Revelation.

The verses where Jesus speaks of "the lightning flashes" simply means that many will not be prepared for the end of the ages. It does not mean that it is going to happen quickly. There will be a sense of apathy among many, and their minds will no longer be focused on the end. Instead, their minds will be caught up on other aspects of this life. They will not be prepared for or be able to see the significance of the events that are unfolding around them. So, when the end of the ages does begin to unfold, they will not be prepared.

Luke 17:22-37 Then he said to the disciples, "The days are coming when you will long to see one of the days of the Son of Man, and you will not see it. They will say to you, 'Look there!' or 'Look here!' Do not go; do not set off in pursuit. For as the lightning flashes and lights up the sky from one side to the other, so will the Son of Man be in his day [other ancient authorities lack *in his day*]. But first he must endure much suffering and be rejected by this generation. Just as it was in the days of Noah, so, too, it will be in the days of the Son of Man. They were eating and drinking and marrying and being given in marriage until the day Noah entered the ark, and the flood came and destroyed all of them. Likewise, just as it was in the days of Lot, they were eating and drinking, buying and selling, planting and building, but on the day that Lot left Sodom it rained fire and sulfur from heaven and destroyed all of them; it will be like that on the day that the Son of Man is revealed. On that day, anyone on the housetop who has belongings in the house must not come down to take them away, and likewise anyone in the field must not turn back.

Remember Lot's wife [Genesis 19:24-26]. Those who try to make their life secure will lose it, but those who lose their life will keep it. I tell you, on that night there will be two in one bed; one will be taken and the other left. There will be two women grinding meal together; one will be taken and the other left. [other ancient authorities add 17.36, *Two will be in the field; one will be taken and the other left.*] Then they asked him, "Where, Lord?" He said to them, "Where the corpse is, there the eagles will gather."

*****

Following are passages from all three books being presented in a parallel form, where Jesus expounds on these events. The first thing Jesus says to draw their attention is that in the very end there will be a complete annihilation of this earth. Understand, Jesus at this point is talking about the final end of this world. After all of the other events that we are about to discuss, this earth will be no more.

Matthew 24:1-2 As Jesus came out of the temple and was going away, his disciples came to point out to him the buildings of the temple. Then he asked them, "You see all these, do you not? Truly I tell you, not one stone will be left here upon another; all will be thrown down."

Mark 13:1-2 As he came out of the temple, one of his disciples said to him, "Look, Teacher, what large stones and what large buildings!" Then Jesus asked him, "Do you see these great buildings? Not one stone will be left here upon another; all will be thrown down."

Luke 21:5-6 When some were speaking about the temple, how it was adorned with beautiful stones and gifts dedicated to God, he said, "As for these things that you see, the days will come when not one stone will be left upon another; all will be thrown down."

***

Jesus now has their attention. The disciples want to understand more, so they question Jesus directly about the end of the ages. He then begins sharing events that will lead up to that final end.

The very first warning that Jesus proclaims to the disciples is to stay awake and be aware of the many false prophets that will come proclaiming that they are representing Jesus. He knew that many would fall prey to the twisted doctrines of these false prophets. He warns the disciples to be aware of this and not to fall for these prophets that pervert the Scriptures for their own profits and benefits. Later, Philippians 1:15-17 speaks about the false prophets that were already appearing within the Early Church. That is why it is important for us to read, study, and pray, embracing the Scriptures each day ourselves. In doing so, our hearts will be guarded from the false prophets that walk so freely among us.

Matthew 24:3-5 When he was sitting on the Mount of Olives, the disciples came to him privately, saying, "Tell us, when will this be, and what will be the sign of your coming and of the end of the age?" Jesus answered them, "Beware that no one leads you astray. For many will come in my name, saying, 'I am the Messiah!' [or *the Christ*] and they will lead many astray."

Mark 13:3-6 When he was sitting on the Mount of Olives opposite the temple, Peter, James, John, and Andrew asked him privately, "Tell us, when will this be, and what will be the sign that all these things are about to be accomplished?" Then Jesus began to say to them, "Beware that no one leads you astray. Many will come in my name and say, 'I am he! [Greek *I am*]' and they will lead many astray."

Luke 21:7-8 They asked him, "Teacher, when will this be, and what will be the sign that this is about to take place?" And he said, "Beware that you are not led astray, for many will come in my name and say, 'I am he! [Greek *I am*]' and, 'The time is near! [or *at hand!*]' Do not go after them."

***

Next, Jesus foretells of the increase in struggles that humankind has and will face through the ages. These struggles, wars, rumors of war, famines, and earthquakes would increase and intensify over the ages. Our present time is a witness to this truth. In our present age, we are witnessing some of the most horrendous devastation within the realm of wars that we have ever seen. The innocent are dying over humankind's greed and need to have more power.

At the time that I am writing this, there are dozens of ongoing wars and regional conflicts happening around the world, with some prominent examples including the Russia-Ukraine war, the ongoing conflict in Syria, the Sudanese civil war, the Myanmar civil war, and conflicts in the Palestine-Israel region. However, the exact number is difficult to pinpoint due to varying definitions of war and the fluid nature of conflicts.

We also see the suffering we have endured through epidemics, pandemics, firearm deaths, suicides, and mental disorders over the last two centuries as each incident has increased dramatically.

On top of that is the effects of global warming: hurricanes, tornadoes, and wildfires. And let us not forget the pollution *we* have created just within the last century by the introduction of the industrial age and with the creation of plastic.

All of these factors caused the creation of the Doomsday Clock by the Bulletin of the Atomic Scientists. The clock presently sits at eighty-five seconds to midnight. That is the closest it has ever been to worldwide destruction.

And this is not even mentioning the famines, droughts, and other natural disasters that have increased significantly. As a whole, we have disrespected the gift of life we have been given upon this wondrous planet and have caused these calamities to fall on us. We are responsible for our own undoing, not God. I encourage you to read the statistics of these struggles and suffering that is found in the reference section at the end of this book.

Note the warning that is given to end two of these three passages: "All this is but the beginning of the birth pangs" (Matthew 24:8 and Mark 13:8). Jesus will expound more upon "the birth pangs" or sufferings, later on in the passages that follow. What we are to understand at the present is this: Right now in our present state, the world has entered into that phase of God's plan in which Jesus stated is just the beginning of birth pangs.

Matthew 24:6-8 "And you will hear of wars and rumors of wars; see that you are not alarmed, for this must take place, but the end is not yet. For nation will rise against nation and kingdom against kingdom, and there will be famines [other ancient authorities add *and pestilences*] and earthquakes in various places: all this is but the beginning of the birth pangs."

Mark 13:7-8 "When you hear of wars and rumors of wars, do not be alarmed; this must take place, but the end is still to come. For nation will rise against nation and kingdom against kingdom; there will be earthquakes in various places; there will be famines. This is but the beginning of the birth pangs."

Luke 21:9-11 "When you hear of wars and insurrections, do not be terrified, for these things must take place first, but the end will not follow immediately." Then he said to them, "Nation will rise against nation and kingdom against kingdom; there will be great earthquakes and in various places famines and plagues, and there will be dreadful portents and great signs from heaven."

✱✱✱

Jesus, then brings the disciples back to their personal present situation. Jesus will depart this earth, and the disciples are warned they will face great persecution and that some will be put to death for their faith. This persecution will intensify to the point that parents, siblings, relatives, and friends will betray them. But, in the midst of this persecution, He assures them that in their endurance, their souls will be eternally saved.

These words that Jesus spoke to the disciples still ring true for those who believe to this day. Though in many parts of the world, the persecution comes with no more than being laughed at, being called a fool, or being scorned, there are still places on this earth where belief in Jesus will lead to death.

Jesus proclaimed a significant truth, recorded in Matthew 24:12: "And because of the increase of lawlessness, the love of many will grow cold." As humankind has progressed over the centuries, from the time of Jesus until now, the hatred and evil within humankind has become more and more exposed. I believe this is the lawlessness Jesus is speaking of. The internet has provided a source for hatred and evil to unite and spread throughout the world. Hearts have grown cold. Lies and deception are rampant. The spirit of the false prophet has become more prevalent and bolder.

Even so, in the midst of it all, there is still a remnant proclaiming the truth. There is always hope in Jesus to hold onto.

> Matthew 24:9-14 "Then they will hand you over to be tortured and will put you to death, and you will be hated by all nations because of my name. Then many will fall away [or *stumble*], and they will betray one another and hate one another. And many false prophets will arise and lead many astray. And because of the increase of lawlessness, the love of many will grow cold. But the one who endures to the end will be saved. And this good news [or *gospel*] of the kingdom will be proclaimed throughout the world, as a testimony to all the nations, and then the end will come."

> Mark 13:9-13 "As for yourselves, beware, for they will hand you over to councils, and you will be beaten in synagogues, and you will stand before governors and kings because of me, as a testimony to them. And the good news [Greek *gospel*] must first be proclaimed to all nations. When they bring you to trial and hand you over, do not worry beforehand about what you are to say, but say whatever is given you at that time, for it is not you who speak but the Holy Spirit. Sibling will betray sibling to death and a father his child, and children will rise against parents and have them put to death, and you will be hated by all because of my name. But the one who endures to the end will be saved."

Luke 21:12-19 "But before all this occurs, they will arrest you and persecute you; they will hand you over to synagogues and prisons, and you will be brought before kings and governors because of my name. This will give you an opportunity to testify. So make up your minds not to prepare your defense in advance, for I will give you words [Greek *a mouth*] and a wisdom that none of your opponents will be able to withstand or contradict. You will be betrayed even by parents and siblings, by relatives and friends, and they will put some of you to death. You will be hated by all because of my name. But not a hair of your head will perish. By your endurance you will gain your souls."

***

Within the following passages, there is a reference to a prophecy recorded in the book of Daniel (chapters 9-12), in which Jerusalem is surrounded by its enemies, and the sacred places are overcome with religious perversion that is unholy in the eyes of God. The verses in the text of Daniel are complex as far as directly stating when this event will occur. Theologians have many theories. The most important aspect of those verses is the actual event: the desolating sacrilege, the perverted use of the most holy of all places. In these passages, Jesus is encouraging us to stay awake and aware of this event. Some point to the destruction of Jerusalem that occurred in 70 CE. We really cannot say for sure. History repeats itself. Even now, as I work on this project, Israel is at war. Who knows where it will lead? We pray and we hope for peace.

What we do know is Jesus teaches that prior to and after the event of the desolating sacrilege, the world will begin a downward spiral. Humankind will experience suffering like it has never experienced. Throughout all continents and countries, there will be great suffering. This is not talking about a single event; Jesus is speaking of events that will occur through the course of centuries that will intensify as the years progress. Remember the warning Jesus gave earlier: "All this is but the beginning of the birth pangs" (Matthew 24:8 and Mark 13:8). As humankind tries to find answers outside of God, greater questions will arise and more calamities will occur. From generation to generation, the world has suffered greatly. From the wars that past generations have endured, the abuse and annihilation of races during these wars, the various plagues and diseases that have cost the lives of loved ones, to the increase of the mental health crisis we have come to face in these modern times, we are experiencing the beginning of the birth pangs. And the suffering will escalate. What we call "the progress of humankind" through technology, manufactured products, and modern warfare will cause more grief and suffering to humankind than it will benefit. We are losing our souls.

Matthew 24:15-21 "So when you see the desolating sacrilege, spoken of by the prophet Daniel, standing in the holy place (let the reader understand), then those in Judea must flee to the mountains; the one on the housetop must not go down to take things from the house; the one in the field must not turn back to get a coat. Woe to those who are pregnant and to those who are nursing infants in those days! Pray that your flight may not be in winter or on a Sabbath. For at that time there will be great suffering, such as has not been from the beginning of the world until now, no, and never will be."

Mark 13:14-19 "But when you see the desolating sacrilege set up where it ought not to be (let the reader understand), then those in Judea must flee to the mountains; the one on the housetop must not go down or enter to take anything from the house; the one in the field must not turn back to get a coat. Woe to those who are pregnant and to those who are nursing infants in those days! Pray that it may not be in winter. For in those days there will be suffering, such as has not been from the beginning of the creation that God created until now and never will be."


Luke 21:20-24 "When you see Jerusalem surrounded by armies, then know that its desolation has come near [or *is at hand*]. Then those in Judea must flee to the mountains, and those inside the city must leave it, and those out in the country must not enter it, for these are days of vengeance, as a fulfillment of all that is written. Woe to those who are pregnant and to those who are nursing infants in those days! For there will be great distress on the earth and wrath against this people; they will fall by the edge of the sword and be taken away as captives among all nations, and Jerusalem will be trampled on by the nations, until the times of the nations are fulfilled."

***

As time moves forward, Jesus reiterates the severity of the suffering by stating that it will become so intense, that if the days of this age were not shortened, it would be impossible for anyone to be saved. The increase of false messiahs and prophets will overwhelm and entice many to be led astray to follow false doctrines, teachings, and perverted gospels. Even to the point that the very elect may be tempted to follow.

Let me stop here and say this: The "elect" are not predestined from birth. As I have stated before, the elect are those who faithfully believe in God with all of their hearts, minds, souls, and spirits. They know that God is, and with the purest heart, they have chosen to believe. All of humankind from birth has the free will to choose to believe or not. God does not predestine anyone to suffer eternal damnation. The paradox comes in that God knows everything, past, present, and the future. And, as I have stated before, God knows the true motives and intentions of your heart. There is no surprise ending for God; there is only the truth.

There are many who ask, "If God is love, why will the suffering be so great and increase?" We are creating our own suffering. Humankind's lust for control, power, and wealth will be its undoing, not God. The evil and suffering around us is not God's doing; it is our own. We are to blame. God's plan was for us to live and thrive in a state of grace. Our selfish and perverted ambitions have brought all of the suffering upon us that we are experiencing. All of this is part of the answer to three of the four questions that I spoke of in Chapter 7.

Returning to these specific verses, Jesus makes a statement that is used by many to point to the "second coming." In Matthew 24:27, Jesus says, "For as the lightning comes from the east and flashes as far as the west, so will be the coming of the Son of Man." It is certain that Jesus is coming to this earth a second time, but it will not be in the way that the modern Evangelical church has proclaimed it for so many years. As we move forward into Revelation, we will see this second coming and how it will unfold.

There is also one more very important message here that Jesus states, "But be alert." Be aware. Be awake. Throughout the ministry of Jesus, these words are consistently reiterated. It is so easy to drift into a state of apathy or complacency, but we cannot. We must always be aware and awake as to what is happening in our world. If we close our eyes to it, we will miss seeing the truth within the Scriptures unfolding.

Matthew 24:22-28 "And if those days had not been cut short, no one would be saved, but for the sake of the elect those days will be cut short. Then if anyone says to you, 'Look! Here is the Messiah!' [or *the Christ*] or 'There he is!'—do not believe it. For false messiahs [or *christs*] and false prophets will appear and produce great signs and wonders, to lead astray, if possible, even the elect. Take note, I have told you beforehand. So, if they say to you, 'Look! He is in the wilderness,' do not go out. If they say, 'Look! He is in the inner rooms,' do not believe it. For as the lightning comes

from the east and flashes as far as the west, so will be the
coming of the Son of Man. Wherever the corpse is, there the
eagles will gather.”


Mark 13:20-23 “And if the Lord had not cut short those days,
no one would be saved, but for the sake of the elect, whom
he chose, he has cut short those days. And if anyone says to
you at that time, ‘Look! Here is the Messiah! [or *the Christ*]’
or ‘Look! There he is!’—do not believe it. False messiahs [or
*christs*] and false prophets will appear and produce signs and
wonders, to lead astray, if possible, the elect. But be alert; I
have already told you everything.”


***


As Jesus continues, He reveals a significant event that will occur prior
to the coming of the Son of Man. “Immediately after the suffering of
those days” indicates that the suffering will precede the coming of Jesus.
What follows is what many call “The Great Cataclysm,” a major cosmic
event like humankind has never seen. At this time, Jesus will appear for all
humankind to see and will come back to this earth to reign for a period of
time. We will discuss the cataclysm and coming of Jesus further as we move
into Revelation.


Matthew 24:29-31 “Immediately after the suffering of those
days the sun will be darkened, and the moon will not give its
light; the stars will fall from heaven, and the powers of heaven
will be shaken. “Then the sign of the Son of Man will appear
in heaven, and then all the tribes of the earth will mourn, and
they will see ‘the Son of Man coming on the clouds of heaven’
with power and great glory. And he will send out his angels

with a loud trumpet call, and they will gather his elect from the four winds, from one end of heaven to the other."

Mark 13:24-27 "But in those days, after that suffering, the sun will be darkened, and the moon will not give its light, and the stars will be falling from heaven, and the powers in the heavens will be shaken. "Then they will see 'the Son of Man coming in clouds' with great power and glory. Then he will send out the angels and gather the [other ancient authorities read *his*] elect from the four winds, from the ends of the earth to the ends of heaven."

Luke 21:25-28 "There will be signs in the sun, the moon, and the stars and on the earth distress among nations confused by the roaring of the sea and the waves. People will faint from fear and foreboding of what is coming upon the world, for the powers of the heavens will be shaken. Then they will see 'the Son of Man coming in a cloud' with power and great glory. Now when these things begin to take place, stand up and raise your heads, because your redemption is drawing near [or *at hand*]."

***

Be aware. Stay awake. Jesus encourages the disciples and all future generations to watch for these signs, these events. As we are able to tell when one season changes to another, we are to be aware of these events and be able to discern their meaning and purpose. They are telling us the end of the ages is near. Jesus informs us that all of these things will take place before the end of the ages. All that we see around us, all that we know on this earth, all of it will pass away, but the word of God, the truth of God will not pass away.

Matthew 24:32-35 "From the fig tree learn its lesson: as soon as its branch becomes tender and puts forth its leaves, you know that summer is near. So also, when you see all these things, you know that he [or *it*] is near, at the very gates. Truly I tell you, this generation will not pass away until all these things have taken place. Heaven and earth will pass away, but my words will not pass away."

Mark 13:28-31 "From the fig tree learn its lesson: as soon as its branch becomes tender and puts forth its leaves, you know that summer is near. So also, when you see these things taking place, you know that he [or *it*] is near, at the very gates. Truly I tell you, this generation will not pass away until all these things have taken place. Heaven and earth will pass away, but my words will not pass away."

Luke 21:29-33 Then he told them a parable: "Look at the fig tree and all the trees; as soon as they sprout leaves you can see for yourselves and know that summer is already near. So also, when you see these things taking place, you know that the kingdom of God is near. Truly I tell you, this generation will not pass away until all things have taken place. Heaven and earth will pass away, but my words will not pass away."

***

Jesus repeats more forcefully what has been stated. The disciples and all who follow must be aware, stay awake, and be on guard. The return of Jesus will come at a time that many will not expect. The hope of the return of Jesus will fade in many and they will lose their faith. But we must stay vigilant for Jesus will return.

Matthew 24:36-44 "But about that day and hour no one knows, neither the angels of heaven, nor the Son [other ancient authorities lack *nor the Son*], but only the Father. For as the days of Noah were, so will be the coming of the Son of Man. For as in the days before the flood they were eating and drinking, marrying and giving in marriage, until the day Noah entered the ark, and they knew nothing until the flood came and swept them all away, so, too, will be the coming of the Son of Man. Then two will be in the field; one will be taken, and one will be left. Two women will be grinding meal together; one will be taken, and one will be left. Keep awake, therefore, for you do not know on what day [other ancient authorities read *at what hour*] your Lord is coming. But understand this: if the owner of the house had known in what part of the night the thief was coming, he would have stayed awake and would not have let his house be broken into. Therefore you also must be ready, for the Son of Man is coming at an hour you do not expect."

Mark 13:32-37 "But about that day or hour no one knows, neither the angels in heaven nor the Son, but only the Father. Beware, keep alert [other ancient authorities add *and pray*], for you do not know when the time will come. It is like a man going on a journey, when he leaves home and puts his slaves in charge, each with his work, and commands the doorkeeper to be on the watch. Therefore, keep awake, for you do not know when the master of the house will come, in the evening or at midnight or at cockcrow or at dawn, or else he may find you asleep when he comes suddenly. And what I say to you I say to all: Keep awake."

Luke 21:34-36 "Be on guard so that your hearts are not weighed down with dissipation and drunkenness and the worries of this life and that day does not catch you unexpectedly, like a trap. For it will come upon all who live on the face of the whole earth. Be alert at all times, praying that you may have the strength to escape all these things that will take place and to stand before the Son of Man."

***

In the next passage concerning the end of the ages, Jesus promises blessings to those who stay aware and awake while doing what is right and good in the eyes of God and damnation to those who turn from their faith and do what is wrong in the eyes of God.

Matthew 24:45-51 "Who, then, is the faithful and wise slave whom his master has put in charge of his household, to give the other slaves [Greek *to give them*] their allowance of food at the proper time? Blessed is that slave whom his master will find at work when he arrives. Truly I tell you, he will put that one in charge of all his possessions. But if that wicked slave says to himself, 'My master is delayed,' and begins to beat his fellow slaves and eats and drinks with drunkards, the master of that slave will come on a day when he does not expect him and at an hour that he does not know. He will cut him in pieces [or *cut him off*] and put him with the hypocrites, where there will be weeping and gnashing of teeth."

****

In this final parable, concerning the end of the ages, Jesus speaks to all those who profess with their mouth that they are believers. But as I have stated before, God knows our hearts, our true motives, and our true characters. In the end, those who profess to be believers will be separated according to the truth within them. The wicked will go away into eternal punishment, but the righteous will receive the blessing of eternal life.

There are many in the Church today who shy away from the word *sin*. They say, "What is sin? What is it in our lives that would cause God to condemn us into eternal damnation?" This parable, among other verses, provides us with just those actions or non-actions that God despises and that I shared in Chapter 5.

> Matthew 25:31-46 "When the Son of Man comes in his glory and all the angels with him, then he will sit on the throne of his glory. All the nations will be gathered before him, and he will separate people one from another as a shepherd separates the sheep from the goats, and he will put the sheep at his right hand and the goats at the left. Then the king will say to those at his right hand, 'Come, you who are blessed by my Father, inherit the kingdom prepared for you from the foundation of the world, for I was hungry and you gave me food, I was thirsty and you gave me something to drink, I was a stranger and you welcomed me, I was naked and you gave me clothing, I was sick and you took care of me, I was in prison and you visited me.' Then the righteous will answer him, 'Lord, when was it that we saw you hungry and gave you food or thirsty and gave you something to drink? And when was it that we saw you a stranger and welcomed you or naked and gave you clothing? And when was it that we saw you sick or in prison and visited you?' And the king will answer them, 'Truly I tell you, just as you did it to one of the least of these brothers

and sisters of mine, you did it to me.' Then he will say to those at his left hand, 'You who are accursed, depart from me into the eternal fire prepared for the devil and his angels, for I was hungry and you gave me no food, I was thirsty and you gave me nothing to drink, I was a stranger and you did not welcome me, naked and you did not give me clothing, sick and in prison and you did not visit me.' Then they also will answer, 'Lord, when was it that we saw you hungry or thirsty or a stranger or naked or sick or in prison and did not take care of you?' Then he will answer them, 'Truly I tell you, just as you did not do it to one of the least of these, you did not do it to me.' And these will go away into eternal punishment but the righteous into eternal life."

***

Following are some verses from other books of the Scriptures that pertain to the end of the ages. These are not the words of Jesus, but they are inspired by God to give us greater insight on the events of those days and provide us with a glimpse of eternity.

The Scriptures tell us that the end of the ages will be preceded by "the last trumpet." Jesus mentions this, as we have read, in Matthew 24:29-31. This final trumpet will also be addressed later in the Book of Revelation. Whether the trumpet will actually be heard by those of us on earth is not absolutely clear. We know that it will be heard in Heaven where God and the heavenly hosts abide, but we cannot say for sure that we will physically hear it on this earth. As we move into Revelation, we will see that there are events marked by declarations or trumpets within the heavenly hosts that are not heard on this earth. The way that the heavenly hosts communicate is according to God's order.

The Scriptures speak of the imperishable and immortal body we will receive as we pass from this life unto the next. The new body will be a spirit body. This is what makes it imperishable and immortal. It is a body which

150

we cannot perceive in our minds with our finite understanding. It will be a body that has no blemish. We will exist in the spirit for we will become spirit beings as I shared in Chapters 1 and 6.

John 16:1-4a "I have said these things to you to keep you from falling away [or *stumbling*]. They will put you out of the synagogues. Indeed, an hour is coming when those who kill you will think that by doing so they are offering worship to God. And they will do this because they have not known the Father or me. But I have said these things to you so that when their hour comes you may remember that I told you about them."

1 Corinthians 15:50-55 What I am saying, brothers and sisters, is this: flesh and blood cannot inherit the kingdom of God, nor does the perishable inherit the imperishable. Look, I will tell you a mystery! We will not all die [Greek *fall asleep*], but we will all be changed, in a moment, in the twinkling of an eye, at the last trumpet. For the trumpet will sound, and the dead will be raised imperishable, and we will be changed. For this perishable body must put on imperishability, and this mortal body must put on immortality. When this perishable body puts on imperishability and this mortal body puts on immortality, then the saying that is written will be fulfilled: "Death has been swallowed up in victory." "Where, O death, is your victory? Where, O death, is your sting?"

***

Here, in the first passage, the verses speak of the trumpet again and how the "dead in Christ will rise first." This is where those who proclaim the idea of a "rapture" establish their doctrine. As I have said, I do not support the idea of taking one verse and establishing a doctrine. As we will see later in Revelation, there will be many gatherings of the righteous and unrighteous that have died. The resurrection of the dead is a truth, but I will not say it is one big event. I will comment on this more within the study of Revelation.

In the second passage, the verses speak of God avenging the righteous who have suffered under the hand of the unrighteous by sending the unrighteous to eternal damnation and punishment. The unrighteous will be separated from the glory and magnificence of a loving God and be cast into eternal punishment. They will know only torture for all of eternity.

Understand, it is not God's choice that these should go to eternal damnation. It is by the choices they have made that send them into an eternity outside of the presence of God. In their earthly life, they chose not to believe or accept the truth of God. That is their own undoing.

1 Thessalonians 4:13-18 But we do not want you to be uninformed, brothers and sisters, about those who have died [Greek *are asleep*], so that you may not grieve as others do who have no hope. For since we believe that Jesus died and rose again, even so, through Jesus, God will bring with him those who have died [Greek *fallen asleep*]. For this we declare to you by the word of the Lord, that we who are alive, who are left until the coming of the Lord, will by no means precede those who have died [Greek *fallen asleep*]. For the Lord himself, with a cry of command, with the archangel's call and with the sound of God's trumpet, will descend from heaven, and the dead in Christ will rise first. Then we who are alive, who are left, will be caught up in the clouds together with them to meet the Lord in the air, and so we will be with the Lord forever. Therefore encourage one another with these words.

2 Thessalonians 1:5-12 This is evidence of the righteous judgment of God and is intended to make you worthy of the kingdom of God, for which you are also suffering. For it is indeed just of God to repay with affliction those who afflict you and to give relief to the afflicted as well as to us, when the Lord Jesus is revealed from heaven with his mighty angels in a fiery flame, inflicting vengeance on those who do not know God and on those who do not obey the gospel of our Lord Jesus. These will suffer the punishment of eternal destruction, separated from the presence of the Lord and from the glory of his might, when he comes to be glorified by his saints and to be marveled at on that day among all who have believed, because our testimony to you was believed. To this end we always pray for you, asking that our God will make you worthy of his call and will fulfill by his power every good resolve and work of faith, so that the name of our Lord Jesus may be glorified in you and you in him, according to the grace of our God and the Lord Jesus Christ.

***

The Scriptures consistently remind us that there is an order to how God will end this creation. As Jesus taught the disciples, there will be a period of time when suffering will increase before the spirit of the false prophet is fully revealed. The spirit of the false prophet has, is, and will be prevalent before it is fully manifested. The following verses refute the idea that the return of Jesus has already happened. The prophecies which have been spoken by Jesus (and I will be discussing more as we go through Revelation) must be fulfilled to keep God's order.

Let me interject here: The spirit of the antichrist spoken of in 1 John and 2 John (1 John 2:18, 1 John 2:22, 1 John 4:3, and 2 John 1:7) is different from the spirit of the false prophet spoken of in Revelation. It is a truth that the spirit of the antichrist is still active in our world, but it was much more prevalent during the immediate years after Jesus. The purpose of the spirit of the antichrist was to extinguish the claim of Jesus Christ being the Son of God and the Messiah. That initial push to erase the claims of Jesus Christ and His disciples failed though it is still found in some religions today.

The spirit of the false prophet that is spoken of in Revelation is a spirit of deception to accommodate sin and compromise the truth of the Scriptures within the Church. Jesus speaks of this deception when He addresses them in the letters to Pergamum and Thyatira found in Revelation 2:12-29. The objective of the spirit of the false prophet is to twist the Scriptures into teachings that are contrary to what Jesus Christ taught. Much like the teachings of the Nicolaitans, Balaam, and Jezebel that Jesus speaks of in those letters. I shared with you these ideas in Chapter 5 and will comment more on them in Chapter 14.

It is the continued popularity of the spirit of the false prophet that ushers in the end of the ages. As there is the spirit of evil, hate, murder, lying, etc., in people, there is the spirit of the false prophet within the Church. This spirit has manifested itself throughout contemporary history by many within the Church. I believe that as Revelation speaks of the two beasts being multiple rulers, kingdoms, and nations throughout history, the spirit of the false prophet is made up of multiple "religious" people and entities throughout the Church's history.

There are two very important verses that I have pointed out to many that ends this passage. Verses 11 and 12 state, "For this reason God sends them a powerful delusion, leading them to believe what is false, so that all who have not believed the truth but took pleasure in unrighteousness will be condemned." We have seen more and more of this during the present trying times. More and more people, both inside and outside the Church, are believing the lie. It has become a sad state of deception that even those who profess to believe are accepting the lie, yet it is prophesied in the words of these verses. God knows our hearts and knows our motives. If you are not sincere in seeking the truth of the Scriptures, you will find yourself believing the lie.

2 Thessalonians 2:1-12 As to the coming of our Lord Jesus Christ and our being gathered together to him, we beg you, brothers and sisters, not to be quickly shaken in mind or alarmed, either by spirit or by word or by letter, as though from us, to the effect that the day of the Lord is already here. Let no one deceive you in any way, for that day will not come unless the rebellion comes first and the lawless one is revealed [Greek *the man of lawlessness*; other ancient authorities read *the man of sin*], the one destined for destruction [Greek *the son of destruction*]. He opposes and exalts himself above every so-called god or object of worship, so that he takes his seat in the temple of God, declaring himself to be God. Do you not remember that I told you these things when I was still with you? And you know what is now restraining him, so that he may be revealed when his time comes. For the mystery of lawlessness is already at work, but only until the one who now restrains it is removed. And then the lawless one will be revealed, whom the Lord Jesus [other ancient authorities lack *Jesus*] will destroy [other ancient authorities read *consume*] with the breath of his mouth, annihilating him by the manifestation of his coming. The coming of the lawless one is apparent in the working of Satan, who uses all power, signs, lying wonders, and every kind of wicked deception for those who are perishing because they refused to love the truth and so be saved. For this reason God sends them a powerful delusion, leading them to believe what is false, so that all who have not believed the truth but took pleasure in unrighteousness will be condemned.

***

## The Authority of Jesus

The following verses are very important as we move into Revelation. From the very words spoken by Jesus, along with the verses found in 1 Corinthians, Ephesians, and Revelation, it is established that, through the life, death, and resurrection of Jesus, the Creator has given Jesus the Beloved "all authority in heaven and on earth." The obedience shown to the Creator and the sacrifice that Jesus made for all humankind on this earth, has afforded Him all authority over this creation. All authority.

But, as the passage in 1 Corinthians states, the Creator has subjected all things to Jesus, meaning absolute authority, except over the Creator who provided that authority. This authority is given to Jesus until all of the enemies of the Creator have been destroyed.

This truth is very significant in understanding Revelation and its visions. The Creator gives Jesus absolute authority for the work that has been done, is being done, and will be done until the end of this age.

Matthew 28:16-20 Now the eleven disciples went to Galilee, to the mountain to which Jesus had directed them. When they saw him, they worshiped him, but they doubted. And Jesus came and said to them, "All authority in heaven and on earth has been given to me. Go therefore and make disciples of all nations, baptizing them in the name of the Father and of the Son and of the Holy Spirit and teaching them to obey everything that I have commanded you. And remember, I am with you always, to the end of the age. [other ancient authorities add *Amen*]."

John 5:25-29 "Very truly, I tell you, the hour is coming and is now here when the dead will hear the voice of the Son of God, and those who hear will live. For just as the Father has life in himself, so he has granted the Son also to have life in himself, and he has given him authority to execute judgment because he is the Son of Man. Do not be astonished at this, for the hour is coming when all who are in their graves will hear his voice and will come out: those who have done good to the resurrection of life, and those who have done evil to the resurrection of condemnation."

1 Corinthians 15:20-28 But in fact Christ has been raised from the dead, the first fruits of those who have died [Greek *fallen asleep*]. For since death came through a human, the resurrection of the dead has also come through a human, for as all die in Adam, so all will be made alive in Christ. But each in its own order: Christ the first fruits, then at his coming those who belong to Christ. Then comes the end, when he hands over the kingdom to God the Father, after he has destroyed every ruler and every authority and power. For he must reign until he has put all his enemies under his feet. The last enemy to be destroyed is death. For "God [Greek *he*] has put all things in subjection under his feet." But when it says, "All things are put in subjection," it is plain that this does not include the one who put all things in subjection under him. When all things are subjected to him, then the Son himself will also be subjected to the one who put all things in subjection under him, so that God may be all in all.

Ephesians 1:20-23 God [Greek *He*] put this power to work in Christ when he raised him from the dead and seated him at his right hand in the heavenly places [Greek *heavenlies*], far above all rule and authority and power and dominion and above every name that is named, not only in this age but also in the age to come. And he has put all things under his feet and has made him the head over all things for the Church, which is his body, the fullness of him who fills all in all.

Revelation 2:26-28a "To everyone who conquers and continues to do my works to the end, I will give authority over the nations, to rule [or *to shepherd*] them with an iron scepter, as when clay pots are shattered - even as I also received authority from my Father."

# THE SIX SECTIONS

As I started this project, I began viewing Revelation in sections. As I have stated, I see Revelation as many different visions, not one continuous one. So, I came up with six sections into which I divided the content of Revelation. These divisions helped me see what was happening within the context of the subject matter.

First Section - The Authority of Jesus
The first section deals with the authority of Jesus. Jesus's authority is displayed throughout Revelation, but these specific verses record the transition of authority that was rewarded Jesus by the Creator for Jesus's obedience and sacrifice thus providing salvation, redemption, and justification for all of humankind. This transition of authority is very important in the progression of Revelation, as you will see moving forward.

Revelation 1:1-20: Introduction and Salutation, A Vision of Christ

Revelation 2:1-29: The Message to Ephesus, The Message to Smyrna, The Message to Pergamum, The Message to Thyatira

Revelation 3:1-22: The Message to Sardis, The Message to Philadelphia, The Message to Laodicea

Revelation 4:1-11: The Heavenly Worship

Revelation 5:1-14: The Scroll and the Lamb

Revelation 6:1-17: The Seven Seals

Revelation 8:1: The Seventh Seal

Second Section – The Gatherings

The second section deals with the "gatherings." I use the term *gathering* to define where a group of people are physically/spiritually brought together in the presence of God or Jesus. As I have stated, the modern Evangelical church often mentions the idea of a "rapture" or the gathering of the saints to be taken up into heaven. Revelation does not have one specific passage that deals directly with this type of event. It does, however, provide us with nine different gatherings that occur as the end of the ages unfolds. Following are those nine gatherings. We will examine each gathering more specifically as they appear within the visions of Revelation.

1 of 9 - Revelation 6:9-11: The Souls of Those Who Had Been Slaughtered

    2 of 9 - Revelation 7:1-8: The 144,000 of Israel Sealed

    3 of 9 - Revelation 14:14-16: Reaping the Earth's Harvest Part 1

    4 of 9 - Revelation 15:2-4: Those Who Had Conquered the Beast

    5 of 9 - Revelation 7:9-17: The Multitude from Every Nation

    6 of 9 - Revelation 14:17-20: Reaping the Earth's Harvest Part 2

    7 of 9 - Revelation 14:1-5: The Lamb and the 144,000

    8 of 9 - Revelation 20:4-6: Gathering at the One Thousand Years

    9 of 9 - Revelation 20:11-15: The Dead Are Judged

***

Third Section – Judgment of Humankind

The third section consists of verses that deal with the judgment of humankind. I see the seven trumpets as consisting of consequences that we have brought on ourselves that God is allowing due to our free will, sins, and destructive behavior on this earth.

From the two witnesses and beyond, I see these visions proclaiming direct judgments from God for the evil in the world.

Revelation 8:1-13: The Golden Censer, The Seven Trumpets

The seven trumpets are warnings to humankind and are the direct consequences of humankind's reckless and abusive treatment of the earth. Humankind reaps what it has sown.

Revelation 9:1-21: The Seven Trumpets Continued

Revelation 11:1-19: The Two Witnesses, The Seventh Trumpet

Revelation 15:1-8: The Angels with the Seven Last Plagues

Revelation 16:1-21: The Bowls of God's Wrath

The seven bowls of God's wrath are a judgment upon the unrighteous directly from God for their rejection of the plan of salvation that They have provided.

Revelation 20:11-15: The Dead Are Judged

***

Fourth Section – The Seven Thunders and the Little Scroll

The fourth section deals with a very small passage of verses that deserve to be set apart. The Seven Thunders are a mystery that I will discuss later in Chapter 17.

Revelation 10:1-11: The Seven Thunders and the Angel with the Little Scroll

***

Fifth Section – The Physical and Spiritual Battles

The fifth section consists of the physical and spiritual battles. These are the battles that are happening within the physical and spiritual world around us. The physical battles are the wars we see in our daily lives. Humankind warring with itself is our lust for greed and power causing destruction and the loss of innocent lives.

The spiritual battles are unseen—the fight between the components of the spiritual world. I believe in angels and demons. I believe we walk among a spiritual battle that is not ours to fight. There is a common phrase among modern Evangelicals about "spiritual warfare." That is another false doctrine that has been spread. Spiritual battles are not ours to fight. Our battle is solely within ourselves, the struggle to believe, have faith, and do what is right in the eyes of God versus what our flesh would rather do. That is a tough enough battle in itself. It is not our place to take on the demons in this world. I leave those battles up to the blood and power of Jesus and the angels.

Both the physical and spiritual battles are the ongoing battle between God and Satan, the war over the dominion of this creation. In the end as we will see, God will win.

Revelation 12:1-18: The Woman and the Dragon, Michael Defeats the Dragon, The Dragon Fights Again on Earth

Revelation 13:1-10: The First Beast

Revelation 13:11-18: The Second Beast and the Image

Revelation 14:1-20: The Lamb and the 144,000, The Messages of the Three Angels, Reaping the Earth's Harvest

Revelation 17:1-18: The Great Whore and the Beast

Revelation 18:1-24: The Fall of Babylon

Revelation 19:1-21: The Rejoicing in Heaven, The Rider on the White Horse, The Beast and Its Armies Defeated

Revelation 20:1-10: The Thousand Years, Satan's Doom

***

Sixth Section – Into Eternity

The sixth section is all about eternity. For those who faithfully believe it is a spiritual eternal home abiding in a state of grace and in the presence of our loving God. For those who do not believe, it is suffering in spiritual torment and darkness, separated from the love of God.

Revelation 21:1-27: The New Heaven and the New Earth, Vision of the New Jerusalem

Revelation 22:1-21: The River of Life, Epilogue and Benediction

# REVELATION TABLE OF CONTENTS

Because it is important that you are assured all of the chapters and verses of Revelation are represented in this book, following is a Table of Contents for every chapter and verse along with the pages on which you will find them. Not a single verse or word is missing.

Revelation 6:1-17
Verses 1-11, Pages 195-197
Verses 12-17, Pages 247-248

Revelation 7:1-17
Verses 1-8, Page 198
Verses 9-17, Pages 231-232

Revelation 8:1-13
Verse 1, Page 250
Verses 2-13, Pages 207-208

Revelation 9:1-21
Verses 1-21, Pages 211-212

Revelation 10:1-11
Verses 1-11, Pages 214-215

Revelation 11:1-19
Verses 1-13, Pages 233-235
Verse 14, Page 236
Verses 15-19, Pages 249-250

Revelation 12:1-18
Verses 1-18, Pages 172-174

Revelation 13:1-18
Verses 1-10, Pages 201-202
Verses 11-18, Page 204

Revelation 14:1-20
Verses 1-5, Pages 252-253
Verses 6-13, Pages 216-217
Verses 14-16, Page 228
Verses 17-20, Page 237

# THE REVELATION OF JOHN [APOCALYPSE] INTRODUCTION

As we begin our journey through Revelation, I would like to point out some things that are significant to its uniqueness.

Jesus is given many names/titles throughout Revelation. I have noted some of those names/titles at the end of this book in the "References" section.

Revelation provides seven different blessings to faithful believers who read its content. Revelation 1:3 is a blessing upon the reader. Revelation 14:13 is a blessing upon the dead that die from then on. Revelation 16:15 is a blessing for the one who stays awake. Revelation 19:9 is a blessing for those who are invited to the marriage of the Lamb. Revelation 20:6 is a blessing and a proclamation of holiness for those who share in the first resurrection. Revelation 22:7 is a blessing to those who keep the prophecy of this book. Revelation 22:14 is a blessing to those who wash their robes. It is not necessary that you fully understand Revelation to receive these blessings. It is only necessary that you read it and believe that it is truth for these blessings to be bestowed upon you.

The journey through Revelation provides you encounters with many different angels. These angels provide the writer with spiritual comfort and on some occasions, understanding of what is being seen or happening. Not all of the visions are clearly revealed, only those that are important for the understanding that we need of God at this time are revealed.

There is much imagery used in Revelation. I am not going to tell you I have figured it all out; I have not. Some of the imagery is understood, such as the dragon being Satan, the devil, as we know it. Some of the imagery, such as the first and second beasts, are explained by one of the angels as being nations and kingdoms that have been, are, and will be. Keep your mind open and your heart prepared in seeking the truth within Revelation. If after the first read you do not understand it, keep reading it and understanding will come with time.

God made us with a free will. God does not dictate or micromanage our behavior. God is in control of the final destiny of this creation in that there is a plan, an order. But as individuals, God allows our free will to drive humankind. Yes, there are times when God will intervene for us as individuals by the grace and mercy in which is the deepest character of God, but that is all. By the design in which God made us, They allow our free will to dictate our future while all along They know how that future will end as I shared previously.

The final important thing I want to point out is the concept of time. There are various references to time in Revelation. Whether it is noted in days, weeks, or years, there is no way that we can positively say that it is accurate as we know time. Why? Because we have no concept of eternity where there is no time. Time does not exist in eternity. All heavenly beings live only in the present. There is no yesterday or tomorrow. There is no past or future. There is only today. There is only the present. There is only *right now*. That is why when the verses in Genesis 1 speak of the earth being created in six days, we cannot view them as the six days that we know. They are merely a reference for separating the events of this creation which was actually billions of years. Think of this. A trillion years as measured by humankind is still today, the present, in eternity. God is always in the present. Grasp that.

In trying to convey this thought, writers in both the Old testament and New Testament wrote: "For a thousand years in your sight are like yesterday when it is past or like a watch in the night" (Psalm 90:4) and "But do not ignore this one fact, beloved, that with the Lord one day is like a thousand years, and a thousand years are like one day" (2 Peter 3:8). It is very important that you remember this in reading Revelation. Do not get caught up in trying to figure time lapses. It is impossible. Read to understand the events and to know them so that when you see them take place, you will know in your heart that the Scriptures are truth and that the end of the ages are upon us.

**Revelation 1:1-8 – Commentary**
**Introduction and Salutation**
The first note I want to make in beginning our journey through Revelation is the alternate translation of *servant*. You will see the word *slave* as the actual English translation for the original Greek text. I see the translators using the word *servant* in these cases due to it having a softer connotation to the word *slave*. As faithful believers, we are submitting our lives, willingly, to a loving God. We are choosing to serve a loving God; there is no obligation or imprisonment per se. We can walk away from that decision at any time. Yet, at the same time our service to God should be one of absolute devotion, never halfhearted. It is a much better choice to be a slave to a loving God doing good for our neighbors than to be a slave to the destructive nature of sin and wickedness.

In verse 3, both the reader and the hearer of Revelation are given the first of seven blessings. This blessing has a condition. The reader and hearer must "keep what is written in it." Revelation provides us with truth in the character of one who believes. It separates those who do what is right in the eyes of God from those who do wrong in the eyes of God. It separates the righteous from the unrighteous. It shows us that displaying the character of doing right outwardly does not make a person righteous inwardly. The right spirit and character of the heart make a person righteous. This is the truth that the reader and hearer must keep in their lives to receive the blessing that is bestowed.

Verses 5 and 6 provide us with the roles of Jesus as the second entity of the Deity as I shared in Chapter 1. In these verses, Jesus is presented as the faithful witness of God, the firstborn of the dead (meaning that Jesus is the resurrection from the dead), the ruler of the kings (political leaders) of the earth, the provider who loves us and redeems us of our sins (for those who faithfully believe) by the blood sacrifice, and the provider of our eternal life within the heavenly kingdom. These are the roles of Jesus, the Beloved.

Verse 8 proclaims the eternal existence of God (the Deity, the Holy Trinity). The Alpha and Omega. The beginning and the end of all things. Eternal, "who is and who was and who is to come." God has no yesterday or tomorrow but only today. For in eternity where there is no time, there is only today, the present.

Revelation 1:1-8 [1] The revelation of Jesus Christ, which God gave him to show his servants [Greek *slaves*] what must soon take place, and he made it known by sending his angel to his servant [Greek *slave*] John, [2] who testified to the word of God and to the testimony of Jesus Christ, even to all that he saw. [3] Blessed is the one who reads the words of the prophecy, and blessed are those who hear and who keep what is written in it, for the time is near.

[4] John to the seven churches that are in Asia: Grace to you and peace from him who is and who was and who is to come and from the seven spirits who are before his throne, [5] and from Jesus Christ, the faithful witness, the firstborn of the dead, and the ruler of the kings of the earth. To him who loves us and freed [other ancient authorities read *washed*] us from our sins by his blood [6] and made us a kingdom, priests

serving [Greek *priests to*] his God and Father, to him be glory
and dominion forever and ever. Amen.

7 Look! He is coming with the clouds; every eye will see him,
even those who pierced him, and all the tribes of the earth
will wail on account of him. So it is to be. Amen.

8 "I am the Alpha and the Omega," says the Lord God, who
is and who was and who is to come, the Almighty.

***

## Revelation 12:1-18 – Commentary
### The Woman and the Dragon
### Michael Defeats the Dragon
### The Dragon Fights Again on Earth

Luke 10:18 He [Jesus] said to them, "I watched Satan fall
from heaven like a flash of lightning."

I have placed Revelation 12:1-18 here, at the beginning, because it
introduces us to the spiritual battle that has been, is, and will continue
to take place until the final battle at the end of the ages. These passages
speak of the fall of Satan from heaven. All of this took place before the
creation of humankind. Satan, after his fall, became a part of God's plan
for humankind. All of this is part of the four questions I shared in Chapter
7. Let us address the verses we see before us at this time.

Revelation 12:1-3 speaks of a portent. A portent is an omen, a premonition, a sign of glory or warning. It is a celestial phenomenon or vision intended for a deeper symbolic meaning.

The woman throughout these verses symbolizes the christening of two primary events: the creation of humankind itself and the introduction of the Messiah, the savior of humankind, the shepherd to all faithful believers, who provides salvation, redemption, and justification for all those who faithfully believe. You can see the figure of the woman as strictly a visual symbol for the beginning of the spiritual struggle on earth or you can equate the woman to be Mary, the mother of Jesus. But the primary focus of these verses is that they establish the intensity of the spiritual struggle of humankind on this earth. The struggle to do what is right and good in the eyes of God while Satan, the force of evil fights to overcome and dominate.

In Revelation 12:3, we are introduced to the dragon. The dragon represents the forces of evil driven by Satan who is the devil. The dragon is all that is Satan. It is symbolic of kingdoms, nations, and rulers throughout the centuries that have continuously denounced God and persecuted, tormented, and oppressed those who faithfully believe. It is the embodiment of Satan and all of the evil that is in the world.

Note: As I shared within the prologue concerning the translations of the Scriptures, there is a translation of a Greek word in verse 10 that I would like to point out. The New Revised Standard Version Updated Edition uses the phrase "brothers and sisters." The actual Greek word that is used here is *adelphoi*. Many of the older translations used the English word *brethren* or *brothers* for the translation of this Greek word. Those translations lean toward masculine nouns/pronouns, when in fact the Greek word *adelphoi* includes both males and females. That is why the more modern translations use "brothers and sisters." The sentence is actually referring to all faithful believers, both male and female. Many early translations were based on masculine nouns/pronouns, when in fact they should have been more gender inclusive as I shared in the prologue.

Revelation 12:7-12 summarizes the rebellion, defeat, and expulsion of Satan, the dragon, and his angels from heaven. They were cast down to earth as their punishment. As noted at the introduction of this section, Luke 10:18, Jesus speaks of seeing Satan fall from heaven.

Isaiah 14:12-15 describes Satan's fall in this way:

> "How you are fallen from heaven, O Morning Star, son of
> Dawn! How you are cut down to the ground, you who laid
> the nations low! You said to yourself, 'I will ascend to heaven;
> I will raise my throne above the stars of God; I will sit on the
> mount of assembly on the heights of Zaphon; I will ascend
> to the tops of the clouds; I will make myself like the Most
> High.' But you are brought down to Sheol, to the depths of
> the Pit.'"

As seen from the verses in Isaiah, Satan desired to be God. This was the lie he told himself. Satan's downfall was his selfish ambition to be God. Satan shared this lie with a horde of other angels, and they followed him believing that they would rule the heavens. This is the same lie that Satan has used throughout the ages to entice the lust of power by humankind to rule. The power to be a god. This same lie is producing much of what we are seeing today: the overwhelming lies and deception within governments and nations to control and have power. It is the spirit of the false prophet promoting lies and deception to obtain power and rule within our communities, both nationally and internationally. You will see this deceptive pattern repeated in our journey through Revelation.

The final verses of 13 through 18 reveal this continuous struggle within humankind. The force of evil to overcome all that is good. This is very real within the age in which we are living. This is what we are facing in our daily lives. But, as illustrated in these verses, God always provides a safe haven for those who faithfully believe. In the midst of the suffering and struggles, our faith in God provides a peace within the storm and a place of rest. This is the hope that sustains us.

### Revelation 12:1-18 – The Woman and the Dragon - [1]
A great portent appeared in heaven: a woman clothed with the sun, with the moon under her feet, and on her head a crown of twelve stars. [2] She was pregnant and was crying out

in birth pangs, in the agony of giving birth. ³ Then another portent appeared in heaven: a great red dragon, with seven heads and ten horns and seven diadems on his heads. ⁴ His tail swept down a third of the stars of heaven and threw them to the earth. Then the dragon stood before the woman who was about to deliver a child, so that he might devour her child as soon as it was born. ⁵ And she gave birth to a son, a male child, who is to rule [or *to shepherd*] all the nations with a scepter of iron. But her child was snatched away and taken to God and to his throne, ⁶ and the woman fled into the wilderness, where she has a place prepared by God, so that there she can be nourished for one thousand two hundred sixty days.

**Michael Defeats the Dragon** - ⁷ And war broke out in heaven; Michael and his angels fought against the dragon. The dragon and his angels fought back, ⁸ but they were defeated, and there was no longer any place for them in heaven. ⁹ The great dragon was thrown down, that ancient serpent, who is called the devil and Satan, the deceiver of the whole world—he was thrown down to the earth, and his angels were thrown down with him.

¹⁰ Then I heard a loud voice in heaven proclaiming, "Now have come the salvation and the power and the kingdom of our God and the authority of his Messiah [Greek *Christ*], for the accuser of our brothers and sisters [Greek "adelphoi" *brothers* or *believers* designating both men and women] has been thrown down, who accuses them day and night before our God. ¹¹ But they have conquered him by the blood of the Lamb and by the word of their testimony, for they did not cling to life even in the face of death. ¹² Rejoice then, you heavens and those who dwell in them! But woe to the earth

and the sea, for the devil has come down to you with great wrath because he knows that his time is short!"

**The Dragon Fights Again on Earth** – [13] So when the dragon saw that he had been thrown down to the earth, he pursued [or *persecuted*] the woman who had delivered the male child. [14] But the woman was given the two wings of the great eagle, so that she could fly from the serpent into the wilderness, to her place where she is nourished for a time, and times, and half a time. [15] Then from his mouth the serpent poured water like a river after the woman, to sweep her away with the flood. [16] But the earth came to the help of the woman; it opened its mouth and swallowed the river that the dragon had poured from his mouth. [17] Then the dragon was angry with the woman and went off to wage war on the rest of her children, those who keep the commandments of God and hold the testimony of Jesus. [18] Then the dragon [Greek *Then he*] took his stand [other ancient authorities read *Then I stood*] on the sand of the seashore.

***

**Revelation 1:9-20 – Commentary**
  **A Vision of Christ**

As I noted in the last section of Chapter 10, the authority of Jesus is very important throughout Revelation. Here as we read Revelation 1:9-20, we are introduced to a glorified Jesus proclaiming, "I am the First and the Last and the Living One. I was dead, and see, I am alive forever and ever, and I have the keys of Death and of Hades." At the beginning of this vision, Jesus acknowledges to the writer the authority which has been established. This proclamation also establishes the role that Jesus the Beloved plays in the Deity, the Holy Trinity. In having risen from the dead, Jesus holds the keys of Death and of Hades: Death being the literal end of this life and Hades being the grave.

Having secured that authority, Jesus instructs the writer to "write what you have seen, what is, and what is to take place after this." The first instructions to write would be the letters to the churches. With this, Jesus proclaims the authority over the Church, not just a single body of faithful believers within a single congregation or denomination, but the Church as the corporate body of all faithful believers.

> Revelation 1:9-20 – A Vision of Christ – [9] I, John, your brother who share with you the persecution and the kingdom and the endurance in Jesus, was on the island called Patmos because of the word of God and the testimony of Jesus [or *testimony to Jesus*]. [10] I was in the spirit [or *in the Spirit*] on the Lord's day, and I heard behind me a loud voice like a trumpet [11] saying, "Write in a book what you see, and send it to the seven churches, to Ephesus, to Smyrna, to Pergamum, to Thyatira, to Sardis, to Philadelphia, and to Laodicea."

> [12] Then I turned to see whose voice it was that spoke to me, and on turning I saw seven golden lampstands, [13] and in the midst of the lampstands I saw one like the Son of Man, clothed with a long robe and with a golden sash across his chest. [14] His head and his hair were white as white wool, white as snow; his eyes were like a flame of fire; [15] his feet were like burnished bronze, refined as in a furnace, and his voice was like the sound of many waters. [16] In his right hand he held seven stars, and from his mouth came a sharp, two-edged sword, and his face was like the sun shining with full force.

$^{17}$ When I saw him, I fell at his feet as though dead. But he placed his right hand on me, saying, "Do not be afraid; I am the First and the Last $^{18}$ and the Living One. I was dead, and see, I am alive forever and ever, and I have the keys of Death and of Hades. $^{19}$ Now write what you have seen, what is, and what is to take place after this. $^{20}$ As for the mystery of the seven stars that you saw in my right hand and the seven golden lampstands: the seven stars are the angels of the seven churches, and the seven lampstands are the seven churches.

# THE LETTERS TO THE CHURCHES

**Revelation 2:1-29 through 3:1-22**

With the letters to the churches, the authority of Jesus as head of the Church is established. Jesus is the Shepherd. There are spiritual guidelines within the letters that the Church is instructed to follow. These letters speak to all faithful believers (and some not so faithful), not denominations, not independents, not affiliates, but to all faithful believers who profess that Jesus is Lord. *That* is the real Church. In reading these verses from the Scriptures, we are made aware of three things: that which is wrong in the eyes of God, that which is right in the eyes of God, and that which displeases God that we must repent of or face eternal consequences. God is a loving God who is always willing to forgive our sins and faults, but we have to be willing to repent of them with a sincere heart. If we do not, we will be found lacking on that day when we stand before the judgment seat and the books are open.

***

**Revelation 2:1-7 – Commentary**
**Ephesus - First Love**

Jesus notes to Ephesus that they are doing well in their outward actions of not tolerating evil, discerning false prophets among the teachers, and having endured the struggles of persecution without growing weary. But inwardly, they are lacking the zeal of their first love of God. They are acting righteously but their hearts are no longer committed to the depth of their relationship with God as they were in the beginning.

When a person is awakened to the grace of God in their lives, there is this immense amount of love for God that swells up inside their heart. I call this the "Grace Revelation." It is the realization that this all-powerful, all-knowing, and all-loving God that has created all things, has revealed Their grace to each of us personally. Grace is the absolute unconditional love of God for Their creation. This grace is available to all people who open themselves up to receive it. That is the only condition. You must open yourself up to receive it. I can confidently say that if you do so with a sincere heart you will have your "Grace Revelation."

It is that initial love that Jesus is speaking of here. That overwhelming sense of having tapped into the love of an eternal God. It is that same love that Jesus spoke of in Mark 12:30 where He states, "You shall love the Lord your God with all your heart and with all your soul and with all your mind and with all your strength." You cannot let that love diminish.

In the Prologue, I stated I do not believe that you have to attend church in order to have a personal relationship with God, but I do believe you have to establish a daily routine of reading the Scriptures, studying the Scriptures, and praying with a sincere heart to have that relationship. Many only see verses of the Scriptures when they attend their local church. Sadly, that is also the only time they pray. They participate in an emotional worship and negate true spiritual worship. You cannot sustain a relationship with God unless that first love continues to burn within your heart every day.

In Philippians 3:10-12, the writer states, "I want to know Christ [Greek *him*] and the power of his resurrection and the sharing of his sufferings by becoming like him in his death, if somehow I may attain the resurrection from the dead. Not that I have already obtained this or have already reached the goal, [or *have already been made perfect*] but I press on to lay hold of that for which Christ [other ancient authorities read *Christ Jesus*] has laid hold of me." That is the love that Jesus is speaking of to the church of Ephesus. That love is an uncompromising and relentless love that longs to commune with God. It is the love of reading and studying the Scriptures finding joy and peace as the verses speak to you. It is that love and passion that drive the spirit within you to always seek and desire to do what is right and good in the eyes of God. That is the spirit of first love which you must embrace and nurture in your daily walk.

In verse 6, Jesus mentions the Nicolaitans, we will learn more about them in the letter to Pergamum.

> Revelation 2:1-7 – The Message to Ephesus – [1] "To the angel of the church in Ephesus write: These are the words of him who holds the seven stars in his right hand, who walks among the seven golden lampstands: [2] "I know your works, your toil and your endurance. I know that you cannot tolerate evildoers; you have tested those who claim to be apostles but are not and have found them to be false. [3] I also know that you are enduring and bearing up for the sake of my name and that you have not grown weary. 4 But I have this against you, that you have abandoned the love you had at first. [5] Remember, then, from where you have fallen; repent and do the works you did at first. If not, I will come to you and remove your lampstand from its place, unless you repent. [6] Yet this is to your credit: you hate the works of the Nicolaitans, which I also hate. [7] Let anyone who has an ear listen to what the Spirit is saying to the churches. To everyone who conquers, I will give permission to eat from the tree of life that is in the paradise of God."

***

**Revelation 2:8-11 – Commentary**
**Smyrna – Be Faithful Until Death**

Jesus acknowledges no faults in the church of Smyrna. The earthly affliction and poverty the church has endured are seen as spiritual riches. The false prophets have made themselves known in Smyrna, but the church rejected them. Jesus warns them of the suffering and affliction they are about to experience and encourages them to be faithful until death.

It is much easier to face death when you are no longer given hope for life than it is to be given a choice of life or death because of your religious belief. I have witnessed many people who have died of cancer. Once all hope of cure is gone, death becomes a comfort. It becomes a source of peace. Especially when you have dealt with your sins and are ready to face God.

It is much harder to face death when you are given a choice of living or dying for what you believe in as so many martyrs have done. Many have endured torture before death for the sake of their faith. When you are confronted with the choice of living if you deny your faith or dying if you hold fast to your faith, death becomes much harder to face, especially if you love this life too much. Peter denied Jesus when faced with that choice the first time (Matthew 26:33–35, Mark 14:29–31, Luke 22:33–34, and John 18:15–27). Later in his life, Peter again faced death for his beliefs and held fast to his faith unto death. Jesus encourages us to be faithful until death. In doing so, the crown of life that awaits us will be far superior to any form of happiness found on this earth.

In verse 11, Jesus refers to the "second death." The "second death" is eternal damnation. It is the reality of living eternally in sorrow and suffering while separated from a loving God. Jesus promises Smyrna that all who hold fast to their faith in this life will not experience the second death.

Revelation 2:8-11 – The Message to Smyrna – [8] "And to the angel of the church in Smyrna write: These are the words of the First and the Last, who was dead and came to life: [9] "I know your affliction and your poverty, even though you are rich. I know the slander on the part of those who say that they are Jews and are not but are a synagogue of Satan. [10] Do not fear what you are about to suffer. Beware, the devil is about to throw some of you into prison so that you may be tested, and for ten days you will have affliction. Be faithful until death, and I will give you the crown of life. [11] Let anyone who has an ear listen to what the Spirit is saying to the churches. Whoever conquers will not be harmed by the second death."

***

**Revelation 2:12-17 – Commentary**

**Pergamum – Balaam and the Sins of Indulgence and Indifference**

Jesus points out the good of some at the church of Pergamum but then points out that there are those among them who are holding to the teaching of Balaam (see Numbers 31:15-16) and the indulgence and indifference of the Nicolaitans.

Balaam refused to listen to God (see the story of Balaam, Numbers 22-31) and went to Balak who had summoned him. Balak wanted Balaam to curse the children of Israel so that he could overcome them in war. Balaam would not curse Israel; he blessed them instead. Balak was furious with Balaam, but to save his own life, Balaam instructed Balak "to put a stumbling block before the people of Israel, so that they would eat food sacrificed to idols and engage in sexual immorality [or *prostitution*]" (Revelation 2:14b).

The Nicolaitans were a false form of Christianity, a "Christian" sect that lived in unrestrained indulgence and indifference to immoral sex and food. They perverted the Scriptures to adhere to their own gluttonous lifestyle while disregarding any form of discipline in these areas. This sect had grown popular in the areas of Ephesus and Pergamum. Jesus commended Ephesus for condemning the works of the Nicolaitans, but corrected Pergamum for having some who were embracing the Nicolaitans teachings. Jesus warns them to repent of these errors. If they do not repent, they will face the eternal consequences.

Revelation 2:12-17 – The Message to Pergamum – [12] "And to the angel of the church in Pergamum write: These are the words of him who has the sharp two-edged sword: [13] "I know

181

where you are living, where Satan's throne is. Yet you are holding fast to my name, and you did not deny your faith in me [or *deny my faith*] even in the days of Antipas my witness, my faithful one, who was killed among you, where Satan lives. <sup>14</sup> But I have a few things against you: you have some there who hold to the teaching of Balaam, who taught Balak to put a stumbling block before the people of Israel, so that they would eat food sacrificed to idols and engage in sexual immorality [or *prostitution*]. <sup>15</sup> So you also have some who hold to the teaching of the Nicolaitans. <sup>16</sup> Repent, then. If not, I will come to you soon and wage war against them with the sword of my mouth. <sup>17</sup> Let anyone who has an ear listen to what the Spirit is saying to the churches. To everyone who conquers I will give some of the hidden manna, and I will give a white stone, and on the white stone is written a new name that no one knows except the one who receives it."

***

## Revelation 2:18-29 – Commentary
### Thyatira – Tolerating the Sins of Jezebel

Jesus disapproves of those in Thyatira who were tolerating the woman Jezebel, a false prophet of her own self-indulgence. Much like the Nicolaitans, Jezebel was enticing members of the church into compromising their faith and accepting the sinful acts of sexual immorality and eating food sacrificed to idols. Jesus warns Thyatira of Jezebel's evil and the suffering that will occur to those who continue in their sins with her. It is here that Jesus makes a declaration that is most important to all of us concerning the day of judgment when we stand before God and the books are open.

I have already stated on several occasions that we will be judged by our inner motives. Motives that only God knows. Jesus reinforces that in verse 23 by saying, "And all the churches will know that I am the one who searches minds and hearts, and I will give to each of you as your works deserve." We can lie to ourselves and to others. We can justify our actions to ourselves and to others. But when the books are open and we stand before God, the true motives of our hearts will be revealed. Nothing will be hidden. That is why Jesus calls us to repent of those things that are wrong in the eyes of God. Repent with a sincere and pure heart and you will be forgiven and those sins will not be counted against you.

Revelation 2:18-29 – The Message to Thyatira – [18] "And to the angel of the church in Thyatira write: These are the words of the Son of God, who has eyes like a flame of fire and whose feet are like burnished bronze: [19] "I know your works: your love, faith, service, and endurance. I know that your latest works are greater than the first. [20] But I have this against you: you tolerate that woman Jezebel, who calls herself a prophet and is teaching and beguiling my servants [Greek *slaves*] to engage in sexual immorality [or *prostitution*] and to eat food sacrificed to idols. [21] I gave her time to repent, but she refuses to repent of her sexual immorality [or *prostitution*]. [22] Beware, I am throwing her on a bed, and those who commit adultery with her I am throwing into great distress, unless they repent of her doings, [23] and I will strike her children dead. And all the churches will know that I am the one who searches minds and hearts, and I will give to each of you as your works deserve. [24] But to the rest of you in Thyatira, who do not hold this teaching, who have not learned what some call 'the deep things of Satan,' to you I say, I do not lay on you any other burden; [25] only hold fast to what you have until I come. [26] To everyone who conquers and continues to do my works to the end, I will give authority over the nations, [27] to rule [or *to shepherd*] them with an iron scepter, as when clay pots are shattered—[28] "even as I also received authority from my Father. To the one who conquers I will also give the morning star. [29] Let anyone who has an ear listen to what the Spirit is saying to the churches."

***

## Revelation 3:1-6 – Commentary
### Sardis – Wake Up!

Jesus addresses the church of Sardis with a very simple but direct message: Wake up! Complacency is one of the greatest problems within the modern church. Having a sense of spiritual security within itself while the world around it is suffering and lost, is a sad state to be in. There are many within the Evangelical Charismatic movement that are caught up in this false sense of spiritual security. They are enthralled in an emotional state of worship rather than a spiritual state of worship. They confuse their emotions with being alive and in touch with God, when, in fact they, are dead in their sense of security and spiritual awareness. They are proud and arrogant in their palace of comfort, not realizing that they are dead to God. They are believing the lie that they are blessed by God when, in fact, they are spiritually lacking.

> Revelation 3:1-6 – The Message to Sardis – [1] "And to the angel of the church in Sardis write: These are the words of him who has the seven spirits of God and the seven stars: "I know your works; you have a name of being alive, but you are dead. [2] Wake up and strengthen what remains and is on the point of death, for I have not found your works perfect in the sight of my God. [3] Remember, then, what you received and heard; obey it and repent. If you do not wake up, I will come like a thief, and you will not know at what hour I will come to you. [4] Yet you have still a few persons in Sardis who have not soiled their clothes; they will walk with me, dressed in white, for they are worthy. [5] If you conquer, you will be clothed like them in white robes, and I will not erase your name from the book of life; I will confess your name before my Father and before his angels. [6] Let anyone who has an ear listen to what the Spirit is saying to the churches."

***

## Revelation 3:7-13 – Commentary
### Philadelphia – Hold Fast

Jesus encourages the church in Philadelphia to hold fast to their faith. Jesus acknowledges to them that He sees their struggles and suffering. But, through their suffering, they have endured, kept the Word, and have not denied Him. They have been faithful.

Because Philadelphia has endured such great anguish, Jesus makes them a promise: "Because you have kept my word of endurance, I will keep you from the hour of trial that is coming on the whole world to test the inhabitants of the earth." Remember what Jesus said earlier in Matthew 24:15-21, Mark 13:14-19, and Luke 21:20-24? He prophesied that "there will be great suffering, such as has not been from the beginning of the world until now, no, and never will be." Jesus promises those in the church of Philadelphia that because of their endurance and faithfulness, they would not have to experience this period of great suffering, "to test the inhabitants of the earth." What a powerful source of comfort for those who have already suffered so much. Jesus is faithful to those who are faithful.

Revelation 3:7-13 – The Message to Philadelphia – [7] "And to the angel of the church in Philadelphia write: These are the words of the Holy One, the True One, who has the key of David, who opens and no one will shut, who shuts and no one opens: [8] "I know your works. Look, I have set before you an open door that no one is able to shut. I know that you have but little power, yet you have kept my word and have not denied my name. [9] I will make those of the synagogue of Satan who say that they are Jews and are not but are lying—I will make them come and bow down before your feet, and they will learn that I have loved you. [10] Because you have kept my word of endurance, I will keep you from the hour of trial that is coming on the whole world to test the inhabitants of the earth. [11] I am coming soon; hold fast to what you have, so that no one takes away your crown. [12] If you conquer, I will make you a pillar in the temple of my God; you will never go out of it. I will write on you the name of my God and the name of the city of my God, the new Jerusalem that comes down from my God out of heaven, and my own new name. [13] Let anyone who has an ear listen to what the Spirit is saying to the churches."

***

### Revelation 3:14-22 – Commentary
### Laodicea – The Lukewarm Church

Jesus confronts the church in Laodicea with a very stern warning: "I know your works; you are neither cold nor hot. I wish that you were either cold or hot. So, because you are lukewarm and neither cold nor hot, I am about to spit you out of my mouth. For you say, 'I am rich, I have prospered, and I need nothing.' You do not realize that you are wretched, pitiable, poor, blind, and naked." With the word *spit*, Jesus is equating the act of vomiting, a total rejection of these people.

The words spoken by Jesus in verse 19 confirm and establish the condition of the heart in which we are expected to repent of our sins. "Be earnest, therefore, and repent." The word *earnest*, defined by *dictionary.com*, means "serious and zealous in intention, purpose, or effort...showing depth and sincerity of feeling." Jesus is calling for repentance with a pure and sincere heart. As I have stated, you can lie to yourself, but Jesus sees through the lies. A halfhearted confession is lukewarm. This is what He is referring to. If you do not repent of your sins with a truly sincere heart, it means nothing and you are worse off than you were before.

Understand this: Jesus knows the struggles we face. We are not perfect, nor will we ever be perfect as long as we are in this flesh. The sin in our lives is not what damns our souls. It is the insincerity or indifference in which we deal with them that damns our souls. God called David "a man after His own heart" (1 Samuel 13:14) because David had a sincere and pure heart before God. David knew his faults, weaknesses, and sins. He confronted them with a sincere heart, desiring to have a pure heart before God. He knew he was not perfect, but he knew when he sinned, he had to confess with the greatest of sincerity to a God who knew his heart and loved him. Again, it is not our sins that damn us; it is the sincerity in which we deal with our sins that determines whether our souls will be eternally damned.

I cannot think of any better description that depicts the condition of the modern Evangelical church here in the United States than these words of Jesus to the church in Laodicea. Over the past decades, the false teachings that have been brought forth from Evangelical pulpits have been so damaging to the work of God. False teachings such as prosperity living, "name-it-claim-it," faith healing, and positive thinking proclaimed by false prophets have resulted in an Evangelical church that is proud, boastful, and out of touch with the truth that Jesus gave us.

Revelation 3:14-22 – The Message to Laodicea – [14] "And to the angel of the church in Laodicea write: The words of the Amen, the faithful and true witness, the origin [or *beginning*] of God's creation: [15] "I know your works; you are neither cold nor hot. I wish that you were either cold or hot. [16] So, because you are lukewarm and neither cold nor hot, I am about to spit you out of my mouth. [17] For you say, 'I am rich, I have prospered, and I need nothing.' You do not realize that you are wretched, pitiable, poor, blind, and naked. [18] Therefore I advise you to buy from me gold refined by fire so that you may be rich, and white robes to clothe yourself and to keep the shame of your nakedness from being seen, and salve to anoint your eyes so that you may see. [19] I reprove and discipline those whom I love. Be earnest, therefore, and repent. [20] Listen! I am standing at the door, knocking; if you hear my voice and open the door, I will come in and eat with you, and you with me. [21] To the one who conquers I will give a place with me on my throne, just as I myself conquered and sat down with my Father on his throne. [22] Let anyone who has an ear listen to what the Spirit is saying to the churches."

***

With these letters, Jesus acknowledges and encourages the churches in Smyrna and Philadelphia for their faithfulness in the midst of struggles and trying times. They are reassured of their coming salvation and the promise of an eternal home in the presence of God for doing what is right and good. Jesus reprimands Ephesus, Pergamum, Thyatira, Sardis, and Laodicea for those things that are wrong and detestable in the eyes of God. They are provided with words of encouragement to repent and do what is right, while also reminding them that if they do not repent with a sincere heart, they will be lost and their eternal salvation will be denied.

# THE HEAVENLY WORSHIP

**Revelation 4:1-11 – Commentary**

In Revelation 4:1-11, we are provided with the writer's vision of the throne of God. It is an awesome vision of magnificence and power. God's throne is surrounded by the glory of power and beauty. We are introduced to the twenty-four elders and to the four living creatures. We see the "seven flaming torches, which are the seven spirits of God," which is a depiction of the all-encompassing, omnipresent attribute of God. It is a wondrous sight to behold.

I cannot tell you who the twenty-four elders are. There are many who have theories, but the most important matter is that they are elders who have been specifically chosen to sit around the throne of God as is noted in Mark 10:35-40.

The four living creatures have faces of a lion, ox, human, and eagle. I see those faces as representation of the attributes of God. As the lion is depicted, God is King. As the ox is depicted, God is strong and powerful. As humankind is depicted, God is all wisdom and knowledge. As the eagle is depicted, God is all majesty. The creatures being full of eyes in front and back, represent the all-seeing God.

What is also important to note is that all of creation is created to worship God. We are to always be in a state of thankfulness and gratitude to a God who loves us and desires for us to live in grace. God is worthy of that reverence.

Revelation 4:1-11 – The Heavenly Worship – [1] After this I looked, and there in heaven a door stood open! And the first voice, which I had heard speaking to me like a trumpet, said, "Come up here, and I will show you what must take place after this." [2] At once I was in the spirit, [or *in the Spirit*] and there in heaven stood a throne, with one seated on the throne! [3] And the one seated there looks like jasper and carnelian, and around the throne is a rainbow that looks like an emerald. [4] Around the throne are twenty-four thrones, and seated on the thrones are twenty-four elders, dressed in white robes, with golden crowns on their heads. [5] Coming from the throne are flashes of lightning and rumblings and peals of thunder, and in front of the throne burn seven flaming torches, which are the seven spirits of God, [6] and in front of the throne there is something like a sea of glass, like crystal.

Around the throne, and on each side of the throne, are four living creatures, full of eyes in front and back: 7 the first living creature like a lion, the second living creature like an ox, the third living creature with a face like a human, and the fourth living creature like a flying eagle. [8] And the four living creatures, each of them with six wings, are full of eyes all around and inside. Day and night without ceasing they sing, "Holy, holy, holy, the Lord God the Almighty, who was and is and is to come."

[9] And whenever the living creatures give glory and honor and thanks to the one who is seated on the throne, who lives forever and ever, [10] the twenty-four elders fall before the one who is seated on the throne and worship the one who lives forever and ever; they cast their crowns before the throne,

singing, [11] "You are worthy, our Lord and God, to receive glory and honor and power, for you created all things, and by your will they existed and were created."

*** 

## Revelation 5:1-14 – Commentary
### The Scroll and the Lamb
### The Promised Authority

The sequence of this vision is one of the most significant in Revelation. It embodies all that Jesus the Beloved is, in receiving all authority that was promised by the Creator to Him as proclaimed in the Scriptures. Here, the writer witnesses the transfer of authority from the Creator to Jesus. Remember what the verses said in 1 Corinthians 15:27-28: "For 'God [Greek *he*] has put all things in subjection under his feet.' But when it says, 'All things are put in subjection,' it is plain that this does not include the one who put all things in subjection under him. When all things are subjected to him, then the Son himself will also be subjected to the one who put all things in subjection under him, so that God may be all in all." The Creator is giving Jesus this authority, but Jesus is still subjected to the authority of the Creator. Each has a distinct role in the Deity.

In Revelation 5:1-5, the writer sees the throne of God. Seated on the throne is the Creator holding a scroll that is secured with seven seals. The sealing of the scroll is significant in that only someone with the proper authority can open it. So, the question is posed: "Who is worthy to open the scroll and break its seals?" It appears that there is no one worthy to break the seals. This brings great sorrow to the writer and he begins to weep. That is when one of the elders proclaim, "Do not weep. See, the Lion of the tribe of Judah, the Root of David, has conquered, so that he can open the scroll and its seven seals." The words "has conquered" refers to the life, death, and resurrection of Jesus which provides salvation, redemption, and justification for all humankind who believe and have faith (see Romans 4:13-25).

In verses 6 and 7, the Lamb, Jesus the Beloved, Messiah and Savior, is standing before the throne. With the description given, Jesus is equated with the Deity having "seven horns and seven eyes, which are the seven spirits of God sent out into all the earth," all-encompassing omnipotence. Jesus then takes the scroll from the Creator, or as promised, the Creator gives Jesus the authority which had been promised, fulfilling the words Jesus spoke, "And Jesus came and said to them, "All authority in heaven and on earth has been given to me" (Matthew 28:18).

Upon this exchange from the Creator to Jesus, the heavenly hosts, thousands upon thousands of angels, break out into a new song of worship. They recognize the authority that has been given to Jesus for the work completed on earth, the provision made for humankind. The heavenly hosts are then joined by "every creature in heaven and on earth and under the earth and in the sea and all that is in them" giving praise, honor, and glory while singing "to the one seated on the throne and to the Lamb." It is a glorious sight to behold for the writer, seeing all of creation recognize, praise, and worship the Creator and Jesus the Beloved.

Revelation 5:1-14 – The Scroll and the Lamb – [1] Then I saw in the right hand of the one seated on the throne a scroll written on the inside and on the back, sealed [or *written on the inside and sealed on the back*] with seven seals, [2] and I saw a mighty angel proclaiming with a loud voice, "Who is worthy to open the scroll and break its seals?" [3] And no one in heaven or on earth or under the earth was able to open the scroll or to look into it. [4] And I began to weep bitterly because no one was found worthy to open the scroll or to look into it. [5] Then one of the elders said to me, "Do not weep. See, the Lion of the tribe of Judah, the Root of David, has conquered, so that he can open the scroll and its seven seals."

[6] Then I saw between the throne and the four living creatures and among the elders a Lamb standing as if it had been

slaughtered, with seven horns and seven eyes, which are the seven spirits of God sent out into all the earth. [7] He went and took the scroll from the right hand of the one who was seated on the throne. [8] When he had taken the scroll, the four living creatures and the twenty-four elders fell before the Lamb, each holding a harp and golden bowls full of incense, which are the prayers of the saints. [9] They sing a new song: "You are worthy to take the scroll and to break its seals, for you were slaughtered and by your blood you ransomed for God saints from [Greek *ransomed for God from*] every tribe and language and people and nation; [10] you have made them a kingdom and priests serving [Greek *priests to*] our God, and they will reign [other ancient authorities read *they reign*] on earth."

[11] Then I looked, and I heard the voice of many angels surrounding the throne and the living creatures and the elders; they numbered myriads of myriads and thousands of thousands, [12] singing with full voice, "Worthy is the Lamb that was slaughtered to receive power and wealth and wisdom and might and honor and glory and blessing!" [13] Then I heard every creature in heaven and on earth and under the earth and in the sea and all that is in them, singing, "To the one seated on the throne and to the Lamb be blessing and honor and glory and might forever and ever!" [14] And the four living creatures said, "Amen!" And the elders fell down and worshiped.

***

**Revelation 6:1-11 – Commentary**
**The First Five Seals**
**Gathering 1 of 9**

Throughout my life, both from my conversations with religious leaders and from television and the movies, the four horses we are about to discuss have been known as "The Four Horses of the Apocalypse." They are widely associated with death and destruction and the end of the world. That is not how I see them. It was in these verses that I began to see Revelation in a different way. Jesus is not unleashing destruction; the Creator is handing Jesus the authority that was promised. Follow me as I explain.

Jesus has been given authority over the earth and humankind. This authority covers a diverse array of countries and people. In my eyes, I see the four horses as representation of various forms of governments/countries in which we have on this earth and the authority that Jesus has over them. I believe the four horses have been active for centuries since the ascension of Jesus (Acts 1:6-11) and the transition of authority that we have seen in the prior verses. As Jesus begins to break each seal, we see the authority being established over these various governments and countries.

Revelation 6:1-2 presents the first horse whose rider has a crown (victorious) and a bow for "conquering and to conquer." The bow is a defensive weapon. The white horse represents good. I see the white horse and its rider as governments and countries that have strength and power which is used to defend the weak and fight against the evil in the world.

Revelation 6:3-4 presents the second horse whose rider has a great sword "to take peace from the earth, so that people would slaughter one another." The sword is an aggressive weapon. I see the bright red horse and rider as the warring governments and countries of evil that desire only to destroy, create wars, and cause conflict among people.

Revelation 6:5-6 presents the third horse whose rider "held a pair of scales in his hand." I see this as the governments and countries that represent commerce and trade. Their people are used for labor to produce materials and products for the majority of the population of the world.

Revelation 6:7-8 presents the fourth horse whose rider is "Death, and Hades followed with him, they were given authority over a fourth of the earth, to kill with sword, famine, and pestilence and by the wild animals of the earth." I see this as governments and countries within the classification of the third world, generally characterized by high rates of poverty, economic or political instability, and high mortality rates.

All four of these forms of governments/countries are under the authority of Jesus, mediator between humankind and the Creator. Does this mean that Jesus controls these government/countries? Are they following His spiritual bidding? No. There is still free will. The authority that Jesus has over these governments/countries is that they are all subject to His spiritual authority. They will all be judged accordingly at the end of the ages as to whether they have done right in the eyes of God or done wrong in the eyes of God. It will be this way until the end of the ages.

Revelation 6:9-11 presents us with the first of nine gatherings in Revelation. These gatherings are of a specific spiritual nature. As Jesus breaks the fifth seal, the writer states, "I saw under the altar the souls of those who had been slaughtered for the word of God and for the testimony they had given." I see these souls as those who died or were martyred for the sake of their faith in God during the Old Testament ages, prior to the coming of Jesus to the earth. These souls are asking, "How long will it be before you judge and avenge our blood on the inhabitants of the earth?" As each one of them is given a white robe, they are told to "rest a little longer, until the number would be complete both of their fellow servants and of their brothers and sisters who were soon to be killed as they themselves had been killed." So, these verses represent the many who have died or been martyred prior to the coming of Jesus along with those who will sacrifice their lives for the sake of their faith from the time of Jesus until the end of the ages.

> Revelation 6:1-11 – The First Five Seals – [1] Then I saw the Lamb break one of the seven seals, and I heard one of the four living creatures call out, as with a voice of thunder, "Come!" [or *"Go!"*] [2] I looked, and there was a white horse! Its rider had a bow; a crown was given to him, and he came out conquering and to conquer.

³ When he broke the second seal, I heard the second living creature call out, "Come!" [or *"Go!"*] ⁴ And out came [or *went*] another horse, bright red; its rider was permitted to take peace from the earth, so that people would slaughter one another, and he was given a great sword.

⁵ When he broke the third seal, I heard the third living creature call out, "Come!" [or *"Go!"*] I looked, and there was a black horse! Its rider held a pair of scales in his hand, ⁶ and I heard what seemed to be a voice in the midst of the four living creatures saying, "A quart of wheat for a day's pay [Greek *a denarius*] and three quarts of barley for a day's pay, [Greek *a denarius*] but do not damage the olive oil and the wine!"

⁷ When he broke the fourth seal, I heard the voice of the fourth living creature call out, "Come!" [or *"Go!"*] ⁸ I looked, and there was a pale green horse! Its rider's name was Death, and Hades followed with him; they were given authority over a fourth of the earth, to kill with sword, famine, and pestilence and by the wild animals of the earth.

The Souls of Those Who Had Been Slaughtered

⁹ When he broke the fifth seal, I saw under the altar the souls of those who had been slaughtered for the word of God and for the testimony they had given; ¹⁰ they cried out with a loud voice, "Sovereign Lord, holy and true, how long will it be

before you judge and avenge our blood on the inhabitants of the earth?" [11] They were each given a white robe and told to rest a little longer, until the number would be complete both of their fellow servants [Greek *slaves*] and of their brothers and sisters [Greek "adelphoi" *brothers* or *believers* designating both men and women] who were soon to be killed as they themselves had been killed.

***

**Revelation 7:1-8 – Commentary**
**The 144,000 of Israel Sealed**
**Gathering 2 of 9**

In Revelation 7:1-3a an interaction is recorded between one angel and the four angels "holding back the four winds of the earth." This interaction is not literal. These angels are not holding back the wind. I see the four winds symbolizing the impending judgment upon the earth once other events have taken place that are prophesied. I see these as the same four angels we will see later in Revelation 9:13-19.

Revelation 7:3b-8 details a special gathering. It is the second of the nine gatherings. It is the gathering of the remnant of Israel. Again, I do not want to get caught up in specific numbers, as the "one hundred forty-four thousand" mentioned. Just note that a large number from "every tribe of the people of Israel" is marked with "a seal on their foreheads." This is the seal of God. They are marked as God's chosen. This does not necessarily mean a visible physical mark; it could simply mean a spiritual mark within their soul. This same "one hundred forty-four thousand" sealed remnant of Israel is mentioned again in Revelation 9:4, 14:1, and 14:3 as we will see later.

I also want to note, as mentioned in 2 Corinthians 1:22, Ephesians 1:13, and Ephesians 4:30, that all believers who hold fast to their faith and do what is right and good in the eyes of God are spiritually marked with a seal, the Presence of the Holy Spirit in their lives. This seal, along with the

197

seal marking the remnant of Israel, declares us all as God's servants and provides us with the same eternal spiritual protection as long as we are faithful.

Revelation 7:1-8 – The 144,000 of Israel Sealed – [1] After this I saw four angels standing at the four corners of the earth, holding back the four winds of the earth so that no wind could blow on earth or sea or against any tree. [2] I saw another angel ascending from the rising of the sun, with the seal of the living God, and he called with a loud voice to the four angels who had been given power to damage earth and sea, [3] saying, "Do not damage the earth or the sea or the trees, until we have marked the servants of our God with a seal on their foreheads."

[4] And I heard the number of those who were sealed, one hundred forty-four thousand, sealed out of every tribe of the people of Israel: [5] From the tribe of Judah twelve thousand sealed, from the tribe of Reuben twelve thousand, from the tribe of Gad twelve thousand, [6] from the tribe of Asher twelve thousand, from the tribe of Naphtali twelve thousand, from the tribe of Manasseh twelve thousand, [7] from the tribe of Simeon twelve thousand, from the tribe of Levi twelve thousand, from the tribe of Issachar twelve thousand, [8] from the tribe of Zebulun twelve thousand, from the tribe of Joseph twelve thousand, from the tribe of Benjamin twelve thousand sealed.

# THE BEASTS, THE IMAGE, THE BRAND, AND THE FIRST FOUR TRUMPETS

**Revelation 13:1-10 – Commentary**

Revelation 13:1-10 introduces us to the first beast. The reason I have placed this vision at this section of our journey is that I see the first beast as representing the Eastern World, which is where humankind came into existence. The sea represents a bottomless pit coming from the earth.

In Revelation 13:1, the beast is described as having "ten horns and seven heads, and on its horns were ten diadems, and on its heads were blasphemous names." As we will discover later in Revelation 17:1-18, the beast symbolizes various kingdoms, nations, governments, and rulers throughout the centuries. I cannot tell you which ones. All we know for certain is that there are a selection of these nations that are driven by the destructive and evil spirit of Satan, the dragon. By the description given, it has ten horns with each horn having ten diadems or crowns; each crown represents a ruler or consecutive reigning rulers. So, we are speaking of many kingdoms, nations, governments, and rulers through the centuries that are past, present, and future as destructive and evil forces. It is important to remember this concerning the timeline of Revelation.

This beast, which is full of evil, has seven heads "and on its heads were blasphemous names." I see those seven blasphemous names as the seven deadly sins; pride, greed, lust, envy, gluttony, anger, and apathy. If "the love of money is a root of all kinds of evil" (1 Timothy 6:10), then pride is the root of all kinds of sin. I see pride as sitting on top as the source of the other six deadly sins. "Pride goes before destruction and a haughty spirit before a fall" (Proverbs 16:18). *Haughty* is defined by *Merriam-Webster* as "blatantly and disdainfully proud: having or showing an attitude of superiority and contempt for people or things perceived to be inferior." Pride and a haughty spirit are the thrust behind the other six deadly sins.

It is from the deception and evil of the first beast that the spirit of the false prophet is born. It was birthed out of the first beast soon after the death, resurrection, and ascension of Jesus and has continued to thrive and grow through the centuries. It is the great lie of deception, both for the non-believer and the believer who is caught up in a deluded spiritual life.

In Revelation 13:5, forty-two months is mentioned, which is the same as 1,260 days, a consistent period mentioned throughout Revelation. Again, it is unnecessary to get caught up in these time lapses as being perfectly accurate; just note that it is a specific period of time. It is a period of time that will have a beginning and an ending in which God knows. Remember, this beast represents many kingdoms, nations, governments, and rulers throughout the centuries. There will be times when the evil will rise up, and there will be times when it is suppressed according to the hearts of humankind and God's plan.

In Revelation 13:8, the Book of Life is mentioned once again. We were introduced to the Book of Life in Revelation 3:5. The Book of Life is mentioned a total of six times in Revelation and one other time in Philippians 4:2-3: "I urge Euodia and I urge Syntyche to be of the same mind in the Lord. Yes, and I ask you also, my loyal companion [or *loyal Syzygus*], help these women, for they have struggled beside me in the work of the gospel, together with Clement and the rest of my coworkers, whose names are in the book of life." As we will see later, the Book of Life is an accounting of those who believe in God and do what is right and good in

Their eyes. Those listed in the Book of Life are faithful in their relationship with God and the salvation that has been provided.

**Revelation 13:1-10 – The First Beast –** [1] And I saw a beast rising out of the sea, with ten horns and seven heads, and on its horns were ten diadems, and on its heads were blasphemous names. [2] And the beast that I saw was like a leopard, its feet were like a bear's, and its mouth was like a lion's mouth. And the dragon gave it his power and his throne and great authority. [3] One of its heads seemed to have received a death blow, but its fatal wound [Greek *the plague of its death*] had been healed. In amazement the whole earth followed the beast. [4] They worshiped the dragon, for he had given his authority to the beast, and they worshiped the beast, saying, "Who is like the beast, and who can fight against it?"

[5] The beast was given a mouth speaking arrogant and blasphemous words, and it was allowed to exercise authority for forty-two months. [6] It opened its mouth to speak blasphemies against God, blaspheming his name and his dwelling, that is, those who dwell in heaven. [7] Also, it was allowed to wage war on the saints and to conquer them [other ancient authorities lack this sentence of *7a*]. It was given authority over every tribe and people and language and nation, [8] and all the inhabitants of the earth will worship it, everyone whose name has not been written from the foundation of the world in the book of life of the Lamb that was slaughtered [or *written in the book of life of the Lamb that was slaughtered from the foundation of the world*].

[9] Let anyone who has an ear listen: [10] If you are to be taken captive, into captivity you go; if you kill with the sword, with the sword you must be killed. Here is a call for the endurance and faith of the saints.

***

## Revelation 13:11-18 — Commentary
### The Second Beast, Image, and the Brand

Revelation 13:11-18 introduces us to the second beast. I see the second beast as the Western World. The second beast comes from the earth of the first beast.

As with the first beast, the second beast represents various rulers and nations since its inception and into the modern ages. In these verses, I see the rise of the false prophet with its boasting and proclamations. The spirit of the false prophet breathes within the governments. It lives behind many of the pulpits within the churches. Today we see false spiritual teachings coming from the pulpits of churches. We hear lies coming from our politicians that spread like wildfire. We are facing chaotic times.

The first beast, the Eastern World, is the history and foundation of the second beast, the Western World. The second beast owes all of its strength and knowledge from what it has learned from the first beast. This is seen as worship in verse 12. But the second beast progresses faster in advancements of power. Here I see how the Western World, especially the United States, has progressed and moved ahead of the Eastern World in technological achievements.

These technological achievements and advancements are perceived as "great signs" in the imagery of this vision. As verse 13 states, "even making fire come down from heaven to earth in the sight of all" could easily describe the creation of the atom bomb and the beginning of the nuclear arms race. Think about it: The United States was the first to achieve sending men to the moon. A tremendous technical accomplishment. As we have moved into the modern age, the United States has been one of the major forces behind the development and use of the internet, software, and artificial intelligence.

Verses 14 and 15 describes the second beast as deceiving "the inhabitants of earth, telling them to make an image for the beast." This portion of the vision sets forth the innovation of the World Wide Web and the use of deep fakes and artificial intelligence as we discussed in Chapter 2. The world has become increasingly reliant upon technology and its advancements. We have entered into a time where the combination of robotics and artificial intelligence is real. In doing so, we have created the "image of the beast," and we are giving it life, breath, and speech. Artificial intelligence is the infrastructure for the image of the beast. It is paving the way for the mark of the beast. It is no longer a science fiction concept that technology could render humanity useless, even unto death, for those who refuse to embrace its superiority. This age of humanity praises and worships the age of technology, even at the cost of losing our souls.

In verses 16 and 17, the imagery perfectly describes the idea of a cashless society. The world is fast approaching a time when buying and selling will all be performed by a digital format and the printing of money will cease. Income and expenditures will solely become digital transfers. All transactions will occur through the world of technology as it becomes more and more reliant on this method. This technology provides the very source of the mark or brand of the beast, where each person is given a brand or chip implanted within their person to buy or sell "so that no one can buy or sell who does not have the brand."

All of our credit cards already have chips on them. Even today, it would be easy to implant a chip within a person for the sake of tracking their finances for buying and selling. This is the "brand" that these verses speak of. It is real and it is available now. The only thing left is to complete the cashless society and all will be reliant on this "brand" to buy or sell.

Verse 18 is once again warning us to stay awake and aware of these events as we progress toward the end of the ages. I cannot tell you what the significance is of the numbers 666 or 616 at this time. The most important thing is to heed the warning of staying awake spiritually, just as Jesus told us to do. Keep your eyes open. I am confident that when the time comes,

we will understand the meaning of those numbers and see them for what
they are.

**Revelation 13:11-18 – The Second Beast, Image, and
the Brand –** [11] Then I saw another beast that rose out of the
earth; it had two horns like a lamb, and it spoke like a dragon.
[12] It exercises all the authority of the first beast on its behalf,
and it makes the earth and its inhabitants worship the first
beast, whose fatal wound [Greek *whose plague of its death*]
had been healed. [13] It performs great signs, even making fire
come down from heaven to earth in the sight of all, [14] and
by the signs that it is allowed to perform on behalf of the
beast it deceives the inhabitants of earth, telling them to make
an image for the beast that had been wounded by the sword
[or *that had received the plague of the sword*] and yet lived, [15]
and it was allowed to give breath [or *spirit*] to the image of
the beast so that the image of the beast could even speak and
cause those who would not worship the image of the beast
to be killed. [16] Also, it causes all, both small and great, both
rich and poor, both free and slave, to be given a brand on the
right hand or the forehead, [17] so that no one can buy or sell
who does not have the brand, that is, the name of the beast or
the number for its name. [18] This calls for wisdom: let anyone
with understanding calculate the number of the beast, for it
is the number for a person. Its number is six hundred sixty-six
[other ancient authorities read *six hundred sixteen*].

***

**Revelation 8:2-13 – Commentary**
  **The Golden Censer**
  **The First Four Trumpets**

It is important to remember as we continue through Revelation, these seven truths that I have shared previously.

- Remember the verses in Matthew 24, Mark 13, and Luke 21 where Jesus told the disciples that there would be increased suffering of all people as the end of the ages grows closer.

- That some of the visions, though seen separately by the writer, occur concurrently.

- That these visions have been, are, and will be until the end of the ages; some are even ongoing.

- That Jesus has been given the authority that He was promised, but as 1 Corinthians 15:27b-28 states, Jesus's authority is still subjected to the Creator who has ultimate authority overall.

- That the first and second beast have been and are currently active. The spirit of the false prophet and the "image of the beast" are all currently active. All of the images seen in these visions are now in place as we draw nearer to the end of the ages.

- Humankind, not God, is responsible for our own undoing. As we continue in Revelation, the visions describe events that take place upon humankind that are allowed by God due to its continued rebellion against God. These destructive circumstances are the consequences of our abuse of the earth and its resources, our abuse of each other, and our abuse of God's grace and provision of salvation. They are the consequences of our corporate sins as humankind. They are not what God desired for us but what we have brought upon ourselves.

- The trumpet is an instrument of warning. In ancient times of battle, it was a call to arms or a call to retreat. Either way, it was used as a warning. The seven trumpets in Revelation are used in the same way. They are a warning to all humankind to heed the signs of destruction that our rebellion has created.

With the first four trumpets, I do not see these images as literal. The hail, fire, blood, great mountain, star from heaven, Wormwood, and the sun, moon, and stars being darkened are symbolic images of the destruction humankind has caused by our abuse of the earth. Global warming is the result of humankind not caring for the world in which we have been given. We are reaping what we have sown.

The beginning of these destructive circumstances, plagues, sicknesses, natural disasters, and persecution, is what the Scriptures refer to as The Great Tribulation/Ordeal. It is a period in which humankind will endure the suffering of which Jesus spoke to the disciples. Many modern Evangelicals teach that faithful believers will be "raptured" up into heaven before all of these catastrophes take place. This teaching is incorrect and is not supported by the Scriptures.

These destructive events have already begun. We are in The Great Tribulation/Ordeal. As we move forward in Revelation, you will see that humankind has now progressed into the prophetic visions that were seen so many centuries ago. These disasters, either natural, galactical, or man-made are now upon us. I will say this again: We, not God, are responsible for this undoing.

During The Great Tribulation/Ordeal, those who are faithful believers will have to endure and be subjected to all of this destruction around us. Our faith will be tested. We will witness and be exposed to all of the suffering during this time, but we must hold fast. God's grace will sustain us through these times.

In verses 2 through 5, we see an assembling of angels around the throne of God. The prayers of the saints have been heard, and The Great Tribulation/Ordeal is imminent. In verse 5, the action of the angel throwing the golden censer down to earth is symbolic of the beginning of this time. The eight verses that follow verse 5 proclaims the harsh consequences of our selfish behavior and humanistic desire to be our own god.

I see the angels and events of verses 6 through 12 as figurative images of all those things we have seen and experienced over the last couple of centuries. We have been warned of global warming and its devastating effect on our planet, yet we have done very little to correct it. We have not listened. We have allowed greed, selfishness, and lust for control to direct this horrendous abuse of the earth. We are paying dearly for it. We have seen and are seeing the very results of this behavior unfold before us and we still do little to correct the errors of our ways.

In verse 13, there is the imagery of those warnings. Warnings that many still refuse to hear. Warnings of yet more destruction to come. Even with all of the scientific evidence we have that we are destroying our planet, we are not listening. We are not heeding the warning with the urgency it requires. Many have chosen to stick their head in the sand and leave it. Shame on those who have done so.

**Revelation 8:2-13 – The Golden Censer –** [2] And I saw the seven angels who stand before God, and seven trumpets were given to them. [3] Another angel with a golden censer came and stood at the altar; he was given a great quantity of incense to offer with the prayers of all the saints on the golden altar that is before the throne. [4] And the smoke of the incense, with the prayers of the saints, rose before God from the hand of the angel. [5] Then the angel took the censer and filled it with fire from the altar and threw it on the earth, and there were peals of thunder, rumblings, flashes of lightning, and an earthquake.

The First Four of Seven Trumpets

[6] Now the seven angels who had the seven trumpets made ready to blow them [other ancient authorities read *made themselves ready to blow*].

[7] The first angel blew his trumpet, and there came hail and fire, mixed with blood, and they were hurled to the earth, and a third of the earth was burned up, and a third of the trees were burned up, and all green grass was burned up.

<sup>8</sup> The second angel blew his trumpet, and something like a great mountain, burning with fire, was thrown into the sea. <sup>9</sup> A third of the sea became blood, a third of the living creatures in the sea died, and a third of the ships were destroyed.

<sup>10</sup> The third angel blew his trumpet, and a great star fell from heaven, blazing like a torch, and it fell on a third of the rivers and on the springs of water. <sup>11</sup> The name of the star is Wormwood. A third of the waters became wormwood, and many died from the water because it was made bitter.

<sup>12</sup> The fourth angel blew his trumpet, and a third of the sun was struck, and a third of the moon, and a third of the stars, so that a third of their light was darkened; a third of the day was kept from shining and likewise the night.

<sup>13</sup> Then I looked, and I heard an eagle crying with a loud voice as it flew in midheaven, "Woe, woe, woe to the inhabitants of the earth, at the blasts of the other trumpets that the three angels are about to blow!"

# MORE TRUMPETS, ANGELS, AND THE SEVEN THUNDERS

**Revelation 9:1-21 – Commentary**

I cannot interpret the images, per se, that we see in Revelation 9:1-21. I am sure theologians have many different interpretations of what the images of the locusts (verses 1 through 12) and the horses (verses 13 through 21) are. I simply see them as representing forms of humankind's inventions of weaponry for war or major natural or man-made disasters. Beyond that, I cannot be more specific as to what they are.

In verse 1, we are introduced to one of the banished angels that had been a part of the rebellion in heaven and has been cast down to earth. We are told in verse 11 that this angel's name means "destruction" and "destroyer." This angel ushers in a period of extreme suffering for those "who do not have the seal of God." This indicates that those who have the seal of God will not be physically affected by the destructive nature of these weapons but will still have to deal with the consequences of those who are affected by them.

Verse 2 mentions that "from the shaft rose smoke like the smoke of a great furnace, and the sun and the air were darkened with the smoke from the shaft." From that and the description that this torment will not kill people but will cause them great suffering, I see this as possibly a chemical or gaseous form of disaster. Whether the source is man-made or natural, it causes great suffering and sickness to the point that people will want to die.

Verse 6 says, "And in those days people will seek death but will not find it; they will long to die, but death will flee from them." I do not believe that this means people will not be dying by other causes. I do not see that death suddenly goes away for this period of time. I see this as imagery to indicate how much suffering this disaster causes, so much so, that people will wish death upon themselves, but death will not come. At least not by this specific calamity. This period of suffering will climax at some point and end the first woe.

Revelation 9:13-19 refers back to 7:1-3 and the four angels "who had been held ready for the hour, the day, the month, and the year, to kill a third of humankind." This vision speaks of modern war and its consequences. I see the three elements of these wars, fire, smoke, and sulfur, being indicative of modern weapons of destruction, primarily bombs and artillery.

Our modern wars not only cause great destruction of physical property with multiple buildings, facilities, and homes being wiped out with a single strike, but the loss of human lives, including the innocent. This is devastating. We have seen millions of people die from one war after another. Wars that the governments and nations may be able to justify but are an abomination in the eyes of God. Wars that are founded on pride, greed, lust, envy, gluttony, anger, and apathy. The seven deadly sins.

Verses 20 through 21 speaks of the condition of those "who were not killed by these plagues," they are those "who do not have the seal of God." Even having witnessed and been exposed to the plagues, those remaining who have turned from God and refused to believe and acknowledge Gods existence still do not repent of their sins. Their hearts are hard. Their pride and arrogance will not allow them to acknowledge the loving God that created them. It is a sad state of spiritual blindness.

This is the second woe, and it continues on through the following visions.

**Revelation 9:1-21 – The Fifth Trumpet - FIRST WOE** – <sup>1</sup> And the fifth angel blew his trumpet, and I saw a star that had fallen from heaven to earth, and he was given the key to the shaft of the bottomless pit; <sup>2</sup> he opened the shaft of the bottomless pit, and from the shaft rose smoke like the smoke of a great furnace, and the sun and the air were darkened with the smoke from the shaft. <sup>3</sup> Then from the smoke came locusts on the earth, and they were given authority like the authority of scorpions of the earth. <sup>4</sup> They were told not to damage the grass of the earth or any green growth or any tree, but only those people who do not have the seal of God on their foreheads. <sup>5</sup> They were allowed to torment them for five months but not to kill them, and the agony suffered was like that caused by a scorpion when it stings someone. <sup>6</sup> And in those days people will seek death but will not find it; they will long to die, but death will flee from them.

<sup>7</sup> In appearance the locusts were like horses equipped for battle. On their heads were what looked like crowns of gold; their faces were like human faces, <sup>8</sup> their hair like women's hair, and their teeth like lions' teeth; <sup>9</sup> they had scales like iron breastplates, and the noise of their wings was like the noise of many chariots with horses rushing into battle. <sup>10</sup> They have tails like scorpions, with stingers, and in their tails is their power to harm people for five months. <sup>11</sup> They have as king over them the angel of the bottomless pit; his name in Hebrew is Abaddon [that is, *Destruction*] and in Greek he is called Apollyon [that is, *Destroyer*].

$^{12}$ The first woe has passed. There are still two woes to come.

## The Sixth Trumpet - SECOND WOE BEGINS

$^{13}$ Then the sixth angel blew his trumpet, and I heard a voice from the horns [other ancient authorities read *four horns*] of the golden altar before God, $^{14}$ saying to the sixth angel who had the trumpet, "Release the four angels who are bound at the great River Euphrates." $^{15}$ So the four angels were released, who had been held ready for the hour, the day, the month, and the year, to kill a third of humankind. $^{16}$ The number of the troops of cavalry was two hundred million; I heard their number. $^{17}$ And this was how I saw the horses in my vision: the riders wore breastplates the color of fire and of sapphire [Greek *hyacinth*] and of sulfur; the heads of the horses were like lions' heads, and fire and smoke and sulfur came out of their mouths. $^{18}$ By these three plagues a third of humankind was killed, by the fire and smoke and sulfur coming out of the horses' [Greek *their*] mouths. $^{19}$ For the power of the horses is in their mouths and in their tails; their tails are like serpents, with heads, and with them they inflict harm.

$^{20}$ The rest of humankind, who were not killed by these plagues, did not repent of the works of their hands or give up worshiping demons and idols of gold and silver and bronze and stone and wood, which cannot see or hear or walk. $^{21}$ And they did not repent of their murders or their sorceries or their prostitution or their thefts.

***

## Revelation 10:1-11 – Commentary
### The Angel with the Little Scroll/Seven Thunders

Revelation 10:1-11 is one of the most intriguing passages in Revelation. It deals with the mystery of God and the limitations of our understanding as humans. As much as I have read and studied the Scriptures, as much time as I have spent meditating and in prayer, the more I understand God, the more I realize that there is so much more to understand. God is expansive, limitless, and far beyond anything that we can imagine. Yet God is personal to each and every one of us. That in itself is an amazing mystery.

If you read the Scriptures straight through, starting in Genesis and continuing through to Revelation, what you will see is a progressive revelation of a most amazing God. God does not change, but we, as humans, must grow and learn. Our understanding of God must progress as we grow and learn. In the beginning of the Old Testament, you might see God one way, and then that perspective changes as you read the New Testament and the life of Jesus. Even with the disciples, every time they thought they had Jesus figured out, He would take them to another level of learning by saying or doing something more profound.

The writer of 1 Corinthians 13:9-12 put it this way: "For we know only in part, and we prophesy only in part, but when the complete comes, the partial will come to an end. When I was a child, I spoke like a child, I thought like a child, I reasoned like a child. When I became an adult, I put an end to childish ways. For now we see only a reflection, as in a mirror, but then we will see face to face. Now I know only in part; then I will know fully, even as I have been fully known." This is that progressive learning that we must embrace and search for, knowing that we will not really have full understanding until we have passed through into eternity.

Revelation 10:1-2 introduces us to an angel with a little scroll who gives a great shout, as a lion roaring. After this shout, the "seven thunders sounded." I see this as seven individual proclamations that came directly from the throne of God. God's voice is often characterized by thunder in Revelation. I believe that God allowed the writer to hear these proclamations to strengthen his faith as a faithful believer and to also help him have a fuller understanding of the many visions he was experiencing. But then the writer was told to seal up the context of these proclamations and not write them down. I believe that these proclamations have something to do with the mystery of God because the very next thing the angel says is, "There will be no more delay, but in the days when the seventh angel is to blow his trumpet, the mystery of God will be fulfilled, as he announced to his servants [Greek *slaves*] the prophets."

The New Testament Epistles speak frequently of the mystery of God being revealed through the birth, death, and resurrection of Jesus. But here, in verses 6 and 7, we are told that there will be no more delay; we are told that the mystery of God will be fulfilled. As I stated earlier, there is a progressive understanding that we as faithful believers must continue to strive toward. This mystery will not be fulfilled and completed until the end of the ages. As the writer stated earlier, "Then I will know fully, even as I have been fully known." There is still so much more for us to learn and understand.

Verses 8 through 11 address the writer. In these verses, I see that the prophetic word is sweet to the mouth of the prophet, but it is bitter to the stomach of those who hear it because it is truth. God's truth reveals all lies. It is a bitter pill to swallow.

**Revelation 10:1-11 – The Angel with the Little Scroll – The Seven Thunders –** [1] And I saw another mighty angel coming down from heaven, wrapped in a cloud, with a rainbow over his head; his face was like the sun and his legs like pillars of fire. [2] He held a little scroll open in his hand. Setting his right foot on the sea and his left foot on the land, [3] he gave a great shout, like a lion roaring. And when he shouted, the seven thunders sounded. [4] And when the seven thunders had sounded, I was about to write, but I heard a voice from heaven saying, "Seal up what the seven thunders have said, and do not write it down." [5] Then the angel whom I saw standing on the sea and the land raised his right hand to heaven [6] and swore by him who lives forever and ever, who created heaven and what is in it, the earth and what is in it, and the sea and what is in it: "There will be no more delay, [7] but in the days when the seventh angel is to blow his trumpet, the mystery of God will be fulfilled, as he announced to his servants [Greek *slaves*] the prophets."

[8] Then the voice that I had heard from heaven spoke to me again, saying, "Go, take the scroll that is open in the hand of the angel who is standing on the sea and on the land." [9] So I went to the angel and told him to give me the little scroll, and he said to me, "Take it and eat; it will be bitter to your stomach but sweet as honey in your mouth." [10] So I took the little scroll from the hand of the angel and ate it; it was sweet as honey in my mouth, but when I had eaten it my stomach was made bitter.

[11] Then they said to me, "You must prophesy again about many peoples and nations and languages and kings."

***

## Revelation 14:6-13 – Commentary
### The Messages of the Three Angels

Revelation 14:6-13 brings us to a very significant place as we move forward to the end of the ages. Three angels provide proclamations from heaven to those on earth. I do not know if these angels will literally be seen or if they are the remnant of the Church by inspiration of the Spirit making these proclamations. Regardless, they are very important proclamations to those who remain on the earth, both the righteous and the unrighteous.

The first proclamation (verses 6 through 7) reiterates what Jesus proclaimed in Matthew 22:36-38, Mark 12:29-30, and Luke 10:26-28: "You shall love the Lord your God with all your heart and with all your soul and with all your mind and with all your strength." It is the first and greatest commandment. Loving God with such intensity is the identical act to fearing or respecting God and giving Them glory and worshipping "him who made heaven and earth, the sea and the springs of water." If you sincerely love God, you will worship Them with that same earnestness.

The second proclamation (verse 8) is the judgment and fall of the great city Babylon. We will learn more about Babylon later.

The third proclamation (verses 9 through 11) is the eternal judgment of "Those who worship the beast and its image and receive the brand on their foreheads or on their hands."

The final proclamation (verses 12 through 13) is a word of encouragement to endure and the second of seven blessings for "those who keep the commandments of God and hold fast to the faith of [or *to their faith in*] Jesus" and "the dead who from now on die in the Lord." As with the first blessing, the second blessing has conditions that we must follow to receive it. That blessing is for those "who from now on die in the Lord."

**Revelation 14:6-13 – The Messages of the Three Angels** – ⁶ Then I saw another angel flying in midheaven, with an eternal gospel to proclaim to those who live [Greek *sit*] on the earth—to every nation and tribe and language and people. ⁷ He said in a loud voice, "Fear God and give him glory, for the hour of his judgment has come, and worship him who made heaven and earth, the sea and the springs of water."

$^8$ Then another angel, a second, followed, saying, "Fallen, fallen is Babylon the great! She has made all nations drink of the wine of the wrath of her prostitution."

$^9$ Then another angel, a third, followed them, crying with a loud voice, "Those who worship the beast and its image and receive the brand on their foreheads or on their hands, $^{10}$ they will also drink the wine of God's wrath, poured unmixed into the cup of his anger, and they will be tormented with fire and sulfur in the presence of the holy angels and in the presence of the Lamb. $^{11}$ And the smoke of their torment goes up forever and ever. There is no rest day or night for those who worship the beast and its image and for anyone who receives the brand of its name."

$^{12}$ Here is a call for the endurance of the saints, those who keep the commandments of God and hold fast to the faith of [or *to their faith in*] Jesus.

$^{13}$ And I heard a voice from heaven saying, "Write this: Blessed are the dead who from now on die in the Lord." "Yes," [other ancient authorities lack *Yes*] says the Spirit, "they will rest from their labors, for their deeds follow them."

# THE GREAT WHORE AND THE BEAST

**Revelation 17:1-18 – Commentary with Verses in Logical Order**

In Revelation 16:19, as we will see later, states, "God remembered great Babylon and gave her the wine cup of the fury of his wrath." There is no question that the city of Babylon existed. It was an ancient city whose ruins are within the boundaries of Iraq. But the following vision is not about that ancient city. This vision is about the modern Babylon, a contemporary nation. The vision of the fall of modern Babylon that is mentioned in Revelation 16:19 is recorded in Revelation 17, 18, and the first part of 19. The fall of modern Babylon is clearly a significant event in that it takes up two and a half chapters of Revelation. It is a turning point in the final days during the end of the ages.

The verses found in Revelation 17 can be confusing due to the timeline moving back and forth between the present, future, and distant future. The actual events in the vision are not communicated in chronological order. So, I will share my commentary on these verses in a logical order with the hope that it will clarify this section of the vision. The verses will then follow in their original order.

***

In verses 1 and 2, one of the seven angels who will carry out the seven final plagues proclaims to the writer the judgment upon "the great whore [or *prostitute*] who is seated on many waters" (this whore symbolizes the modern Babylon).

> Revelation 17: 1-2 – [1] Then one of the seven angels who had the seven bowls came and said to me, "Come, I will show you the judgment of the great whore [or *prostitute*] who is seated on many waters, [2] with whom the kings of the earth have engaged in sexual immorality [or *prostitution*] and with the wine of whose prostitution the inhabitants of the earth have become drunk."

***

In verses 3 through 18, the vision indicates four groupings of people. Again, I cannot give you specifics on the exact countries/nations each portrays, but by reading you will see what is important for us to understand. We see the woman, the waters, seven heads/mountains (which are part of the beast), and the beast itself representing these four groupings of people.

The woman in verse 3 represents a single nation of people, the modern Babylon. This woman is an entirely separate entity from the beast. The nation that the woman represents is proud and arrogant and has a lot of power and wealth.

In verse 15, we are provided with an explanation of the waters. The angel explains that, "the waters that you saw, where the whore [or *prostitute*] is seated, are peoples and multitudes and nations and languages." I see these people as that which constitutes the nation that the whore (which is the modern Babylon) represents. It is a single nation filled with diverse cultures and people.

Verse 18 declares, "The woman [the whore] you saw is the great city [the modern Babylon] that rules [has great authority and power] over the kings of the earth." Many of the other nations, represented by the seven heads and ten horns (as seen later), have relations with this powerful nation by way of being allies or economic partners. But they do not necessarily like this nation; they tolerate it for its power and wealth.

The nation represented by the woman, as described in verses 4 and 5, stands alone within the world by its wealth, lavish indulgence, selfish pleasures, reckless behavior, and commercialism. It is a capitalistic nation. By comparison to the others, it is a very rich nation. Many believe that the United States is the modern Baylon. I see this as true in that, with the fall of modern Babylon found in the Western World, all of the attention goes back to the Eastern World where the final battles, both physical and spiritual, will take place.

Verse 6 states, "And I saw that the woman was drunk with the blood of the saints and the blood of the witnesses to Jesus." I do not see this as the nation has put these witnesses to death as much as I see that this nation has blasphemed the name of God and the testimony of Jesus horrendously. It is viewed as an abomination in the eyes of God. At the same time, I do not count out the idea of this nation, sometime in the future, becoming intolerant to those who truly believe in the Scriptures and do not adhere to the way it has chosen to pervert the Scriptures and so they put the faithful believers to death.

> Revelation 17: 3, 15, 18, 4, 5, 6 – [3] So he carried me away in the spirit [or *in the Spirit*] into a wilderness, and I saw a woman sitting on a scarlet beast that was full of blasphemous names, and it had seven heads and ten horns.

> [15] And he said to me, "The waters that you saw, where the whore [or *prostitute*] is seated, are peoples and multitudes and nations and languages."

[superscript 18] "The woman you saw is the great city that rules over the kings of the earth."

[superscript 4] The woman was clothed in purple and scarlet and adorned with gold and jewels and pearls, holding in her hand a golden cup full of abominations and the impurities of her prostitution, [superscript 5] and on her forehead was written a name, a mystery: "Babylon the great, mother [or *Babylon, the great mother*] of whores [or *prostitutes*] and of earth's abominations." [superscript 6] And I saw that the woman was drunk with the blood of the saints and the blood of the witnesses to Jesus. When I saw her, I was greatly amazed.

***

The beast in verses 7 and 8 represents multiple countries. This is the same beast that is spoken of in Revelation 13:1. The beast that was, is not, and is to come having a wound that healed. The beast is a separate entity from the whore. It is also a separate entity to the seven heads and ten horns as we will see. That is important to understand. Found within the core of this beast is the spirit of the false prophet.

The beast will "go to destruction" at the end of the ages. But as it makes its final appearance on this earth, many non-believers, "whose names have not been written in the book of life from the foundation of the world," will follow it.

Revelation 17:7-8 – [superscript 7] But the angel said to me, "Why are you so amazed? I will tell you the mystery of the woman and of the beast with seven heads and ten horns that carries her. [8] The beast that you saw was and is not and is about to ascend from the bottomless pit and go to destruction. And the inhabitants of the earth, whose names have not been written in the book of life from the foundation of the world, will be amazed when they see the beast, because it was and is not and is to come."

***

The seven heads or kings in verses 9 and 10 "are seven mountains on which the woman is seated." I do not see this as literal mountains. I see this as other strong nations that have allied with the woman.

The angel explains that when this vision comes to be five of these kings will have fallen, one will be living and the other is yet to come. The king that is yet to become king will remain only a little while.

Revelation 17:9-10 – [9] "This calls for a mind that has wisdom: the seven heads are seven mountains on which the woman is seated; also, they are seven kings, [10] of whom five have fallen, one is living, and the other has not yet come, and when he comes he must remain only a little while."

***

The beast itself, in verse 11, represents an eighth country/nation that is associated with the seven. This is the country that will "go to destruction" at the end of the ages.

Revelation 17:11 – [11] "As for the beast that was and is not, it is an eighth, but it belongs to the seven, and it goes to destruction."

***

The ten horns are ten countries/nations that are yet to come, in verses 12 and 13 and will receive power and authority alongside the beast, the eighth nation, for a short time. (Again, there is no way to be able to determine how long a short time is.)

Revelation 17:12-13 – [12] "And the ten horns that you saw are ten kings who have not yet received a kingdom, but they are to receive authority as kings for one hour, together with the beast. [13] These are united in yielding their power and authority to the beast..."

***

With verses 16 and 17, the angel then returns to the continuation of the destruction of Babylon. Verse 16 speaks of the ten nations (horns) uniting with the nation represented by the beast and "will hate the whore [or *prostitute*; the nation that is the modern Babylon]; they will make her desolate and naked; they will devour her flesh and burn her up with fire."

It is important to note what verse 17 states: "For God has put it into their hearts to carry out his purpose by agreeing to give their kingdom [that is the kingdom of modern Babylon] to the beast, until the words of God will be fulfilled." This is all a part of God's plan for the end of the ages. God's purpose is to allow the ten nations along with the beast to overcome the whore, the modern Babylon, its government, and to rule over its people. This is God's plan unfolding.

> Revelation 17:16-17 – [16] "And the ten horns that you saw, they and the beast will hate the whore [or *prostitute*]; they will make her desolate and naked; they will devour her flesh and burn her up with fire. [17] For God has put it into their hearts to carry out his purpose by agreeing to give their kingdom to the beast, until the words of God will be fulfilled."

***

Finally, as noted in verse 14, these ten countries/nations will be united under the direction of the country/nation that the beast represents for the purpose of waging "war on the Lamb." This war will be the battle of Armageddon that is to come, as we will see later on.

> Revelation 17:14 – [14] "They will wage war on the Lamb, and the Lamb will conquer them, for he is Lord of lords and King of kings, and those with him are called and chosen and faithful."

***

**Revelation 17:1-18 – Verses in Original Order – The Great Whore and the Beast –** [1] Then one of the seven angels who had the seven bowls came and said to me, "Come, I will show you the judgment of the great whore [or *prostitute*] who is seated on many waters, [2] with whom the kings of the earth have engaged in sexual immorality [or *prostitution*] and with the wine of whose prostitution the inhabitants of the earth have become drunk." [3] So he carried me away in the spirit [or *in the Spirit*] into a wilderness, and I saw a woman sitting on a scarlet beast that was full of blasphemous names, and it had seven heads and ten horns. [4] The woman was clothed in purple and scarlet and adorned with gold and jewels and pearls, holding in her hand a golden cup full of abominations and the impurities of her prostitution, [5] and on her forehead was written a name, a mystery: "Babylon the great, mother [or *Babylon, the great mother*] of whores [or *prostitutes*] and of earth's abominations." [6] And I saw that the woman was drunk with the blood of the saints and the blood of the witnesses to Jesus.

When I saw her, I was greatly amazed. [7] But the angel said to me, "Why are you so amazed? I will tell you the mystery of the woman and of the beast with seven heads and ten horns that carries her. [8] The beast that you saw was and is not and is about to ascend from the bottomless pit and go to destruction. And the inhabitants of the earth, whose names have not been written in the book of life from the foundation of the world, will be amazed when they see the beast, because it was and is not and is to come.

[9] "This calls for a mind that has wisdom: the seven heads are seven mountains on which the woman is seated; also, they are seven kings, [10] of whom five have fallen, one is living, and the other has not yet come, and when he comes he must remain only a little while. [11] As for the beast that was and is not, it is an eighth, but it belongs to the seven, and it goes to destruction. [12] And the ten horns that you saw are ten kings who have not yet received a kingdom, but they are to receive authority as kings for one hour, together with the beast. [13] These are united in yielding their power and authority to the beast; [14] they will wage war on the Lamb, and the Lamb will conquer them, for he is Lord of lords and King of kings, and those with him are called and chosen and faithful."

[15] And he said to me, "The waters that you saw, where the whore [or *prostitute*] is seated, are peoples and multitudes and nations and languages. [16] And the ten horns that you saw, they and the beast will hate the whore [or *prostitute*]; they will make her desolate and naked; they will devour her flesh and burn her up with fire. [17] For God has put it into their hearts to carry out his purpose by agreeing to give their kingdom to the beast, until the words of God will be fulfilled. [18] The woman you saw is the great city that rules over the kings of the earth."

# BABYLON, PLAGUES, AND TWO WITNESSES

**Revelation 18:1-8 – Commentary**

In Revelation 18:1-8, we see the prophetic proclamation of the fall of Babylon, the great nation. Verses 1 through 3 proclaim the sins of Babylon.

In verse 4, another voice from heaven speaks. I see this as a proclamation to all faithful believers to separate themselves from the sins of the world. Though they are in the world, they cannot be of the world that indulges in the sins that displease God. If we do not heed this warning, we will share in Babylon's demise.

In verses 5 through 8, that same voice proclaims the final judgment upon Babylon.

**Revelation 18:1-8 – Babylon –** [1] After this I saw another angel coming down from heaven, having great authority, and the earth was illumined by his splendor. 2 He called out with a mighty voice, "Fallen, fallen is Babylon the great! It has become a dwelling place of demons, a haunt of every foul spirit, a haunt of every foul bird, a haunt of every foul and hateful beast [other ancient authorities read *a haunt of every foul and hateful bird*]. [3] For all the nations have fallen [other ancient authorities read *all the nations have drunk*] from the wine of the wrath of her prostitution, and the kings of the earth have engaged in sexual immorality [or *prostitution*] with her, and the merchants of the earth have grown rich from the power [or *resources*] of her luxury."

<sup>4</sup> Then I heard another voice from heaven saying, "Come out of her, my people, so that you do not take part in her sins and so that you do not share in her plagues, <sup>5</sup> for her sins are heaped high as heaven, and God has remembered her iniquities. <sup>6</sup> Render to her as she herself has rendered, and repay her double for her deeds; mix a double dose for her in the cup she mixed. <sup>7</sup> As she glorified herself and lived luxuriously, so give her a like measure of torment and grief. Since in her heart she says, 'I rule as a queen; I am no widow, and I will never see grief,' <sup>8</sup> therefore her plagues will come in a single day—pestilence and mourning and famine—and she will be burned with fire, for mighty is the Lord God who judges her."

***

## Revelation 14:14-16 – Commentary
### Gathering 3 of 9
### Reaping the Earth's Harvest

I see Revelation 14:14-20 as two separate events, so I have set them apart from each other. I see this vision as the separation of the righteous from the unrighteous. I will explain.

In Matthew 25:31-46, Jesus shared the parable of the sheep and the goats. The judgment of the righteous (the sheep) and the unrighteous (the goats). In John 4:35 Jesus states, "Do you not say, 'Four months more, then comes the harvest'? But I tell you, look around you, and see how the fields are ripe for harvesting."

Another parable that alludes to this specific time in Revelation and the events/judgment to come is Matthew 13:24-30, which states, "The kingdom of heaven may be compared to someone who sowed good seed in his field, but while everybody was asleep an enemy came and sowed weeds among the wheat and then went away. So when the plants came up and bore grain, then the weeds appeared as well. And the slaves of the householder came and said to him, 'Master, did you not sow good seed in your field? Where, then, did these weeds come from?' He answered, 'An enemy has done this.' The slaves said to him, 'Then do you want us to go and gather them?' But he replied, 'No, for in gathering the weeds you would uproot the wheat along with them. Let both of them grow together until the harvest, and at harvest time I will tell the reapers, Collect the weeds first and bind them in bundles to be burned, but gather the wheat into my barn.'"

I see Revelation 14:14-16 as representing the "reaping of the harvest" of the righteous, the gathering of the sheep, and the separation of the wheat (righteous) from the weeds (unrighteous). It is the third of nine gatherings.

**Revelation 14:14-16 – Reaping the Earth's Harvest – Part 1 –** [14] Then I looked, and there was a white cloud, and seated on the cloud was one like the Son of Man, with a golden crown on his head and a sharp sickle in his hand! [15] Another angel came out of the temple, calling with a loud voice to the one who sat on the cloud, "Use your sickle and reap, for the hour to reap has come, because the harvest of the earth is fully ripe." [16] So the one who sat on the cloud swung his sickle over the earth, and the earth was reaped.

***

**Revelation 15:1-8 – Commentary**
**Gathering 4 of 9**
**The Angels with the Seven Last Plagues**

As we move into the following visions, the suffering for those who have rejected God becomes more intense. They have refused to acknowledge God and accept the truth and the provision of Their salvation. As we read earlier in 2 Thessalonians 2:9-12, "The coming of the lawless one is apparent in the working of Satan, who uses all power, signs, lying wonders, and every kind of wicked deception for those who are perishing because they refused to love the truth and so be saved. For this reason, God sends them a powerful delusion, leading them to believe what is false, so that all who have not believed the truth but took pleasure in unrighteousness will be condemned."

This judgment from God does not come lightly. It is not the direction God had chosen for humankind to take. It is the path that the deceived have chosen. As I have said before, it is not God's doing; it is their own undoing for rejecting the truth of God.

So, as the end of the ages draws nearer, God unleashes earthly suffering and torment on those who have rejected Their truth. Death and destruction will reign for a period of time and as Jesus had prophesied to His disciples, there will be suffering and sorrow like has never been seen upon the earth.

At the same time this is happening to those who have rejected the truth, those who believe and have embraced the truth of God will be unharmed. They will be gathered and protected by the grace and mercy of a loving God.

In Revelation 15:1 we are introduced to the seven angels who will set forth the sorrow and plagues on those who refuse to believe.

Revelation 15:2-4 accounts for those "who had conquered the beast and its image and the number of its name." Those who had endured the temptations of the beast and its image and had stood faithful are gathered in the presence of God to worship Them. This is the fourth of nine gatherings.

In Revelation 15:5-9, the vision turns toward the sacred temple and reveals the seven angels with the seven last plagues. With the proclamations of the seven angels with the seven last plagues, the visions shift from humankind's destruction of itself to God's judgment upon humankind for their rejection of God's truth.

**Revelation 15:1-8 – The Angels with the Seven Last Plagues –** [1] Then I saw another portent in heaven, great and amazing: seven angels with seven plagues, which are the last, for with them the wrath of God is ended.

[2] And I saw what appeared to be a sea of glass mixed with fire and those who had conquered the beast and its image and the number of its name standing beside the sea of glass with harps of God in their hands. [3] And they sing the song of Moses, the servant [Greek *slave*] of God, and the song of the Lamb: "Great and amazing are your deeds, Lord God the Almighty! Just and true are your ways, King of the nations [other ancient authorities read *the ages*]! [4] Lord, who will not fear and glorify your name? For you alone are holy. All nations will come and worship before you, for your judgments have been revealed."

[5] After this I looked, and the temple of the tent [or *tabernacle*] of witness in heaven was opened, [6] and out of the temple came the seven angels with the seven plagues, robed in pure bright linen [other ancient authorities read *stone*], with golden sashes across their chests. [7] Then one of the four living creatures gave the seven angels seven golden bowls full of the wrath of God, who lives forever and ever; [8] and the temple was filled with smoke from the glory of God and from his power, and no one could enter the temple until the seven plagues of the seven angels were ended.

***

**Revelation 7:9-17 – Commentary**
**Gathering 5 of 9**
**The Multitude from Every Nation**

Revelation 7:9-17 deals with the fifth of nine gatherings in Revelation. I have chosen to place this vision here because of the reference by the angel in verse 14 that "These are they who have come out of the great ordeal [or *great tribulation*]." I see this "great multitude that no one could count, from every nation, from all tribes and peoples and languages, standing before the throne and before the Lamb" as a witness to the remnant of faithful believers who endure the Great Tribulation/Ordeal and hold fast to their faith. Again, I see much of these visions as happening concurrently or consecutively, I believe that right before Jesus returns to this earth, these events will unfold successively and orderly.

In verse 9, note that once again, the throne of God and the Lamb are distinguished as two separate entities as I addressed in Chapter 1.

Verses 15 through 17 are our hope. It is the hope we must all cling to during these trying times. It is the hope that we are promised if we endure and hold fast to our faith. Reading these verses always strengthens my faith and provides great peace to my heart.

**Revelation 7:9-17 – The Multitude from Every Nation**
– [9] After this I looked, and there was a great multitude that no one could count, from every nation, from all tribes and peoples and languages, standing before the throne and before the Lamb, robed in white, with palm branches in their hands. [10] They cried out in a loud voice, saying, "Salvation belongs to our God who is seated on the throne and to the Lamb!"

$^{11}$ And all the angels stood around the throne and around the elders and the four living creatures, and they fell on their faces before the throne and worshiped God, $^{12}$ singing, "Amen! Blessing and glory and wisdom and thanksgiving and honor and power and might be to our God forever and ever! Amen."

$^{13}$ Then one of the elders addressed me, saying, "Who are these, robed in white, and where have they come from?" $^{14}$ I said to him, "Sir, you are the one who knows." Then he said to me, "These are they who have come out of the great ordeal [or *great tribulation*]; they have washed their robes and made them white in the blood of the Lamb. $^{15}$ For this reason they are before the throne of God and worship him day and night within his temple, and the one who is seated on the throne will shelter them. $^{16}$ They will hunger no more and thirst no more; the sun will not strike them, nor any scorching heat, $^{17}$ for the Lamb at the center of the throne will be their shepherd, and he will guide them to springs of the water of life, and God will wipe away every tear from their eyes."

***

**Revelation 11:1-13 – Commentary**
**The Two Witnesses**

I have discussed these passages over the years with several people. I have heard many ideas of who the two witnesses are. It is all speculation. The most important aspect of this vision is being aware of the actual event and knowing what is happening.

Verses 1 and 2 allude to the event Jesus spoke of to the disciples concerning the desolating sacrilege spoken of in Matthew 24:15-21, Mark

13:14-19, and Luke 21:20-24: "For it is given over to the nations, and they will trample over the holy city for forty-two months." Again, the number of days is not as important as the actual event.

At this time, two witnesses will rise up and prophesy to those who are left on the earth. Now, it is true that thirty to even sixty years ago, television could have broadcast these witnesses to be seen around the world, but today, with social media and the accessibility of the internet, this event of the two witnesses could be seen instantly, live, all over the world. Do you see the significance of the technology we now have in fulfilling the Scriptures? These two witnesses will perform powerful miracles and perform great signs while the world is watching. They will have authority to cause tremendous suffering and plagues. All the while, they will be testifying to those left on this earth of the salvation provided by God.

Because of this, the world will hate them. The vision reveals that the first beast will rise up against them and kill them according to God's plan. It states that these two witnesses will not be provided a proper burial, but instead the world will look upon their dead bodies and rejoice. They will celebrate the death of these two witnesses by the beast with gift giving and revelry.

After a period of days, God will breathe life back into the two witnesses and they will rise up to be taken into heaven in front of all the world. "At that moment there was a great earthquake." I see this earthquake as the same earthquake that is spoken of in Revelation 6:12 and 16:18.

Verse 13 states, "And the rest were terrified and gave glory to the God of heaven." I see those who are glorifying God as those who are sealed by God and who have the Presence of the Holy Spirit in their lives. As I stated earlier, those that are here on earth and sealed by God will see the judgment of God upon the unrighteous all around them, but they themselves will not be harmed.

**Revelation 11:1-13 - The Two Witnesses –** [1] Then I was given a measuring rod like a staff, and I was told, "Come and measure the temple of God and the altar and those who worship there, [2] but do not measure the court outside the temple; leave that out, for it is given over to the nations, and

they will trample over the holy city for forty-two months. ³
And I will grant my two witnesses authority to prophesy for
one thousand two hundred sixty days, wearing sackcloth."

⁴ These are the two olive trees and the two lampstands that
stand before the Lord of the earth. ⁵ And if anyone wants
to harm them, fire pours from their mouth and consumes
their foes; anyone who wants to harm them must be killed in
this manner. ⁶ They have authority to shut the sky, so that no
rain may fall during the days of their prophesying, and they
have authority over the waters to turn them into blood and
to strike the earth with every kind of plague, as often as they
desire.

⁷ When they have finished their testimony, the beast that
comes up from the bottomless pit will wage war on them
and conquer them and kill them, ⁸ and their dead bodies
will lie in the street of the great city that is prophetically
[or *allegorically*; Greek *spiritually*] called Sodom and Egypt,
where also their Lord was crucified. ⁹ For three and a half days
members of the peoples and tribes and languages and nations
will gaze at their dead bodies and refuse to let them be placed
in a tomb, ¹⁰ and the inhabitants of the earth will gloat over
them and celebrate and exchange presents, because these two
prophets tormented the inhabitants of the earth.

¹¹ But after the three and a half days, the breath [or *the
spirit*] of life from God entered the two witnesses [Greek
*them*], and they stood on their feet, and those who saw them
were terrified. ¹² Then they [other ancient authorities read

*1]* heard a loud voice from heaven saying to them, "Come up here!" And they went up to heaven in a cloud while their enemies watched them. [13] At that moment there was a great earthquake, and a tenth of the city fell; seven thousand people were killed in the earthquake, and the rest were terrified and gave glory to the God of heaven.

# BOWLS OF GOD'S WRATH AND THE FALL OF BABYLON

**Revelation 11:14 – Commentary**

I see the following several passages of verses happening consecutively. First, the angel announces that the second woe has passed and the third is coming very soon.

**Revelation 11:14 – The Second Woe Has Passed –** [14]

The second woe has passed. The third woe is coming very soon.

***

**Revelation 14:17-20 – Commentary**
**Gathering 6 of 9**

As mentioned in my commentary of Revelation 14:14-16, I see verses 17 through 20 as a separate harvest as mentioned in the parables. This is the harvesting of the "goats" or the "weeds." They are the unrighteous, those who have turned their backs on God and followed their own selfish desires. This is the sixth of nine gatherings.

Verse 19 mentions "the great winepress of the wrath of God." This is the same winepress that is mentioned in Revelation 19:15b: "He will tread the winepress of the fury of the wrath of God the Almighty." This is all in reference to the final spiritual conflict that happens later, the battle of Gog and Magog.

**Revelation 14:17-20 – Reaping the Earth's Harvest – Part 2 –** [17] Then another angel came out of the temple in heaven, and he, too, had a sharp sickle. [18] Then another angel came out from the altar, the angel who has authority over fire, and he called with a loud voice to him who had the sharp sickle, "Use your sharp sickle and gather the clusters of the vine of the earth, for its grapes are ripe." [19] So the angel swung his sickle over the earth and gathered the vintage of the earth, and he threw it into the great winepress of the wrath of God. [20] And the winepress was trodden outside the city, and blood flowed from the winepress, as high as a horse's bridle, for a distance of about one thousand six hundred stadia [or *about two hundred miles*].

***

**Revelation 16:1-16 – Commentary**
**The Bowls of God's Wrath**

Remember what Jesus said in Matthew, Mark, and Luke where He stated, "For at that time there will be great suffering, such as has not been from the beginning of the world until now, no, and never will be?" Revelation 16:1-21 speaks of that time when God will unleash judgment upon those who have rejected Their truth and believed the deceptions and lies of Satan.

Verses 2 through 10 describe the first five plagues. In the midst of these plagues is a proclamation from the angel and the altar: "Yes, O Lord God, the Almighty, your judgments are true and just!" The angels and all of the heavenly hosts know that God is just in Their judgments. God knows our hearts. They know the sincere and innocent. They know the deceived and the evil souls. God does not punish those who do what is right in Their eyes. These plagues do not harm those who are redeemed by God's salvation and carry Their seal. God is a loving God to those who earnestly seek Them and love Them. God will deliver faithful believers from these horrid plagues.

Verses 8 through 10 share the response of those who are suffering from the first four plagues, they "cursed the God of heaven because of their pains and sores, and they did not repent of their deeds." Their hearts are so hard from the sins in their lives that they are unable to recognize the salvation available and repent. Their pride and arrogance are too great to acknowledge they are wrong in having rejected God.

In verses 12 through 16, the sixth angel appears. Within these verses is a subject matter that all of us have heard of in our lives. So many equate Armageddon as the final battle of all time because they have not read the Scriptures with understanding. These verses do not reflect the actual battle of Armageddon; they describe the preparation for the battle, not the battle itself. The battle of Armageddon comes later. That battle will occur "on the great day of God the Almighty."

Verses 13 and 14 proclaim that the writer sees "three foul spirits like frogs coming from the mouth of the dragon, from the mouth of the beast, and from the mouth of the false prophet." In this segment there is the dragon (Satan), the first beast, and the spirit of the false prophet. The foul spirts they spew out are lies spoken to deceive the nations and gather them in preparation for the battle of Armageddon.

Verse 15 is, once again, Jesus proclaiming a warning of His coming and the third of seven blessings, "Blessed is the one who stays awake and is clothed [Greek *and keeps his robes*], not going about naked and exposed to shame." Jesus reiterates His call for us to stay awake, be alert, keep our eyes open and our hearts focused on what is happening around us and in the world, so we will know and be aware of the signs as the end of the ages draws near.

**Revelation 16:1-16 – The Bowls of God's Wrath –** [1] Then I heard a loud voice from the temple telling the seven angels, "Go and pour out on the earth the seven bowls of the wrath of God."

[2] So the first angel went and poured his bowl on the earth, and a foul and painful sore came on those who had the brand of the beast and who worshiped its image.

[3] The second angel poured his bowl into the sea, and it became like the blood of a corpse, and every living thing in the sea died.

[4] The third angel poured his bowl into the rivers and the springs of water, and they became blood. [5] And I heard the angel of the waters say, "You are just, O Holy One, who are and were, for you have judged these things; [6] because they shed the blood of saints and prophets, you have given them blood to drink. It is what they deserve!"

[7] And I heard the altar respond, "Yes, O Lord God, the Almighty, your judgments are true and just!"

$^8$ The fourth angel poured his bowl on the sun, and it was allowed to scorch people with fire; $^9$ they were scorched by the fierce heat, but they cursed the name of God, who had authority over these plagues, and they did not repent and give him glory.

$^{10}$ The fifth angel poured his bowl on the throne of the beast, and its kingdom was plunged into darkness; people gnawed their tongues in agony $^{11}$ and cursed the God of heaven because of their pains and sores, and they did not repent of their deeds.

## The Preparation for the Battle of Armageddon

$^{12}$ The sixth angel poured his bowl on the great River Euphrates, and its water was dried up in order to prepare the way for the kings from the east. $^{13}$ And I saw three foul spirits like frogs coming from the mouth of the dragon, from the mouth of the beast, and from the mouth of the false prophet. $^{14}$ These are demonic spirits, performing signs, who go abroad to the kings of the whole world, to assemble them for battle on the great day of God the Almighty. $^{15}$ ("See, I am coming like a thief! Blessed is the one who stays awake and is clothed [Greek *and keeps his robes*], not going about naked and exposed to shame.") $^{16}$ And the demonic spirits [Greek *they*] assembled the kings [Greek *them*] at the place that in Hebrew is called Harmagedon [or *Armageddon*].

*******

**Revelation 16:17-21 – Commentary**

Over the next several pages, I see the visions from Revelation 6:12-17, 11:15-19, 16:17-21, 18:9-24, and 19:1-10 happening concurrently or consecutively. These events will draw to a conclusion the plagues, the fall of Babylon, the opening of the sixth seal, the warning of the seventh trumpet, and the conclusion of the third woe.

Revelation 16:17 makes a proclamation much like Jesus did in John 19:30 where He proclaimed, "It is finished." Here a loud voice proclaims, "It is done!" As Jesus proclaimed from the cross that His work on this earth was now finished, the voice from the throne proclaims the wrath of God is completed.

With verses 18 through 21 we see the final plague cast down upon the earth, along with a proclamation of what we are about to see, the fall of Babylon.

In verses 18 and 19, the writer witnesses a great earthquake, "such as had not occurred since people were upon the earth." I see this earthquake and the earthquake seen in the visions of Revelation 6:12-17 and Revelation 11:15-19 as one and the same.

**Revelation 16:17-21 –** [17] The seventh angel poured his bowl into the air, and a loud voice came out of the temple, from the throne, saying, "It is done!" [18] And there came flashes of lightning, rumblings, peals of thunder, and a violent earthquake, such as had not occurred since people were upon the earth, so violent was that earthquake. [19] The great city was split into three parts, and the cities of the nations fell. God remembered great Babylon and gave her the wine cup of the fury of his wrath. [20] And every island fled away, and no mountains were to be found, [21] and huge hailstones, each weighing about a hundred pounds [Greek *weighing about a talent*], dropped from heaven on people, until they cursed God for the plague of the hail, so fearful was that plague.

***

## Revelation 18:9-24 – Commentary
### God Remembered Babylon – The Fall of Babylon

Verses 9 through 19 record the lamentations and sorrow of those who had participated in the indulgences of Babylon as they look upon its destruction. The many kings/leaders of the nations who had reveled in the excessive luxuries of Babylon, merchants who traded merchandise with it, the shipmasters and seafarers who had participated in the shipments of merchandise and materials, all are mournful for the trade they have lost with the fall of the great Babylon.

Verses 20 through 24 proclaim the quick and decisive destruction of the great Babylon and announces that it is no more.

**Revelation 18:9-24 – God Remembered Babylon – The Fall of Babylon –** [9] And the kings of the earth, who engaged in sexual immorality [or *prostitution*] and lived in luxury with her, will weep and wail over her when they see the smoke of her burning; [10] they will stand far off, in fear of her torment, and say, "Alas, alas, the great city, Babylon, the mighty city! For in one hour your judgment has come."

[11] And the merchants of the earth weep and mourn for her, since no one buys their cargo any more, [12] cargo of gold, silver, jewels and pearls, fine linen, purple, silk and scarlet, all kinds of scented wood, all articles of ivory, all articles of costly wood, bronze, iron, and marble, [13] cinnamon, spice, incense, myrrh, frankincense, wine, olive oil, choice flour and wheat,

242

cattle and sheep, horses and chariots, slaves—and human lives [or *chariots, and human bodies and souls*]. <sup>14</sup> "The fruit for which your soul longed has gone from you, and all your delicacies and your splendor are lost to you, never to be found again!"

<sup>15</sup> The merchants of these wares, who grew wealthy from her, will stand far off, in fear of her torment, weeping and mourning aloud, <sup>16</sup> "Alas, alas, the great city, clothed in fine linen, in purple and scarlet, adorned with gold, with jewels, and with pearls! <sup>17</sup> For in one hour all this wealth has been laid waste!" And all shipmasters and seafarers, sailors and all whose trade is on the sea, stood far off <sup>18</sup> and cried out as they saw the smoke of her burning, "What city was like the great city?" <sup>19</sup> And they threw dust on their heads as they wept and mourned, crying out, "Alas, alas, the great city, where all who had ships at sea grew rich by her wealth! For in one hour she has been laid waste."

<sup>20</sup> Rejoice over her, O heaven, you saints and apostles and prophets! For God has condemned her condemnation of you.

<sup>21</sup> Then a mighty angel took up a stone like a great millstone and threw it into the sea, saying, "With such violence Babylon the great city will be thrown down and will be found no more; <sup>22</sup> and the sound of harpists and entertainers and of flutists and trumpeters will be heard in you no more, and an artisan of any trade will be found in you no more, and the sound of the millstone will be heard in you no more, <sup>23</sup> and

the light of a lamp will shine in you no more, and the voice of bridegroom and bride will be heard in you no more, for your merchants were the magnates of the earth, and all nations were deceived by your sorcery. [24] And in you [Greek *her*] was found the blood of prophets and of saints and of all who have been slaughtered on earth."

***

**Revelation 19:1-10 – Commentary**
  **The Rejoicing in Heaven**

Revelation 19:1-3 records the response from a "great multitude" in heaven concerning the fall of Babylon. They are rejoicing over the righteous judgment of Babylon. This is something that so many struggle with. God is love and yet They allow such harsh judgment. But it is our own doing that justifies God's judgment. We bring it upon ourselves. The great multitude cries, "Hallelujah." Hallelujah literally means "Praise Yah(Weh)," which is known more broadly as "Praise Jehovah." Jehovah is a form of the Hebrew name of God.

Verses 4 and 5 see the twenty-four elders and four living creatures worshipping God along with a call for all to worship and praise God. This is followed by verses 6 through 8 where, once again the great multitude in heaven gives praise and worship to God along with proclaiming the coming of the marriage of the Lamb. The marriage of the Lamb is symbolic of the final act in which all faithful believers are united with Jesus at the end of the ages within the surroundings of the new heaven and new earth.

Verse 9 proclaims the fourth of seven blessings. "Blessed are those who are invited to the marriage supper of the Lamb." This is a true statement. We are all invited to the marriage supper of the Lamb, but not all accept that invitation, confirming the free will choice in which God gave us. Jesus spoke of this in His parable "The Wedding Banquet" recorded in Matthew 22:1-14 and Luke 14:15-24. The invitation is there; we must be willing to accept it.

**Revelation 19:1-10 – The Rejoicing in Heaven –** $^1$ After this I heard what seemed to be the loud voice of a great multitude in heaven, saying, "Hallelujah! Salvation and glory and power to our God, $^2$ for his judgments are true and just; he has judged the great whore [or *prostitute*] who corrupted the earth with her prostitution, and he has avenged on her the blood of his servants [Greek *slaves*]."

$^3$ Once more they said, "Hallelujah! The smoke goes up from her forever and ever." $^4$ And the twenty-four elders and the four living creatures fell down and worshiped God who is seated on the throne, saying, "Amen. Hallelujah!" $^5$ And from the throne came a voice saying, "Praise our God, all you his servants [Greek *slaves*] and [other ancient authorities lack *and*] all who fear him, small and great."

$^6$ Then I heard what seemed to be the voice of a great multitude, like the sound of many waters and like the sound of mighty thunderpeals, crying out, "Hallelujah! For the Lord [other ancient authorities add *our*] God the Almighty reigns. $^7$ Let us rejoice and exult and give him the glory, for the marriage of the Lamb has come, and his bride has made herself ready; $^8$ to her it has been granted to be clothed with fine linen, bright and pure"—for the fine linen is the righteous deeds of the saints.

$^9$ And the angel said [Greek *he said*] to me, "Write this: Blessed are those who are invited to the marriage supper of the Lamb." And he said to me, "These are true words of God." [10] Then I fell down at his feet to worship him, but he said to me, "You must not do that! I am a fellow servant [Greek *slave*] with you and your brothers and sisters [Greek "adelphoi" *brothers* or *believers* designating both men and women] who hold the testimony of Jesus [or *to Jesus*]. Worship God! For the testimony of Jesus [or *to Jesus*] is the spirit of prophecy."

# THE FINAL SEALS AND TRUMPET

**Revelation 6:12-17 – Commentary**

As we were told by Jesus in Matthew 24:29-31, Mark 13:24-27, and Luke 21:25-28, there will be a cosmic cataclysm that occurs right before His coming back to this earth. Up until this vision, all of the plagues and destruction that are prophesied happen on the earth. But this vision deals with the cosmic cataclysm that Jesus prophesied that would occur right before His return to this earth. This is the authority that Jesus holds: the sixth seal is broken.

Verse 12 describes the earthquake that I see as being intertwined with the earthquake spoken of in Revelation 16:18 and 11:19. Verses 12 through 14 describe the cosmic cataclysm that Jesus prophesied would happen, displaying His authority and power over nature.

Verses 15 through 17 describe the humbling of the powerful and the fear of non-believers as they realize that "the great day of their [other ancient authorities read *his*] wrath has come, and who is able to stand?" It is a powerful revelation for them as it is now too late to rectify within their souls.

**Revelation 6:12-17 – The Sixth Seal –** [12] When he broke the sixth seal, I looked, and there was a great earthquake; the sun became black as sackcloth, the full moon became like blood, [13] and the stars of the sky fell to the earth as the fig tree drops its winter fruit when shaken by a gale. [14] The sky vanished like a scroll rolling itself up, and every mountain and island was removed from its place. [15] Then the kings of the earth and the magnates and the generals and the rich and the powerful and everyone, slave and free, hid in the caves and among the rocks of the mountains, [16] calling to the mountains and rocks, "Fall on us and hide us from the face of the one seated on the throne and from the wrath of the Lamb, [17] for the great day of their [other ancient authorities read *his*] wrath has come, and who is able to stand?"

***

## Revelation 11:15-19 – Commentary
### The Seventh Trumpet
### Third Woe – Has Passed

The seventh and final trumpet sounds. Matthew 24:31, 1 Corinthians 15:52, and 1 Thessalonians 4:16 speak of this final trumpet sound as being the proclamation of the return of Jesus to this earth.

Along with this trumpet sound, verse 15 proclaims that all creation has become "the kingdom of our Lord and of his Messiah [Greek *Christ*]." Note the two significant entities mentioned as I shared in Chapter 1.

Verses 16 through 18 describe, once again, the twenty-four elders proclaiming praise and worshipping the Lord God Almighty. It is they who pronounce the final judgment. It is a three-fold judgment that will occur. It is a judgment of the dead. It is a judgment "for rewarding your servants [Greek *slaves*], the prophets and saints and all who fear your name, both small and great." But it is the third judgment that has stuck in my heart over the years.

In verse 18, it is clearly proclaimed that there will be a judgment set aside that is "for destroying those who destroy the earth." The earth does not belong to us. The earth was given to us by a loving God who wanted us to care for it and respect it. It was Their gift to us to live on in a state of grace. But we have slowly destroyed it. It has been scientifically proven that all of the things we believed were created for the progress of our well-being

248

and our benefit has harmed the fragile earth that we have been given to care for. The so-called progress we have made creating a luxurious life of self-indulgence has caused havoc to this wondrous planet. The system of Capitalism we have created only benefits the ultra-rich. For this we all will be held accountable on that day if we have not repented of our ways before then.

As with the introduction of the seven trumpets in Revelation 8:5, in 11:19 at the conclusion of the seven trumpets, there is a display of God's power and majesty.

Though it is not actually stated in the Scriptures, this concludes the third woe.

**Revelation 11:15-19 – The Seventh Trumpet and Third Woe –** [15] Then the seventh angel blew his trumpet, and there were loud voices in heaven, saying, "The kingdom of the world has become the kingdom of our Lord and of his Messiah [Greek *Christ*], and he will reign forever and ever."

[16] Then the twenty-four elders who sit on their thrones before God fell on their faces and worshiped God, [17] singing, "We give you thanks, Lord God Almighty, who are and who were, for you have taken your great power and begun to reign. [18] The nations raged, but your wrath has come, and the time for judging the dead, for rewarding your servants [Greek *slaves*], the prophets and saints and all who fear your name, both small and great, and for destroying those who destroy the earth."

[19] Then God's temple in heaven was opened, and the ark of his covenant was seen within his temple, and there

were flashes of lightning, rumblings, peals of thunder, an earthquake, and heavy hail.


***


**Revelation 8:1 – Commentary**
**The Seventh Seal**
The seventh seal is broken and for a brief time there is silence in heaven. All who inhabit heaven come to a silence. A moment of peace. A time of rest before the reveal of Jesus in the skies before all of humankind.


**Revelation 8:1 – The Seventh Seal –** [1] When the Lamb broke the seventh seal, there was silence in heaven for about half an hour.

# THE RIDER, THE THOUSAND YEARS, AND SATAN'S DOOM

**Revelation 19:11-16 – Commentary**

The following verses from the Scriptures announce, what I see, as the second coming of Jesus as He prophesied that He would come again. This is Jesus, the Christ, "Faithful and True," "The Word of God," and "King of kings and Lord of lords." This is the Messiah for whom the children of Israel have been waiting. Israel did not accept Jesus the first time when He came to earth as a humble servant to the people for their salvation, but now He returns in power and majesty to establish rule over His people. This second return is for the salvation of the chosen, the remnant of Israel.

Verse 15 states, "He will tread the winepress of the fury of the wrath of God the Almighty" as was mentioned earlier in Revelation 14:17-20.

**Revelation 19:11-16 – The Rider on the White Horse**
– [11] Then I saw heaven opened, and there was a white horse! Its rider is called Faithful and True, and in righteousness he judges and wages war. [12] His eyes are like [other ancient authorities omit *like*] a flame of fire, and on his head are many diadems, and he has a name inscribed that no one knows but

himself. [13] He is clothed in a robe dipped in [other ancient authorities read *sprinkled with*] blood, and his name is called The Word of God. [14] And the armies of heaven, wearing fine linen, white and pure, were following him on white horses. [15] From his mouth comes a sharp sword with which to strike down the nations, and he will rule [or *will shepherd*] them with a scepter of iron; he will tread the winepress of the fury of the wrath of God the Almighty. [16] On his robe and on his thigh he has a name inscribed, "King of kings and Lord of lords."

***

### Revelation 14:1-5 – Commentary
#### Gathering 7 of 9

As Jesus returns to the earth, the 144,000 that had been sealed by God "who had his name and his Father's name written on their foreheads" joins Jesus at Mount Zion. These are the same 144,000 that were sealed in Revelation 7:1-8. They are the chosen remnant of Israel. They are the seventh of nine gatherings.

### Revelation 14:1-5 – The Lamb and the 144,000 – [1]

Then I looked, and there was the Lamb, standing on Mount Zion! And with him were one hundred forty-four thousand who had his name and his Father's name written on their foreheads. [2] And I heard a voice from heaven like the sound of many waters and like the sound of loud thunder; the voice I heard was like the sound of harpists playing on their harps, [3] and they sing a new song before the throne and before the four living creatures and before the elders. No one could learn that song except the one hundred forty-four thousand who have been redeemed from the earth. [4] It is these who have not defiled themselves with women, for they are virgins; these follow the Lamb wherever he goes. They have been redeemed from humankind as first fruits for God and the Lamb, [5] and in their mouth no lie was found; they are blameless.

***

## Revelation 19:17-21 – Commentary
### The Beast and Its Armies Defeated

Remember the sixth angel that poured out the bowl of God's wrath in Revelation 16:12-16? In those verses, it described the preparations for the battle of Armageddon by drying up the great River Euphrates "in order to prepare the way for the kings from the east" (verse 12b). "And the demonic spirits [Greek *they*] assembled the kings [Greek *them*] at the place that in Hebrew is called Harmagedon [or *Armageddon*]" (verse 16).

Here, in Revelation 19:17-21, we have the actual battle of the armies that were assembled in Armageddon to fight against Jesus and His army. At the conclusion of the battle, the (first) beast and the false prophet are captured and thrown "alive into the lake of fire that burns with sulfur." Once again, the beast represents the nations driven by evil and the false prophet represents those who have spread the lies perverting the truth found within the Scriptures. All of the kings, their armies, and their followers are defeated by Jesus and His army at this great battle that many call Armageddon.

**Revelation 19:17-21 – The Beast and Its Armies Defeated –** [17] Then I saw an angel standing in the sun, and with a loud voice he called to all the birds that fly in midheaven, "Come, gather for the great supper of God, [18] to eat the flesh of kings, the flesh of captains, the flesh of the mighty, the flesh of horses and their riders—flesh of all, both free and slave, both small and great." [19] Then I saw the beast and the kings of the earth with their armies gathered to wage war against the rider on the horse and against his army. [20] And the beast was captured, and with it the false prophet who had performed in its presence the signs by which he deceived those who had received the brand of the beast and those who worshiped its image. These two were thrown alive into the lake of fire that burns with sulfur. [21] And the rest were killed by the sword of the rider on the horse, the sword that came from his mouth, and all the birds were gorged with their flesh.

***

## Revelation 20:1-3 – Commentary
### The Thousand Years

The most important aspect of these verses that needs to be noted is that when the time comes, when God's plan for humankind is almost completed and Jesus returns to this earth with all of His authority, it takes only one angel to bind and imprison Satan into the pit. This adversary that the world has determined to be so powerful is bound and imprisoned by a single angel. There is no other authority that is greater than God. It is only humankind's lack of discipline and devotion that gives Satan such an appearance of power.

Remember, the thousand years may not be a literal thousand years as we know it. It will be a period of time determined by God. During this time in which Satan is bound, I see evil as being suppressed by the power of Jesus's presence, but there is still evil in the depth of the hearts of humankind. I see demonic spirits being held in check by the authority of Jesus, for even though He is present on this earth, all evil is still yet to be destroyed and eternally cast into damnation. The final spiritual battle is yet to come.

**Revelation 20:1-3 – The Thousand Years – [1]** Then I saw an angel coming down from heaven, holding in his hand the key to the bottomless pit and a great chain. [2] He seized the dragon, that ancient serpent, who is the devil and Satan, and bound him for a thousand years [3] and threw him into the pit and locked and sealed it over him, so that he would deceive the nations no more, until the thousand years were ended. After that he must be let out for a little while.

***

## Revelation 20:4-6 – Commentary
### Gathering 8 of 9

Revelation 20:4-6 provides a very powerful vision pertaining to the first resurrection of the dead. Jesus has returned to earth to reign for a period of time. The writer notes four important elements in this vision. I will break them down accordingly.

1.) 4a: "Then I saw thrones, and those seated on them were given authority to judge." This is in preparation for the great judgment and concludes the Great Tribulation/Ordeal.

2.) 4b through 5a: "I also saw the souls of those who had been beheaded for their testimony to Jesus [or *for the testimony of Jesus*] and for the word of God. They had not worshiped the beast or its image and had not received its brand on their foreheads or their hands. They came to life and reigned with Christ a thousand years. (The rest of the dead did not come to life until the thousand years were ended.)" This is the eighth of nine gatherings.

3.) 5b: "This is the first resurrection." This is the resurrection of the dead in which the writer of 1 Thessalonians 4:16 spoke of.

4.) 6: "Blessed and holy are those who share in the first resurrection. Over these the second death has no power, but they will be priests of God and of Christ, and they will reign with him a thousand years." This is the fifth of seven blessings and a proclamation of holiness for those who share in the first resurrection. What a powerful vision.

**Revelation 20:4-6** — <sup>4</sup> Then I saw thrones, and those seated on them were given authority to judge. I also saw the souls of those who had been beheaded for their testimony to Jesus [or *for the testimony of Jesus*] and for the word of God. They had not worshiped the beast or its image and had not received its brand on their foreheads or their hands. They came to life and reigned with Christ a thousand years. <sup>5</sup> (The rest of the dead did not come to life until the thousand years were ended.) This is the first resurrection. <sup>6</sup> Blessed and holy are those who share in the first resurrection. Over these the second death has no power, but they will be priests of God and of Christ, and they will reign with him a thousand years.

***

## Revelation 20:7-10 – Commentary
### Satan's Doom

Revelation 20:7-10 records the final spiritual battle on this earth and the judgment of Satan and his demons.

In verse 7, Satan is released from his prison and allowed to roam the earth with his demons to deceive the nations one final time. He gathers a vast army to fight against Jesus and His chosen. Once Satan's army has surrounded "the beloved city," "fire came down from heaven [other ancient authorities read *from God, out of heaven, or out of heaven from God*] and consumed them." All of Satan's demons and his followers are consumed by the holy fire of God.

Verse 10 records the final destination of Satan, his eternal damnation along with the beast and the false prophet in the lake of fire and sulfur. There they will suffer in darkness and shame, forever being separated from the God who created them and loved them. Their decisions, their selfish choice to indulge in rebellion, greed, and the lie will torment them eternally.

**Revelation 20:7-10 – Satan's Doom –** [7] When the thousand years are ended, Satan will be released from his prison [8] and will come out to deceive the nations at the four corners of the earth, Gog and Magog, in order to gather them for battle; they are as numerous as the sands of the sea. [9] They marched up over the breadth of the earth and surrounded the camp of the saints and the beloved city. And fire came down from heaven [other ancient authorities read *from God, out of heaven, or out of heaven from God*] and consumed them. [10] And the devil who had deceived them was thrown into the lake of fire and sulfur, where the beast and the false prophet were, and they will be tormented day and night forever and ever.

# JUDGMENT AND THE NEW HEAVEN AND EARTH

**Revelation 20:11-15 – Commentary**

Revelation 20:11-15 records the final of the nine gatherings. In verse 11, the writer sees a "great white throne and the one who sat on it." Read the implications of the next line slowly. The throne of God is seen and "the earth and the heaven fled from his [Greek *the*] presence, and no place was found for them." Read that line again. The Creator will bring to conclusion the creation we all know, even the heavens. It will be removed from Their presence and will exist no more. Do you see the power behind that verse. When it is time, *all* the heavens and earth will be no more. Just like that.

All of the dead are gathered from the beginning of time. All of the dead, for "the sea gave up the dead who were in it, Death and Hades gave up the dead who were in them." All will be raised to face the final judgment of their eternal souls. The flesh that we live in is mortal, but our souls are immortal. Our souls will be given an immortal "body," a spirit body for all eternity. It will be this body that will live forever in the presence of God or be damned forever in the lake of fire, eternal darkness, away from the presence of a loving God. This is the second "death," eternal punishment as recorded in verse 14.

In verse 12, the writer records two types of books being opened: "And books were opened. Also another book was opened, the Book of Life. And the dead were judged according to their works, as recorded in the books." We will all stand before the judgment seat and account for whether we have walked in the truth of God's existence and the salvation They have provided or whether we have believed the lie and lived in accordance to our own selfish ambitions.

The second part of verse 12 starts: "And books were opened." I see these "books" as the secrets within our souls that have not been covered by the forgiveness that God provides a repentant heart. They are our inward motives and thoughts for all of our actions on this earth. God knows them all as I shared in Chapter 6. Understand that everything in the deepest parts of our souls will be revealed that has not been forgiven. As I have said, you can get away with lying to yourselves or to others, but you will not get away with the lie on the day of judgment.

If you have faithfully believed in God, accepted the salvation that They have provided, and repented of all the wrong you have done, all is forgiven and is not recorded in those books. The books will be filled only with those things you have done right in the eyes of God. That is the premise behind the Thread of Truth that I shared in Chapter 3. Because of having lived your life doing what is good and right in the eyes of God and accepting Their salvation, your name will also be found in the Book of Life and you will enter into an eternal life under God's state of grace, forever living within Their presence.

If the books reveal selfish, sinful motives, and a life rejecting God's salvation, your name will not be found in the Book of Life and you will be cast into the eternal fire of dark damnation, forever existing in a state of torment and anguish away from the presence of a loving God.

Finally, in verse 14, Death and Hades are thrown into the lake of fire. Death and Hades will be no more for all souls will exist in an eternal state of grace or damnation from that time forth.

**Revelation 20:11-15 – The Dead Are Judged –** [11] Then I saw a great white throne and the one who sat on it; the earth and the heaven fled from his [Greek *the*] presence, and no place was found for them. [12] And I saw the dead, great and small, standing before the throne, and books were opened. Also another book was opened, the book of life. And the dead were judged according to their works, as recorded in the books. [13] And the sea gave up the dead who were in it, Death and Hades gave up the dead who were in them, and all were judged according to what they had done. [14] Then Death and Hades were thrown into the lake of fire. This is the second death, the lake of fire, [15] and anyone whose name was not found written in the book of life was thrown into the lake of fire.

***

**Revelation 21:1-27 – Commentary**
**The New Heaven and the New Earth**
**Vision of the New Jerusalem**
Revelation 21:1-7 reiterates the promises of God for those who believe and hold fast to their faith. These verses establish the creation of a new heaven and new earth where God dwells among those who were mortals but have now taken on immortality. Verses 4 through 7 echoes the verses found in Revelation 7:15-17, the hope in which we all have with God strongly promising in verse 5: "Write this, for these words are trustworthy and true."

Verse 6 repeats the final declaration of the promise as Jesus proclaimed in John 19:30 with "It is finished!" and the voice from the throne in Revelation 16:17 saying, "It is done!" Here the writer records that "the one who was seated on the throne said, 'It is done! I am the Alpha and the Omega, the Beginning and the End.'" The Creator proclaims the work and purpose of this creation have been completed.

In verse 7, God reaffirms what They promised Cain in Genesis 4 if he did what was right. It is the Thread of Truth: "Those who conquer will inherit these things, and I will be their God, and they will be my children."

And in verse 8, God clarifies those things which are not right in Their eyes and that do not please Them: "But as for the cowardly, the faithless [or *the unbelieving*], the polluted, the murderers, the sexually immoral [or *prostitutes*], the sorcerers, the idolaters, and all liars, their place will be in the lake that burns with fire and sulfur, which is the second death."

Verses 9 through 27 provide a verbal painting of the brilliance and beauty of the new Jerusalem, the place of eternal heavenly worship, peace, and life. I believe the writer described well what he saw in this vision, but I do not believe anyone could truly describe with words the magnificence and majesty of what our eternal home will look like. Our vocabulary is too limited and our minds are too narrow to fully understand how wondrously stunning it will be. I have seen the beauty that God has created on this earth. I have seen the breath-taking wonders of nature that have not been destroyed by man. There are places that are so beautiful to behold, all you can do is stand in awe as you gaze at what is before you. Knowing that this exists on this earthly dwelling confirms in my heart that our heavenly home will be even grander to behold.

Verse 27 reminds us, after describing the splendor of heaven, that "nothing unclean will enter it, nor anyone who practices abomination or falsehood, but only those who are written in the Lamb's book of life." Only those who have done what is right and good in the eyes of God on this earth will receive this eternal blessing.

**Revelation 21:1-27 – The New Heaven and the New Earth –** [1] Then I saw a new heaven and a new earth, for the first heaven and the first earth had passed away, and the sea was no more. [2] And I saw the holy city, the new Jerusalem, coming down out of heaven from God, prepared as a bride adorned for her husband. [3] And I heard a loud voice from the throne saying, "See, the home [Greek *the tabernacle*] of God is among mortals. He will dwell [Greek *will tabernacle*] with them; they will be his peoples [other ancient authorities read *people*], and God himself will be with them and be their God [other ancient authorities lack *and be their God*]; ⁴ he will wipe every tear from their eyes.

Death will be no more; mourning and crying and pain will be no more, for [other ancient authorities lack *for*] the first things have passed away."

⁵ And the one who was seated on the throne said, "See, I am making all things new." Also he said, "Write this, for these words are trustworthy and true." ⁶ Then he said to me, "It is done! I am the Alpha and the Omega, the Beginning and the End. To the thirsty I will give water as a gift from the spring of the water of life. ⁷ Those who conquer will inherit these things, and I will be their God, and they will be my children. ⁸ But as for the cowardly, the faithless [or *the unbelieving*], the polluted, the murderers, the sexually immoral [or *prostitutes*], the sorcerers, the idolaters, and all liars, their place will be in the lake that burns with fire and sulfur, which is the second death."

**Vision of the New Jerusalem**

⁹ Then one of the seven angels who had the seven bowls full of the seven last plagues came and said to me, "Come, I will show you the bride, the wife of the Lamb." ¹⁰ And in the spirit [or *in the Spirit*] he carried me away to a great, high mountain and showed me the holy city Jerusalem coming

down out of heaven from God. [11] It has the glory of God and a radiance like a very rare jewel, like jasper, clear as crystal. [12] It has a great, high wall with twelve gates, and at the gates twelve angels, and on the gates are inscribed the names that are the names [other ancient authorities lack *that are the names*] of the twelve tribes of the Israelites: [13] on the east three gates, on the north three gates, on the south three gates, and on the west three gates. [14] And the wall of the city has twelve foundations, and on them are the twelve names of the twelve apostles of the Lamb.

[15] The angel [Greek *He*] who talked to me had a measuring rod of gold to measure the city and its gates and walls. [16] The city has four equal sides, its length the same as its width, and he measured the city with his rod, twelve thousand stadia [or *fifteen hundred miles*]; its length and width and height are equal. [17] He also measured its wall, one hundred forty-four cubits [or *that is, almost seventy-five yards*] by human measurement, which the angel was using. [18] The wall is built of jasper, while the city is pure gold, clear as glass. [19] The foundations of the wall of the city are adorned with every jewel; the first was jasper, the second sapphire, the third agate, the fourth emerald, [20] the fifth onyx, the sixth carnelian, the seventh chrysolite, the eighth beryl, the ninth topaz, the tenth chrysoprase, the eleventh jacinth, the twelfth amethyst. [21] And the twelve gates are twelve pearls, each of the gates is a single pearl, and the street of the city is pure gold, transparent as glass.

[22] I saw no temple in the city, for its temple is the Lord God the Almighty and the Lamb. [23] And the city has no need of sun or moon to shine on it, for the glory of God is its light,

and its lamp is the Lamb. $^{24}$ The nations will walk by its light, and the kings of the earth will bring their glory into it. $^{25}$ Its gates will never be shut by day—and there will be no night there. $^{26}$ People will bring into it the glory and the honor of the nations. $^{27}$ But nothing unclean will enter it, nor anyone who practices abomination or falsehood, but only those who are written in the Lamb's book of life.

***

**Revelation 22:1-21 – Commentary**
**The River of Life**
**Epilogue and Benediction**

Genesis 2:1-14 describes the Garden of Eden having a river flowing through it and the tree of life. In Revelation 22:1-2, the writer is shown "the river of the water of life, bright as crystal, flowing from the throne of God and of the Lamb." On both sides of the river is the tree of life. So, at the beginning of our world there was a river and a tree of life and at the beginning of the new heaven and earth there will be a river of life with a tree of life on either side. The difference will be that "nothing accursed will be found there any more."

Verse 7 provides us with the sixth of seven blessings: "Blessed is the one who keeps the words of the prophecy of this book." Revelation is a book of profound truth. Those who have no understanding look at it as a book of destruction and a God of plagues and anger. But to those of us who understand, it is a book of hope and promise if we hold fast to what we believe and stay faithful until the end.

It is significant that we understand, as the angel told the writer of these visions in verse nine, that angels are no more than we are; they are servants of a loving God. Though they have spiritual powers that we do not have in our mortal bodies, when we are transformed into our immortal bodies, we will all be equal as servants of a loving God.

Verse 11 provides us with the final instance of what I call the "Thread of Truth." The portion of the verse states, "And the righteous still do right." Doing what is right and good in the eyes of God is our calling.

In verse 12, Jesus reiterates the coming judgment. We will all be judged "according to everyone's work." All of our motives and intentions of the heart will be exposed.

Verse 14 records the final of seven blessings along with the promise and hope of all faithful believers: "Blessed are those who wash their robes [other ancient authorities read *do his commandments*], so that they will have the right to the tree of life and may enter the city by the gates."

In verse 16 we find the final declaration of Jesus proclaiming for the ages: "It is I, Jesus, who sent my angel to you with this testimony for the churches. I am the root and the descendant of David, the bright morning star." So, we all conclude as the writer says, "Come, Lord Jesus!"

**Revelation 22:1-21 – The River of Life –** [1] Then the angel [Greek *He*] showed me the river of the water of life, bright as crystal, flowing from the throne of God and of the Lamb [2] through the middle of the street of the city. On either side of the river is the tree of life [or *the Lamb. In the middle of the street of the city, and on either side of the river, is the tree of life*] with its twelve kinds of fruit, producing its fruit each month, and the leaves of the tree are for the healing of the nations. [3] Nothing accursed will be found there any more. But the throne of God and of the Lamb will be in it, and his servants [Greek *slaves*] will worship him; [4] they will see his face, and his name will be on their foreheads. [5] And there will be no more night; they need no light of lamp or sun, for the Lord God will be their light, and they will reign forever and ever.

⁶ And he said to me, "These words are trustworthy and true, for the Lord, the God of the spirits of the prophets, has sent his angel to show his servants what must soon take place."

⁷ "See, I am coming soon! Blessed is the one who keeps the words of the prophecy of this book."

## Epilogue and Benediction

⁸ I, John, am the one who heard and saw these things. And when I heard and saw them, I fell down to worship at the feet of the angel who showed them to me, ⁹ but he said to me, "You must not do that! I am a fellow servant with you and your brothers and sisters the prophets and with those who keep the words of this book. Worship God!"

¹⁰ And he said to me, "Do not seal up the words of the prophecy of this book, for the time is near. ¹¹ Let the evildoer still do evil, and the filthy still be filthy, and the righteous still do right, and the holy still be holy."

¹² "See, I am coming soon; my reward is with me, to repay according to everyone's work. ¹³ I am the Alpha and the Omega, the First and the Last, the Beginning and the End."

<sup>14</sup> Blessed are those who wash their robes [other ancient authorities read *do his commandments*], so that they will have the right to the tree of life and may enter the city by the gates. <sup>15</sup> Outside are the dogs and sorcerers and sexually immoral [or *prostitutes*] and murderers and idolaters and everyone who loves and practices falsehood.

<sup>16</sup> "It is I, Jesus, who sent my angel to you with this testimony for the churches. I am the root and the descendant of David, the bright morning star."

<sup>17</sup> The Spirit and the bride say, "Come." And let everyone who hears say, "Come." And let everyone who is thirsty come. Let anyone who wishes take the water of life as a gift.

<sup>18</sup> I warn everyone who hears the words of the prophecy of this book: if anyone adds to them, God will add to that person the plagues described in this book; <sup>19</sup> if anyone takes away from the words of the book of this prophecy, God will take away that person's share in the tree of life and in the holy city, which are described in this book.

<sup>20</sup> The one who testifies to these things says, "Surely I am coming soon."

Amen. Come, Lord Jesus!

<sup>21</sup> The grace of the Lord Jesus be with all the saints. Amen. [other ancient authorities lack *all* or *the saints* or *Amen*]

***

## IN CONCLUSION

The book of Revelation provides us with so much information concerning the end of the ages. Understanding it does not come with one setting. Even after years of reading it and studying it I am only able to understand it within the realm in which I have just shared with you. Embracing the primary events and recognizing them is the most important lesson. Following is what I see has happened, is happening, and will happen before the end of the ages.

I believe the first beast (Eastern World) and the second beast (Western World) are alive and well.

I believe that Artificial Intelligence is the infrastructure of the image of the beast. I believe once Artificial Intelligence becomes fully operational around the world, the image of the beast will be complete.

It is a very real concept that with the exhaustive information provided to Artificial Intelligence, this image of the beast will have the ability to know who is loyal to the governing body and who is not. It will also have the ability to bring death upon all who are not loyal.

We are only years away from a cashless society. With the surging popularity of digital currency, we may very well enter into a cashless society within ten to twenty years. Once that has been established, the reality of a "mark of the beast" follows. Either you cooperate with a governing body and receive some form of mark or chip on your person or you will not be able to buy or sell goods.

I believe that the United States is the modern Babylon and with the present atmosphere the current rule of government is establishing, those who were once our allies are now reaching a strong sense of distaste for us. What was once a trusted ally and trade partner, the United States has become arrogant in its dealings with the rest of the world. This sets up the fall of the modern "Great Babylon" as described in Revelation chapters 17 through 19a.

I believe we have entered into the Great Tribulation/Ordeal. Circumstances will only get worse from here. God will protect the eternal soul of those that are covered by the blood of Jesus Christ and the power of the Presence of the Holy Spirit. Hold fast to your faith.

What it all comes down to is staying awake and aware of all that is happening. All the chaos around the world at this present time is solely our fault. This was not the plan God had for this creation; it is the way we have chosen to go. We are now seeing the fruit of our poor choices and bad decisions. May God protect the faithful believers and keep us safe from the evil one.

God is still in control of Their plan. We have to recognize Their majesty and accept Their judgment for it is pure and just. God's will, *will* be done on this earth as it is in heaven. God's plan *will* come to pass. God's prophecies *will* be fulfilled.

Amen.

# HOW TO READ THE SCRIPTURES

The Scriptures, which we know as The Holy Bible, are powerful tools of knowledge and understanding about a loving God. It is a guide for learning. As I stated earlier in this writing, I do not believe you have to go to church to be a faithful believer, but I do believe you have to read the Scriptures, pray, and commune with God on a daily basis. It is not the length of time as much as the sincerity of your heart within that time.

Each morning, I devote a specific time to read, study, and pray. I then commune with God throughout the day. God knows our thoughts and hearts. God's Presence is always with us. Throughout the day I give thanks, praise, and worship God. Throughout the day I communicate with God in the Spirit. I do these things because my belief and faith in God is sincere.

In my forty-plus years working in music retail and professional live audio, I met many fans of artists/bands. They were devoted. Quite a few had every recording the artist/band had produced. Some had seen their favorite artist/band perform live anywhere from twenty to over one hundred times. They were devoted and loyal because that artist/band had spoken to their life.

How much more should we be devoted to the God who has given us life? God doesn't expect us to be fanatical, proclaiming Their name on all of our social media and everywhere we go. That is what has damaged the name of God and the salvation of God in this country so much. What

God expects from us is time devoted to Them in that "secret" place where we sincerely commune with Them. What God expects from us out in the world is to demonstrate the love of Jesus to the world by doing those things that are good and right in Their eyes. Doing those things, not preaching those things. Demonstrating the love of Jesus daily to a hurting world. God will see those things and They will be pleased. God's peace will rest in our lives.

Seek the truth; know the truth; live the truth. The truth is found in the Scriptures. If you devote time to reading them and studying them, God will show you Their truth. I hope you will do so.

My personal choices of the translations I recommend reading and studying are the *New Revised Standard Version Updated Edition* or the *New International Version*.

I have a specific formula for reading the Scriptures that I would like to share with you. It has been successful in my life so I have passed it along to anyone who would receive it. Starting out, read the Gospel of John and the book of First John straight through three times. The Gospel of John and the book of First John is all the truth you need to know about the salvation of God. The love of God is revealed in its fullness within these two writings.

After reading those three times read the Gospels of Matthew, Mark, Luke, and John straight through three times. Again, don't be rushed. Pray and read for understanding.

After you have done that, begin reading the Book of Acts and then the rest of the New Testament.

Then read the New Testament from Matthew to Revelation all the way through. When you are comfortable in your reading of the New Testament, then begin the Old Testament.

In reading the Old Testament, I encourage you to read Psalms, Proverbs, Ecclesiastes, and the Song of Solomon first. There is great wisdom found in those books.

After you have read those, you can begin reading in Genesis and read through Exodus. I would not be concerned with reading Leviticus, Numbers, and Deuteronomy at this time. I would wait to read those after you feel comfortable with your New Testament knowledge.

You can then begin reading Joshua and go all the way through to Malachi in the Old Testament. The stories of old chronicled in Joshua through the Song of Solomon are really amazing. From Isaiah to Malachi are the prophets of old. The faith that those prophets possessed was most excellent.

After you have read the Scriptures and become familiar with the truth that God reveals to you in them, you can bounce back and forth between the New and Old Testament to reread the books you have found that speak to you the most. Make a habit of reading the Scriptures and praying daily. I am confident that in doing so, God's peace will rest on you, your faith will be strengthened, and you will find the truth that you have been seeking.

I leave you with the most powerful prayer recorded in the Scriptures. Right before Jesus was arrested and crucified, He prayed for the disciples and all faithful believers who would follow. That includes us. I often read it to remind myself just how much God loves us and cares for us. It is words to strengthen and encourage. It is words of hope.

> **John 17:1-26** After Jesus had spoken these words, he looked up to heaven and said, "Father, the hour has come; glorify your Son so that the Son may glorify you, since you have given him authority over all people [Greek *flesh*], to give eternal life to all whom you have given him. And this is eternal life, that they may know you, the only true God, and Jesus Christ, whom you have sent. I glorified you on earth by finishing the work that you gave me to do. So now, Father, glorify me in your own presence with the glory that I had in your presence before the world existed.

> "I have made your name known to those whom you gave me from the world. They were yours, and you gave them to me, and they have kept your word. Now they know that everything you have given me is from you, for the words that you gave to me I have given to them, and they have received

them and know in truth that I came from you, and they have believed that you sent me. I am asking on their behalf; I am not asking on behalf of the world but on behalf of those whom you gave me, because they are yours. All mine are yours, and yours are mine, and I have been glorified in them. And now I am no longer in the world, but they are in the world, and I am coming to you. Holy Father, protect them in your name that you have given me, so that they may be one, as we are one. While I was with them, I protected them in your name that [other ancient authorities read *protected in your name those whom*] you have given me. I guarded them, and not one of them was lost except the one destined to be lost [Greek *except the son of destruction*], so that the scripture might be fulfilled. But now I am coming to you, and I speak these things in the world so that they may have my joy made complete in themselves [or *among themselves*]. I have given them your word, and the world has hated them because they do not belong to the world, just as I do not belong to the world. I am not asking you to take them out of the world, but I ask you to protect them from the evil one [or *from evil*]. They do not belong to the world, just as I do not belong to the world. Sanctify them in the truth; your word is truth. As you have sent me into the world, so I have sent them into the world. And for their sakes I sanctify myself, so that they also may be sanctified in truth.


"I ask not only on behalf of these but also on behalf of those who believe in me through their word, that they may all be one. As you, Father, are in me and I am in you, may they also be in us [Other ancient authorities read *be one in us*], so that the world may believe that you have sent me. The glory that you have given me I have given them, so that they may be one, as we are one, I in them and you in me, that they may become completely one, so that the world may know that you have sent me and have loved them even as you have loved me. Father, I desire that those also, whom you have given me, may be with me where I am, to see my glory, which you have given me because you loved me before the foundation of the world.

"Righteous Father, the world does not know you, but I know you, and these know that you have sent me. I made your name known to them, and I will make it known, so that the love with which you have loved me may be in them and I in them."

# REFERENCES AND OTHER IMPORTANT INFORMATION

## REFERENCES

Websites
-www.biblegateway.com
-www.biblehub.com
-www.dictionary.com
-www.merriam-webster.com

Bible Translations
-English Standard Version
-King James Version
-New American Standard Bible
-New Revised Standard Version Updated Edition
-New International Version, 1984
-New International Version – Current Edition
-New King James Version

Names/Titles of Jesus in the Book of Revelation
1.Jesus Christ (Revelation 1:1)

2.Faithful Witness (Revelation 1:5)

3.First Born of the Dead (Revelation 1:5)

4.Ruler of the Kings of the Earth (Revelation 1:5)

5.Alpha and Omega, Almighty (Revelation 1:8)

6.Son of Man (Revelation 1:13)

7.First and the Last (Revelation 17)

8.The Living One (Revelation 1:18)

9.Him who holds the seven stars (Revelation 2:1)

10.[Him] who walks among the seven golden lampstands (Revelation 2:1)

11.Him who has the sharp double-edged sword (Revelation 2:12)

12.Son of God (Revelation 2:18)

13.The one who searches minds and hearts (Revelation 2:23)

14.Him who has the seven spirits of God and the seven stars (Revelation 3:1)

15.The Holy One, the True One (Revelation 3:7)

16.The Amen (Revelation 3:14)

17.The faithful and true witness (Revelation 3:14)

18.Lion of the tribe of Judah, the root of David (Revelation 5:5)

19.A lamb standing (Revelation 5:6)

20.Lord of Lords and King of Kings (Revelation 17:14)

21.The Lamb (Revelation 19:7, 9)

22.Faithful and True (Revelation 19:11)

23.The Word of God (Revelation 19:13)

24.Christ (Revelation 20:4)

25.The beginning and the end (Revelation 22:13)

26.The root and the descendant of David (Revelation 22:16)

27.The bright morning star (Revelation 22:16)

## STATISTICS OF GLOBAL SUFFERINGS AND STRUGGLES

Following is just a handful of statistics that outline the suffering and struggles we are facing right now in our world.

## GLOBAL WARMING – NASA

Global warming is the long-term heating of Earth's surface observed since the pre-industrial period (between 1850 and 1900) due to human activities, primarily fossil fuel burning, which increases heat-trapping greenhouse gas levels in Earth's atmosphere. This term is not interchangeable with the term *climate change*.

Since the pre-industrial period, human activities are estimated to have increased Earth's global average temperature by about 1 degree Celsius (1.8 degrees Fahrenheit), a number that is currently increasing by more than 0.2 degrees Celsius (0.36 degrees Fahrenheit) per decade. The current warming trend is unequivocally the result of human activity since the 1950s and is proceeding at an unprecedented rate over millennia.

## HURRICANES – GLOBALCHANGE.GOV

The intensity, frequency, and duration of North Atlantic hurricanes, as well as the frequency of the strongest (Category 4 and 5) hurricanes, have all increased since the early 1980s. The relative contributions of human and natural causes to these increases are still uncertain. Hurricane-associated storm intensity and rainfall rates are projected to increase as the climate continues to warm.

## TORNADOES – NATIONAL OCEANIC AND ATMOSPHERIC ADMINISTRATION

- The frequency of tornado outbreaks with 16 or more EF-1+ tornadoes is increasing. Before 1980, on average, there were about 3.5 days per year with 16+ tornadoes. Since 2000, this number has doubled to 7 days per year.

- The number of EF-1+ tornadoes that occur on tornado days is increasing. On average, 3.6 tornadoes per tornado day were observed from 1954 to 1974 compared to 4.4 tornadoes per tornado day from 1996 to 2016.

- Research suggests there is a greater risk of more off-season tornadoes in a warmer future climate. This could mean more tornadic activity at a time of year when people are least expecting it. Results are inconclusive for whether tornadoes could become more or less frequent during the traditional severe weather season.

## WILDFIRES – WORLD RESOURCES INSTITUE

The latest data on forest fires confirms what we've long feared: Forest fires are becoming more widespread, burning at least twice as much tree cover today as they did two decades ago.

Using data from researchers at the University of Maryland, recently updated to cover the years 2001 to 2023, we calculated that the area burned by forest fires increased by about 5.4 percent per year over that time period. Forest fires now result in nearly 6 million more hectares of tree cover loss per year than they did in 2001— an area roughly the size of Croatia.

Fire is also making up a larger share of global tree cover loss compared to other drivers like mining and forestry. While fires only accounted for about 20 percent of all tree-cover loss in 2001, they now account for roughly 33 percent.

This increase in fire activity has been starkly visible in recent years. Record-setting forest fires are becoming the norm, with 2020, 2021 and 2023 marking the fourth, third and first worst years for global forest fires, respectively.

Nearly 12 million hectares—an area roughly the size of Nicaragua—burned in 2023, topping the previous record by about 24 percent. Extreme wildfires in Canada accounted for about two thirds (65 percent) of the fire-driven tree cover loss last year and more than one-quarter (27 percent) of all tree-cover loss globally.

## POLLUTION – NASA and EPA

According to data from NASA and the EPA, since the start of the Industrial Revolution around 1700, atmospheric carbon dioxide levels have increased by roughly 50 percent, meaning the current $CO_2$ concentration is now 150 percent of what it was in the pre-industrial era;

this increase is primarily attributed to human activities like burning fossil fuels.

## PLASTIC WASTE – MONTEREY BAY AQUARIUM

How big is our plastic problem?

From the time people started making plastic in the 1950s through 2017, we have produced more than 9 billion tons. Plastic is now commonly used in everything from packaging to clothing, building construction and electronic devices—just about anything you can think of.

The problem is most of this plastic ends up as waste. In fact, the average American disposes of 290 pounds of plastic waste every year.

You may think a lot of plastic gets recycled and made into new products, but in fact, most does not. Only 5 percent of the plastic ever made has been recycled. The rest is either incinerated or ends up in landfills or as litter in the natural environment—including the ocean.

In fact, scientists estimate that around 12 million tons (US) of plastic make their way from land into the sea every year. That's like dumping a garbage truck full of plastic into the ocean every 45 seconds.

And once the plastic pollution is in the landfill or ocean, it lasts for a long time—possibly forever. Since plastic only started being mass-produced in the 1950s, we don't really know how long it lasts in the environment.

## WARS – OUR WORLD AND DATA and WIKIPEDIA

There have been approximately 97 wars around the world since 1700 CE resulting in approximately 163,000,000 deaths of military personnel and civilians. That is 163,000,000 fathers, mothers, sons, and daughters without counting the loss of their families. And that is a low figure.

## EPIDEMICS AND PANDEMICS – NATIONAL INSTITUTES OF HEALTH

Since 1700, there have been approximately ninety-two epidemics and pandemics around the world costing the lives of 92,000,000 people.

## FIREARM DEATHS IN THE UNITED STATES – PER CDC WONDER

In 2022, between 48,117 to 48,204 people died by firearms in the United States—an average of one death every 11 minutes. That is a 35 percent increase from 2012 with 33,563 deaths.

## SUICIDES – CDC WORLDWIDE – WORLD HEALTH ORGANIZATION

- More than 720,000 people die due to suicide every year.

- Suicide is the third leading cause of death among 15 to 29-year-olds.

- Seventy-three percent of global suicides occur in low- and middle-income countries.

- The reasons for suicide are multi-faceted, influenced by social, cultural, biological, psychological, and environmental factors present across the life-course.

- For every suicide, there are many more people who attempt suicide. A prior suicide attempt is an important risk factor for suicide in the general population.

## MENTAL DISORDERS – WORLD HEALTH ORGANIZATION

- In 2019, 1 in every 8 people, or 970 million people around the world were living with a mental health disorder, with anxiety and depressive disorders the most common.

- In 2019, 301 million people were living with an anxiety disorder including 58 million children and adolescents.

- In 2019, 280 million people were living with depression, including 23 million children and adolescents.

• In 2019, 40 million people experienced bipolar disorder.

## DOOMSDAY CLOCK – BULLETIN OF THE ATOMIC SCIENTISTS ORIGINAL TEXT

The Doomsday Clock is a design that warns the public about how close we are to destroying our world with dangerous technologies of our own making. It is a metaphor, a reminder of the perils we must address if we are to survive on the planet.

When the Doomsday Clock was created in 1947, the greatest danger to humanity came from nuclear weapons, in particular from the prospect that the United States and the Soviet Union were headed for a nuclear arms race. The Bulletin considered possible catastrophic disruptions from climate change in its hand-setting deliberations for the first time in 2007.

The members of the Science and Security Board have been deeply worried about the deteriorating state of the world. That is why we set the Doomsday Clock at two minutes to midnight in 2019 and at 100 seconds to midnight in 2022. Last year, we expressed our heightened concern by moving the clock to 90 seconds to midnight—the closest to global catastrophe it has ever been—in large part because of Russian threats to use nuclear weapons in the war in Ukraine.

On January 28. 2025, we set the Doomsday Clock at 89 seconds to midnight. In setting the Clock one second closer to midnight, we sent a stark signal: Because the world is already perilously close to the precipice, a move of even a single second should be taken as an indication of extreme danger and an unmistakable warning that every second of delay in reversing course increases the probability of global disaster.

As of January 7, 2026, it is now 85 seconds to midnight. A year ago, we warned that the world was perilously close to global disaster and that any delay in reversing course increased the probability of catastrophe. Rather than heed this warning, Russia, China, the United States, and other major countries have instead become increasingly aggressive, adversarial, and nationalistic. Hard-won global understandings are collapsing, accelerating a winner-takes-all great power competition and undermining the international cooperation critical to reducing the risks of nuclear war, climate change, the misuse of biotechnology, the potential threat of artificial intelligence, and other apocalyptic dangers. Far too many leaders have grown complacent and indifferent, in many cases adopting rhetoric and policies that accelerate rather than mitigate these existential risks. Because of this failure of leadership, the Bulletin of the Atomic Scientists Science and Security Board today sets the Doomsday Clock at 85 seconds to midnight, the closest it has ever been to catastrophe.